THE THIRD EYE

THE THIRD EYE
A Spiritual Laser for Stimulating Inner Awakening

Prof. (Dr.) Jai Paul Dudeja

GenNext Publication

ISBN: **978-93-5324-155-1** (HB)

First Published, 2019

Published by

GenNext Publication
5, Ansari Road
Daryaganj, New Delhi-110002
Phone: 9811692060
E-mail: gennextpublication@hotmail.com

Printed at: G. Print Process, Delhi.

Contents

List of Figures

Preface

My dear Readers,

I am feeling extremely happy and blessed to see this book titled, ***"THE THIRD EYE: A Spiritual Laser for Stimulating Inner Awakening"*** in your hands. I believe that you have chosen to get this book for not only to go through it out of curiousity and to quench your intellectual thirst, but also to receive the blessings of God Almighty through this book by practicing this technique for your inner awakening and transforming yourself to the state of Higher Consciousness.

The third eye is the gate that opens to the space of higher consciousness and to the inner worlds. It is also the main organ through which the spiritual energy can be awakened and regulated. The third eye (also known as the inner eye or the mind's eye) is a mystical concept referring to an invisible eye, which provides perception beyond the ordinary sight. The "Third Eye" is the seat of intuitive wisdom, of subtle information and spiritual or occult power. The third eye acts as a 'switch', which can stimulate the seeker to the transcendental state of consciousness. It is the spiritual laser for stimulating your inner awakening; it is the beacon that guides you to your true destination – the long-awaited home you have been so passionately longing for. It is the lighthouse of consciousness, which the truth-seekers wish to rely upon.

Each one of us possesses the 'Third Eye', but without the grace of the spiritual master (Guru) or without the suitable spiritual technique, the third eye remains underdeveloped. Conclusively it is the Dharma (duty) of every human on this planet to awaken or open his/her third eye during this lifespan itself in order to reap innumerable benefits in physical, mental, emotional, psychological, spiritual and astral planes.

It is not only our dharma; it should be our right to avail the infinite blessings from God Almighty by opening our third eye. The current book is a sincere effort to introduce the topic of third eye to the readers along with the techniques of opening the third eye and the benefits accrued there from.

Besides the extensive coverage on the well-known 'Third Eye of Lord Shiva' (in Hinduism), this book describes the third eye, its location, the technique of its awakening in other faiths and religions also, viz., Buddhism, Taoism, Jainism, Christianity, Kashmir Shaivism, Sufism, Sikhism, Gnosticism, the 'Eye of Horus', and the Eye of Ra etc. Thus this is a truly multi-religious and multi-faith book, which will definitely draw the attention of all the readers across the Globe interested in this important spiritual subject. Further, this book stepwise explains various techniques for opening one's third eye. The last chapter of this book lists many benefits accrued to those seekers whose third eye is either fully opened or in the process of awakening. All these aspects are comprehensively covered in the **eighteen chapters,** supported by **85 figures** in this book.

A large number of original *Sanskrit mantras* (hymns), written in Devanagri as well as Roman scripts along with their meanings (in English) have been included in this book in order to give authenticity and scholasticism to this book. A sincere effort has been made to ensure that this book appeals equally well to the scholars, the seekers and the common people having a simple knowledge of English language and believing in the vast spiritual treasure hidden in their ancient scriptures.

The **first chapter** gives a fairly detailed 'Introduction to the Third Eye'. This chapter will ignite the interest in the readers, particularly the uninitiated ones to this field, to go through the rest of the book with enhanced enthusiasm. Throughout this book, various terms will be used to explain the phenomenon of opening of the third eye. It is therefore appropriate to explain these terms in the **second chapter** of this book itself. Some of these terms are: various chakras (spiritual energy centres), Kundalini (spiritual energy), channels (naadis) for the transport of kundalini through various chakras, pranayama (breathing techniques), prana vayus etc. It is believed that once the reader goes through this chapter, it will be easy for him/her to appreciate the rest of the chapters. The **third chapter** describes the Ajna Chakra (or the Brow Chakra or the sixth chakra) which many people, particularly the Hindus believe, is the seat of the "Third Eye'. This point is located on the forehead in between the two eyebrows. It is believed that a meditation or focus on this location opens the third eye of the practioner. A majority of people in the world belonging to other faiths and religions believe that the 'Pineal Gland' (a physically real entity) is located at the same place as that of Ajna Chakra, described above. In fact many such people are of view that the Pineal Gland itself is the Third Eye. This issue is covered in details in the **fourth chapter** of this book. There is yet another group of mystics who believe that the opening of the third eye precedes the opening of Alta Major Cenre, which is located at the back on the neck. This issue is dealt with in the **fifth chapter** of this book. There is yet another school of mystic thoughts who opine that there is an intimate correlation between the Thalamus and the Third Eye. In fact some of them believe that the third eye is located at the same place as that of Thalamus. Some of these people go to the extent of claiming that the Thalamus itself is the Third Eye. These views are discussed in the **sixth chapter** of this book. The **seventh, eighth, ninth, tenth, eleventh, twelfth, thirteen, fourteenth, and fifteenth chapters** in this book describe about the Third Eye in Hinduism (Lord Shiva), Kashmir Shaivism, Buddhism, Taoism, Jainism, Christianity (Single Eye), Theosophy, The Eye of Horus, and the third eye in other faiths and religions (Sufism, Sikhism, Ancient American countries, Unicorn, and Gnosticism), respectively. The **sixteenth chapter** of this book is a food for those hungry spiritual tourists who wish to know and do a pilgrimage to some Shiva temples and the 'Third Eye Shrines' located in various countries in the world. Besides receiving spiritual vibrations at each of these temples and shrines, the tourists will be impressed by the architectural design of these buildings. In some of the previous chapters, we have mentioned about different locations of the Third Eye. The question then arises as to where actually the third eye is located and what are the various techniques for opening the third eye. This topic is covered in the **seventeenth chapter** of this book. The **eighteenth (the final) chapter** is a sincere effort to market about the benefits accrued to the practioners whose third eye has either been opened or in the process of getting awakened.

It is my sincere desire that the present book will benefit a large number of readers and the seekers. I sincerely hope that this book will be a GPS for those readers who are pilgrims to the path of fulfilment, higher consciousness and enlightenment.

I would gratefully and open heartedly love to receive any encouraging/critical comments as well as the feedback from my dear readers at my Email ID: drjpdudeja@gmail.com.

Prof. (Dr.) Jai Paul Dudeja
Director,
Amity University Haryana,
Gurugram, India

2019

Acknowledgements

I would sincerely like to express my heartfelt gratitude to the following divine souls who have helped me during the preparation of manuscript of this book:

Currently one of the most inspiring spiritual masters in the world in the area of 'Third Eye Awakening', in particular the third eye of Lord Shiva, is the most revered **Sadguru Jaggi Vasudev ji**, founder of Isha Foundation, Bangalore. My heartfelt Pranaam to Sadguru whose blessings and the spiritual eye has guided me to author this book.

The trigger to write this book was ignited by **Master Del Pe** of the MDP village, Cervantes, Philippines, with whom I had interactive meetings during Sep 28 - Oct 1, 2018 in Philippines, where I was invited to participate in the Second International Convention on Higher Consciousness (ICHC-2018). These meetings, followed by my study of his book on 'Third Eye' (2010), stimulated me to author this book based on the spiritual wisdom given to us for the past thousands of years by our ancient scriptures.

I have drawn infinite inspiration from **Dr. Ashok K Chauhan**, Hon'ble Founder President, Amity Education Group, whose unflinching faith for the awakening of third eye of every individual was inspirational for me to write this book.

Next, I feel indebted with gratitude to **Dr. Aseem K Chauhan**, Hon'ble Chancellor of Amity University Haryana, Gurgaon, who provided me a free and fearless environment to explore newer avenues of knowledge and disciplines at this University, both within and outside my core competence area of Laser Physics & Technology.

Further, my heartfelt admiration and gratitude goes to **Prof. (Dr.) P B Sharma**, Hon'ble Vice Chancellor of Amity University Haryana, Gurgaon, who is a doyen of multidisciplinary science, technology and innovation, and who always inspires, motivates, and appreciates any kind of technical or non-technical work, which enhances the quality of human life on this planet.

Last but certainly not the least my greatest admiration is reserved for **Mrs. Rita Dudeja**, **my wife**, my best friend and my constant source of encouragement, for all my ventures and endeavours like this and many others.

Prof. (Dr.) Jai Paul Dudeja
Director,
Amity University Haryana,
Gurugram, India

2019

Chapter - 1

Introduction to the Third Eye

1.1 What is 'Third Eye'?

The third eye is the gate that opens to the space of consciousness and to the inner worlds. It is also the main organ through which the spiritual energy can be awakened and regulated. The "Third Eye" is the seat of intuitive wisdom, of clairvoyance (clear seeing beyond the unseeable), of subtle information and spiritual or occult power. In Sanskrit, the 'Third Eye' is known by many terms like: Trinetra, Ajna chakra, Mahanadi, Bhrumadhya, Tapah loka, Shiva loka etc. In the Indian mythology it is *jnana-chakshu*: the eye of knowledge and wisdom, the seat of the *antar-guru*, or 'teacher inside'. The third eye (also known as the inner eye or mind's eye) is a mystical concept referring to an invisible eye, which provides perception beyond the ordinary sight. People have always been fascinated by as well as afraid of Lord Shiva's third eye. As one visualises it, the third eye stands on his forehead between the two eyebrows, according to a majority of believers. As per mythology, the third eye can also unleash fire and destruction causing the world to end, besides bringing the welfare of all humans.

As per spiritual teachings, we all have the power to invoke our third eye, thereby achieving enlightenment. Third eye is an intra-organ, a subtle or non-physical organ that all human beings possess. It is called the 'Third Eye' because the moment it is activated, one is able to see without and beyond one's two physical eyes. Blindfolded reading or reading without the need of the two eyes – is one of the visible side-effects of initiation into third-eye-awakening.

Many people also look at the third eye as a tool of the rejection of worldly desires. Spiritual Gurus tell their followers to focus on the 'third eye' as part of the meditation process, thereby achieving the stage of higher consciousness and enlightenment. So, as against the common belief, the third eye does not alone suggest Shiva's anger and also his power to destroy. In fact, it suggests a way towards wisdom, knowledge, higher consciousness and enlightenment.

There are five sensors in a human being. One can see, smell, hear, taste and touch through one's eyes, nose, ears, tongue, and hands, respectively. But there is a **sixth sense.** Through this, one can open the gateway to the subtler realms of existence. One can develop an inner eye and view the invisible world, consisting of multiple dimensions, alternate realities, subtler planes, spiritual world filled with light, perception of the past, present and future of a person, and parallel universes of incredible wonders. In each one of us, there exists this third eye. Once awakened it is far brighter than the millions of physical eyes put together.

Whenever there is any physical object to be seen in the line of sight, the physical eyes see it and transmit this signal to the brain. The brain then deciphers and identifies that object and its attributes. Similarly, when the hands touch something, this sensation is transmitted to the brain. So in each case of the five sensors, it is the signals transmitted to the brain, which are the perceiving, deciding and the identifying factors. These five sensors, without the brain, have no meanings on their own. Now let us assume that all these sensors are temporarily blocked and only the third eye is awakened. It then means that only the 'mind's eye' is functioning, which will perform the role of all these sensing and even beyond.

The third eye acts as a 'switch', which can stimulate the seeker to the transcendental state of consciousness. Whereas the two physical eyes cannot see (look) either the past or the future, the third eye is an organ of inner vision which embraces eternity. When the third eye is awakened, it sets into motion several labyrinths of energy. This helps in correcting a number of physical and emotional disorders in the seeker and leads to transform him/her to a blissful state of mind. The Upanishads describe a human being as a city with ten gates. Nine gates (two eyes, two nostrils, two ears, mouth, urethra, and anus) lead to the outside world. The **tenth gate**, the third eye, opens onto the inner worlds: revealing the whole spectrum of the levels of consciousness.

Any opening (or entrance) is generally referred to an entry point. The openings in a human body have a vital role in our life. These (nine) openings have a major contribution to our daily existence. We can see using our physical eyes (two), hear anything audible through our ears (two), breathe through our nose (two nostrils), taste through our tongue, touch through any one or both of our hands, and defecate and urinate through our rectum and orifice respectively. The nostril also discharges wastage when we are affected by the cold. Our ears also discharge ear wax; our mouths also dissipate when we have a cough or vomit.

The mention of these nine gates of the human body is also recorded in the 'Talks between Narada and King Prachinabarhi in Srimad Bhagavatam', as given here below:

अक्षिणी नासिके कर्णौ मुखं शिश्नगुदाविति ।
द्वे द्वे द्वारौ बहिर्याति यस्तदिन्द्रियसंयुतः ।। 4.29.8 ।।

akṣiṇī nāsike karṇau mukhaṁ śiśna-gudāv iti
dve dve dvārau bahir yāti yas tad-indriya-saṁyutaḥ. (4.29.8)

Meaning: The eyes, nostrils and ears are pairs of gates situated in one place. The mouth, genitals and rectum are also different gates. Being placed into a body having these nine gates, the living entity acts externally in the material world and enjoys sense objects like form and taste.

- Talks between Narada and King Prachinabarhi of Shrimad Bhagavatam; 4.29.8

All of these functions of the *'Nava Dwaras'* (nine gates) are initiated through our brains. It is obvious that we already know their uses but the significance of each of these (nine) gates emerges when these combine with our sensation. According to medical science, our vision, hearing, breathing, tasting, and defecation are all interconnected through our brain. Hence, the psychology suggests that the maximum utilization of our senses can also be obtained if our mind is able to reach the zenith through Nava Dwaras. If we focus at this from a different perspective, we can deduce that our five senses of gathering knowledge are the combination of our eyes, ears, nose, and tongue combining with our flesh. Similarly, our anus, genital, mouth combined with our arms and legs creates action or work. The birth and death of a person are also related to the number 9. It is estimated that a child takes around 9 months to be born which is known as Nava Maasa. Our mind is always in charge of monitoring these nine gates. If we consistently meditate or do yoga, we shall be successful in maintaining these gates properly.

The third eye refers to the tenth gate that leads to the inner realms and spaces of higher consciousness.

Figure 1.1: The third eye located slightly above the midpoint between the two eyebrows

Hinduism has several scriptures which have commented about the Nava Dwaras. There have been several explanations provided which generally portrays the human soul to be a living element in the middle of nine gates. The actions of the body are conducted by its certain natural modes but our soul has the capability to go beyond these boundaries, if required. According to Lord Krishna, our soul has the ability to step outside and revive back to its original destination. During this time, the sensation of the Nava Dwara is considered to be numb. As a result, when an individual reaches to Krishna consciousness, he is completely detached from the physical actions. Therefore, in this controlled order, he lives gladly within the region of nine gates.

These nine gates are also mentioned in the *Shvetasvatara Upanishad*, Chapter 3, and Verse 18, as given below:

नवद्वारे पुरे देही हंसो लेलायते बहिः ।
वशी सर्वस्य लोकस्य स्थावरस्य चरस्य च ।।
– श्वेताश्वतरोपनिषद्तृतीयोऽध्याय, १८

navadvāre pure dehī haṁso lelāyate bahiḥ |
vaśī sarvasya lokasya sthāvarasya carasya ca ||
– Shvetasvatara Upanishad, Ch.3, Verse 18

Meaning: It is He (Hamsah, the Soul), who resides in the body, the city of nine gates. He is the soul that sports in the outside world. He is the master of the whole world: animate and inanimate.

(The Shvetasvatara Upanishad belongs to the Taittiriya School of the Krishna Yajur Veda. It derives its name from the sage who taught it. This Upanishad is regarded as one of the authoritative works which form the Vedanta philosophy. Its mantras are quoted profusely in all Vedantic treatises.)

These nine gates of the city (Pur, like Jaipur, Udaipur, Bilaspur etc.) are also mentioned in Chapter 5, Verse 13 of Srimad Bhagavad Gita, as given below:

सर्वकर्माणि मनसा सन्न्यस्यास्ते सुखं वशी ।
नवद्वारे पुरे देही नैव कुर्वन्न कारयन् ।।
– (श्रीमद्भगवद गीता, 5.13)

Sarvakarmaani manasaa sannyasyaaste sukham vashee;
Navadwaare pure dehee naiva kurvan na kaarayan.
– (Srimad Bhagavad Gita, 5.13)

Meaning: Mentally renouncing all actions and self-controlled, the embodied one rests happily in the nine-gated city, neither acting nor causing others (body and senses) to act.

Sri Aurobindo's interpretation of this shloka, in Srimad Bhagavad Gita, is:

The embodied soul perfectly controlling its nature, having renounced all its actions by the mind (inwardly, not outwardly), sits serenely in its nine-gated city neither doing nor causing to be done.

(The Bhagavad Gita, भगवद्गीता, "The Song of God", often referred to as the Gita, is a 700- verse Hindu scripture in Sanskrit that is part of the Hindu epic Mahabharata (chapters 23–40 of the 6th book of Mahabharata). The Gita is set in a narrative framework of a dialogue between Pandava prince Arjuna and his guide and charioteer Krishna. At the start of the Dharma Yuddha (righteous war) between Pandavas and Kauravas, Arjuna is filled with the moral dilemma and despair about the violence and death the war will cause to his family members (both Pandavas and Kauravas). He wonders if he should renounce and for this, he seeks Krishna's counsel, whose answers and discourse constitute the Bhagavad Gita. Krishna counsels Arjuna to "fulfil his Kshatriya (warrior) duty to uphold the Dharma" through "selfless action". Krishna-Arjuna dialogue covers a broad range of spiritual topics, touching upon ethical dilemmas and philosophical issues that go far beyond the war Arjuna faces. The Bhagavad Gita presents a synthesis of Hindu ideas about dharma, theistic bhakti, and the yogic paths to moksha. The synthesis presents four paths to spirituality – jnana, bhakti, karma, and raja yogas. These incorporate ideas from the Sankhya-Yoga and Vedanta philosophies. The Bhagavad Gita is the best known and the most famous of Hindu texts, with a unique pan-Hindu influence. Gita calls for selfless action. It inspired many leaders of the Indian independence movement including Bal Gangadhar Tilak and Mahatma Gandhi. Gandhi referred to the Gita as his "spiritual dictionary".)

Buddhism has a similar perspective of the nine openings. The striving to reach the tenth gate is also mentioned in it. There have been several reports that monks use Nava Dwaras as a medium to cure illness. The state of nirvana might also be achieved by using Nava Dwaras as a reference during meditation. Nava Dwaras has been present in Buddhism from the very beginning.

Sikhism also has a belief on Nava Dwaras but it says further that the tenth gate opens only in the entry point (at the feet) of God.

Srimad Bhagavad Gita, in Chapter 8, verse 12, mentions about closing all these gates (which connect us with the external world) and opening the 'third eye' to attain yogic concentration:

सर्वद्वाराणि संयम्य मनो हृदि निरुध्य च।
मूर्ध्न्याधायात्मनः प्राणमास्थितो योगधारणाम्।।
– (श्रीमद्भगवद गीता, 8.12)

sarva-dvārāṇi sanyamya mano hṛidi nirudhya cha
mūrdhnyādhāyātmanaḥ prāṇam āsthito yoga-dhāraṇām.
– (Srimad Bhagavad Gita, 8.12)

Meaning: Having closed all the gates, confined the mind in the heart and fixed the life-breath in the head, engaged in the practice of concentration,

OR: Restraining all the gates of the body and fixing the mind in the heart region, and then drawing the life-breath to the head, one should get established in steadfast yogic concentration.

The Third Eye is non-functioning in the ordinary sense, it cannot see unless the physical eyes become unseeing. The same energy must move into third eye. It needs energy to function and the same energy has to be redirected. Hinduism locates the third eye around the middle of the forehead, just above the crossroads of eyebrows. On contrary to this theory, Theosophy located the third eye in back of the head. As per this theory the third eye was placed in the back of the head during ancient period of human era. Gradually it atrophied (decreased in size) as humans evolved and sunk into the pineal gland. The location of the third eye by some people is physically called the pineal gland, a small organ at the very top of the spine as it enters the brain. What makes the pineal gland so special is that a vast amount of energy and blood flows through it more than any other gland in the human body. It is now believed that it helps to regulate the functions of the pituitary gland. Pineal gland and the Pituitary gland are depicted in the following figure.

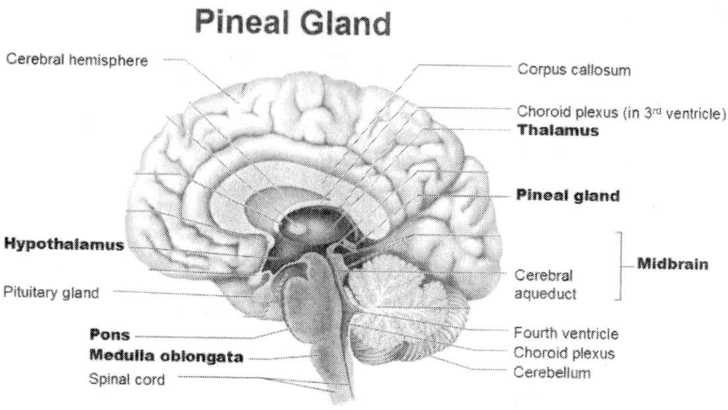

Figure 1.2: Location of Pineal Gland in the brain

When we see through the physical eyes, we can see through the physical body. The third eye is not a part of physical body; but subtle body. That is why the physiologists do not believe that there is an existence of the third eye. With the third eye functioning, we can enter into a different dimension and see things which are invisible to the physical eyes but visible to the subtle eye. With the third eye, we look at the person's soul, at the spirit, not at the physical body through the physical eyes. We cannot see the soul with the physical eyes. The opening of the third eye transforms us into a new world, a subtle world. We start seeing things we have never seen. The third eye is a symbol of enlightenment. It is the *Ajna chakra*, sixth chakra also known as brow chakra or the brow centre. Ajna chakra is also known as the 'Chakra Raja' – the king of chakras, because all the different energy centres in the human body are ruled by this chakra. This is commonly denoted with a dot, eye or a mark on the forehead of deities or enlightened beings. This symbol is called the 'Third Eye' or the 'Eye of Wisdom'. In theosophy, the third eye is referred as the pineal gland. Third Eye is our Inner Vision.

The energy of the third eye is really the same as that which moves in the two ordinary eyes-the same energy. It begins to move in a new centre. The third eye is already there but non-functioning and it cannot see unless these ordinary eyes become unseeing. The third eye is not really a part of physical body. It is a part of the second body which is hidden; it is the subtle body, the *Sukshma*, where life force resides. It has a corresponding spot in the physical body, but is not a part of it. That's why physiology cannot believe that there exists a third eye or anything like it; because your skull can be analysed, penetrated, x-rayed, and there is no physical point, which can be said as third eye.

How is the third eye related with this technique of looking? If your two eyes stop completely, if they become unseeing, static like stones, with no movement in these eyes, the energy stops flowing through them. The energy flows; that is why they move. This energy is the same that flows in our whole body i.e. life force, the very basis of life (most people name it the soul of body). Eyes can be static but energy can never be static. When these two eyes are closed to the energy, if suddenly the doors are closed and energy cannot move through these eyes, this energy tries to find a new path and the third eye is just near, just between the two eyebrows, half an inch deep. It is just like closing one hole from where the water flows and then the water will find another hole to flow out.

Third eye means the spiritual eye. It can perceive only the spiritual realities. Third eye is the seat of intuition. Some claim that it is possible to cultivate the capabilities of 'third eye' to increase, augment and deepen its range of sensitivity and perception. Some associate 'third eye' with pineal gland or hypothalamus, which number of western traditions identify as the seat of the soul. The 'Third eye' is a mystical and esoteric concept. Some believe that it leads one to the inner realms and spaces of higher consciousness.

The third eye generates the supreme insight of the infinite self, when directed inwards. When we say, third eye has opened; it is a state of enlightenment that has been attained. It is associated with psychic perception, higher insights, creativity, magnetic forces and the light. Our dreams, intuitive vision, wisdom & imagination, non-verbal communication all stems from the third eye. The third eye can be said as deeper truth, a link between the "visible" and the "invisible", or between the 'seen' and the 'unseen'. It is the gate and link to a man and his vast cosmic connection. The mystical powers remain dormant simply because they have not been called into action and realities remain far from the truth. Quoting Gita's episode of vishwaroopa darshan, Lord Krishna grants *divya chakshu* to his beloved devotee Arjuna for a brief period to experience his vast & infiniteness.

1.2 'Third Eye' of Lord Shiva

While Lord Shiva's third eye is regarded as a symbol of power and destruction by some people, many look at it as the eye of spiritual wisdom and knowledge. It is considered that Shiva's third eye helps Him see beyond the obvious, something not visible to the other two eyes. His third eye is also regarded as a symbol of power in Shiva to protect the good from the bad. It is said that as the third eye opens, all the evil and the ignorance is destroyed. So, in a sense, the third eye implies the destruction of the bad and the evil.

Among many adjectives and attributes associated to Lord Shiva, He is also known is Tryambakam, (*'Try'* means Three + *'Ambakam'* means Eyes), that is, "One who has three eyes" referring to Rudra or Lord Shiva, Who shares the same attributes.

त्रि अम्बकं इति त्रयम्बकं।
Triambakamiti trayambakam

Meaning: The three-eyed one is trayambaka

Firstly, in His 'vishwaroopa' or universal form, the three eyes symbolically signify the sun, moon and fire. Sunlight during the day, moonlight at night and fire in their absence signify illumination. Secondly, the pair of eyes gives sight to the material world and its experiences. The third eye is symbolic of 'atma-jnana' or knowledge of the Self through which one sees the higher reality. This is also known as 'The eye of wisdom' or the 'jnana chakshu' (or the third eye, or the eye at the centre of the forehead, just between the two eyebrows). This is the centre of knowledge, the wisdom, and the deep concentration.

The following Mantra (known as: "Maha Mrityunjaya Mantra"), mentioned in the Rig Veda (Mandala VII, Hymn 59), also describes the three-eyed "Lord Shiva":

ॐ त्रयम्बकं यजामहे सुगन्धिं पुष्टिवर्धनम्।
उर्वारुकमिव बन्धनान् मृत्योर्मुक्षिय मामृतात्।।

Om trayambakam yajamahe sugandhim pushtivardhanam;
Urvarukamiv bandhanan mrityormukshiya mamratat.

Meaning: I worship the three-eyed One (that is, Lord Shiva); Who is fragrant and Who nourishes all beings. May I be liberated from the bondage of mortality (death), similar to a ripe cucumber leaving effortlessly from its Creeper (a plant with long, flexible and thin stem that grows, typically along the ground or up a building, by slowly spreading out). May I never be separated from the immortality.

This third eye is the faculty of intuition and insight (insight; inner vision; subtle perception) which allows us to realise Shiva (our Essential Nature). Besides our two fleshy eyes, each of us has a third eye which lies dormant unless it is awakened by the practices of Yoga or any other transformative system. When it is awakens, we can live in the world of mundane affairs (with the two fleshy eyes) whilst remaining in contact with the Roots of our Being (with the third eye).

Shiva Purana also mentions about Triyambakam as given below:

त्रयम्बकं यजामहे च त्रैलोक्यपितरं प्रभुम्।
त्रिमण्डलस्य पितरं त्रिगुणस्य महेश्वरम्।।

Trayambakam yajamahe cha trailokyapitaram prabhum.
Trimandalasya pitaram trigunasya maheshwaram.
– (Shiva Purana Rudra Samhita chapter 38)

Meaning: We worship Lord Shiva having three eyes, who is the Lord of three worlds and the master of three gunas.

Further, in Linga Purana, it is mentioned that:

त्रयाणामपि लोकानां गुणानामपि यः प्रभुः।
वेदानामपि देवानां ब्रह्मक्षत्रविशामपि।
अकारोकारमकाराणां मात्राणामपि वाचक।।
तथा सोमस्य सूर्यस्य वह्नेरग्नित्रयस्य च।
अंबा उमा महादेवो ह्यंबकस्तु त्रियंबक।।
– (Linga Purana II.54)

Trayanaamapi lokaanaam gunaamapi yah prahuh.
Vedanamapi devanaam brahmakshatravishaamapi.
Akaarokaaramkaaraanaam maatraanaamapi vaachaka.
Tatha somasya surasya vahneragnitryasya cha.
Amba uma mahadevo hyambakastu triyambakam.
– (Linga Purana II.54)

Meaning: The word 'Tryambaka' has been defined as the one, who happens to be the Lord of the three worlds, three gunas, three Vedas, three gods, three castes— He is revealed by the three syllables 'a', 'u', 'm'. He is the Lord of three fires, viz.: the sun, the moon and the fire. He represents Amba, Uma and Mahadeva. Thus, the Lord of all the sets of three is known as Tryambaka.

All Hindu Gods have two eyes except Lord Shiva. The Lord Shiva is called as Trayambaka Deva for having the third eye. In the two main eyes of the Lord Shiva, the right side eye is named as Sun and the left side eye is named as Moon. These two eyes are used for the continuation of universe; hence these eyes emit less power so as to meet the universal requirements. The third eye of Lord Shiva, situated at the centre of forehead, is known as the symbol of spiritual power and the 'eye of wisdom'.

Lord Shiva's third eye has always fascinated people. It stands there dramatically on his forehead, ready to release a missile of fire and destroy the world. Some of the inscriptions obtained in Mohenjo Daro and Harappa describe Shiva as Munkan, Minkan, Bidukan and Orkan which mean respectively three-eyed, fish-eyed, open-eyed and one-eyed.

Many people assume that, for this attribute of having the third eye, Lord Shiva is called the `destroyer'. They also assume that this eye opens when Shiva is angry. Typically, in modern dance ballets based on Shiva's sacred lore, one often finds drums beating frantically and the actor playing Shiva dancing fiercely, going all around the stage rather energetically, expressing Shiva's rage and sorrow at the death of his spouse, Sati, threatening to destroy all by opening his third eye, until all the gods salute him, sing songs to his glory and beg him to calm down.

Shiva is the Aadi Yogi, and He is always meditating from times immemorial. So, His third eye, also called the 'Ajna Chakra', is activated and is the indication of the immense Yogic energy. The bead of a Rudraksha mala (rosary of the 108-beads which are made from rudraksha) represents the third eye on the forehead of Lord Shiva.

We all are the children of Lord Shiva and we have found our existence from a tiny part that came from Him. Like him, all of us have a **third eye** that helps awaken us and enlightens our path. The master of our life, Lord Shiva is an incarnation of mediation in the real sense and so learning to meditate on Lord Shiva clears the darkness from our eyes and enables us to take the best decisions in our life's affairs.

1.3 'Third Eye' as mentioned in other faiths besides Hinduism

The third eye is called *urna* or *urnakosha* or *ushnisha* in Sanskrit, *unna* in Pali, *byakugo* in Japan, and *Trinetra or Trayambakam* ('three-eyed") - a reference to Lord Shiva. In Hinduism and Buddhism, the third eye is a symbol of enlightenment. They refer to it as eye of knowledge. Hindus believe that the opening of Shiva's third eye causes the eventual destruction of the physical universe. Third Eye once awakened, you will be able to see, hear and feel which you cannot do with your five senses.

The third eye is symbolized by the "Eye of Providence" in apyramid's capstone on the U.S. one-dollar bill. It is portrayed in myths and fables as Cyclops. Some UFO researchers believe the third eye to be a vestigial organ of the extra-terrestrial human ancestors. (A vestigial organ is an anatomical feature or behaviour, which no longer seems to have a purpose in the current form of an organism of the given species. These vestigial structures were the organs, which performed some important function at one point in the past.) The third eye is represented in the Kabbalah as 2 of the 10 Sephiroth (lights) on the Tree of Life: *Binah* and *Hokhmah,* which embody wisdom and understanding. (Kabbalah is the ancient Jewish tradition of the mystical interpretation of Bible, initially transmitted orally and using esoteric methods).

In **Buddhism,** the third eye is regarded as the eye of consciousness. Buddhist teachings ask followers to look at the world not visible through their physical eyes. The third eye is about concentrating one's mind, as a gateway to the inner realm and higher consciousness. In other words, it helps reach the stage of enlightenment. The third eye, or the "Eye of Wisdom", in Buddhism, the urna, is denoted by a dot, or mark on the forehead in the deities of Shiva or Buddha.

You may have come across many Buddha statues and Buddha heads in which a small hairy dot appears between the eyes of the figure. This particular dot is known to have existed in many statues and stupas in the iconography from different nations such as Nepal, India, Burma, Thailand, etc. If we go through the teachings of the Buddha, or the Buddhist teachings; the hatred, delusion, clinging and greed cause suffering in the world. The Eightfold path of the Buddha has been a great way of ridding oneself of these traits and obtaining a higher peace in one's life and reality. Buddhist symbols for greed include mirrors, eyes and the power of the vision.

Figure 1.3: Third Eye displayed between the two eyebrows of Lord Buddha

The eyes of the Buddha reminds the followers of Buddhism to have ethical behaviour, practice meditation, make ritual offerings and have the feeling of generosity in life so as to let go of the greed from their lives. In the same way, the dot, which represents the Third eye of the

Buddha for the Buddhists, was adopted by the followers of Buddhism as well as Hinduism and Taoism in various Asian countries. The Buddhists take the Third eye as the symbol of spiritual awakening of knowledge and wisdom. While the Hindus have a belief of the third eye being a channel to the inner and hidden power, the western symbolize the third eye as the symbol of second sight or clairvoyance.

The third eye in the statues of Buddha and Buddha head statues represents an abstract concept referring to a speculative invisible eye which provides perception of the reality beyond ordinary vision of the people. It signifies the entrance which leads us to the true and inner reality of higher consciousness. Generally, in modern spiritual philosophy, the third eye usually represents a state of enlightenment or awakening which evocates the mental images and brings our deeply personal, spiritual and psychological significance. Often related and associated with religious visions, the third eye is believed to indulge us to improve our extrasensory perception and brings out our ability to observe the vibes, precognition and even supernatural experience.

In **Taoism** or Daoism and many traditional Chinese religious sects such as Chan (a cousin to the Zen school), "third eye training" involves focusing attention on the point between the eyebrows with the eyes closed, and while the body is in various qigong postures. The goal of this training is to allow students to tune in to the correct "vibration" of the universe and gain a solid foundation on which to reach more advanced meditation levels.

Taoism teaches us that the third eye, also called the 'mind's eye', is one of the main energy centres of the body located at the 'sixth chakra' forming a part of the main meridian: the line joining the left and the right hemispheres of the head, and is given the name 'muddy pellet'. The Taoist concept of dantian as energy centres is similar to the Indian yoga concept of chakras as key points where prana is stored. The major difference, however, is that Taoist dantian are the major energetic storage mechanisms whereas the yogic chakras are not so much storage centres, but energetic vortices which act as input and output ports. There are three dantians: lower, middle and the upper. Out of these, the upper dantian (or Shang Dantian), at the forehead between the eyebrows or third eye, which is also called "muddy pellet", associated with the pineal gland.

Figure 1.4: Muddy Pellet or Third Eye (Dantian)

The Third Eye is a natural part of every person. One way to think of the third eye is as a "**meta**" organ that consists of your mind and all of your senses working together as a larger, more powerful sensory organ, so that the pineal gland then acts as a focal point to create a vision. The Third Eye is a very clever bit of natural evolution that allows you to see the patterns in your life. Even more amazing, your third eye can reveal these patterns to you by overlaying this information on the top of your other senses.

According to the **Christianity**, the concept of the third eye is a metaphor for the non-dualistic thinking: the way mystics see. The mystics employ the first two eyes for sensory input from the sight; the 'third eye' is the eye of the reason, meditation and reflection and referred to as having the mind of Christ. There is a theory that Jesus spent much of his early life in India, the centre of the Hindu religion. Jesus speaks of a "single eye" and calls it the "light of the body" and says that if you see this "single eye" your body will be full of light. Jesus, the Nazarene also said that if we can trust the veracity of the Gospels, even the New Testament, "If thine eye be single, thy whole body shall be full of light." He experienced it. "If Thine eye be single" means when Thy third eye opens. This seems to be a clear reference to the third eye. Since the single eye is full of light and the pineal gland regulates the light reception in the brain, and since the pineal gland is where the two halves of the brain meet and become one, it is believed that we can assume that Jesus was speaking of the pineal gland when he made reference to the single/third eye. Many of the mystery schools often coded the information in the form of a pine cone (pineal gland). We can see this prominently in the Vatican as one of the largest statues to nature. It also retains a dominant role on the staff of the Pope. The entwined snakes on Osiris' staff are reminiscent of the kundalini forces entwining up the spinal cord to end in the pineal gland.

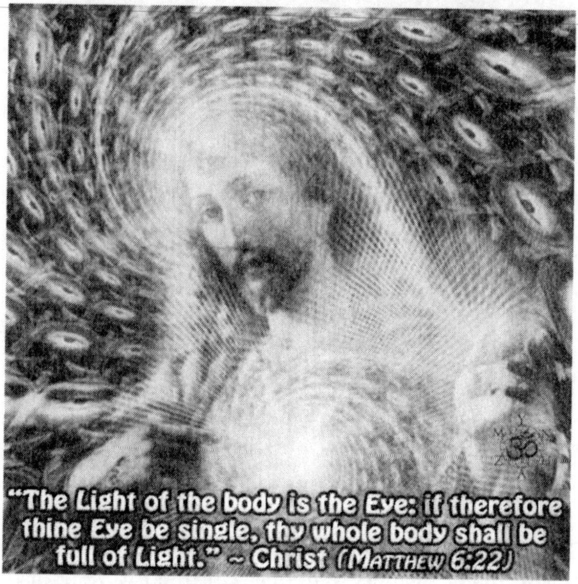

Figure 1.5: Single Eye or Third Eye in Christianity

In **Sufism,** the third eye is called **'Khafi'**. There is a term called 'Lataif' in Sufism, which means the subtle centres or elements of creation or psycho spiritual energy centres (like chakras in Hinduism). The concept of Lataif is drawn from the Holy Quran by Sufis. All Sufis distinguish Lataif-as-Sitta, the six subtleties namely Latifat-an-Nafsi, Latifat-al-Qalbi, Latifat-as-Sirri, Latifat-ar-Ruhi, Latifat-al-Khafi, and Latifat-al-Akhfa. Out of this, Latifat-al-Khafi means inexplicable, arcane or latent subtlety. It represents intuition. **Khafi is located in the**

middle of the forehead between the eyes or on the point of third eye. Its colour is black or the darkest blue. Some people believe that it is located to the right of the chest and it is the darkest green in colour. Some Sufis compare it with Kitab-e-Marqoom the divine codices. The invocation or activation of this latifa leads to the realm of unification with ultimate reality. Khafi is a 'meta' organ, which means that the khafi consists of collective and coherent functioning of all the senses and the mind for a higher consciousness.

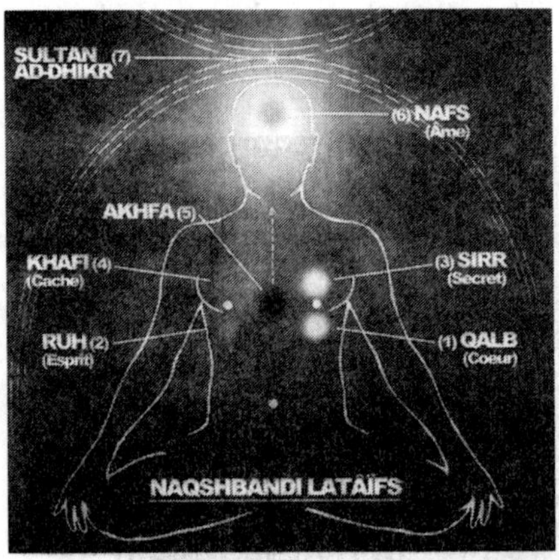

Figure 1.6: Third Eye in Sufism (Khafi)

Being similar to a pinecone in shape (thus its name), the pineal gland is constructed in a three-dimensional Fibonaccian spiral (that is close to a Golden Mean spiral). This shape in sacred geometry is considered a portal system onto itself, helping a person transcend dimensions in many mystery schools. A prime example of this is the mystical group called the **Sufi**. They do a spiral dance to get close to God and the heavens. Inside the pineal gland not only do we find the manufacturing of several 'mind altering' hormones such as melatonin, serotonin and possibly the psychedelic dimethyltryptamine (DMT), we find extremely coherent water with piezoelectric crystals. This extremely coherent water, encased in a sacred geometry chamber, has deep interest to us. The piezoelectric quality of this chamber is a great candidate for an event horizon to project us into other dimensions. This could be a connection to many things including: dreams, astral projection, remote viewing, visions and even the connection to higher self, the soul/spirit worlds. Some authorities have gone as far as calling it a Star Gate.

According to **Jainism,** all living beings are surrounded by leshya-aura; only the emancipated are freed from it forever. Black, blue, and grey; again, red, lotus-coloured and white---These are the qualitative names of leshya in order. The first three leshyas are unchaste, their fruit are inauspicious too. The colour, taste and the smell of these are also repugnant. The other three leshyas are pleasant: They bring an awakening in life as the passions subside.

Figure 1.7: Third Eye in Jainism

Vedic Chakras of Hindu tradition and Leshyas of Jainism are similar concepts. If we look into the scriptures of Jainism such as Bhagawati Sutra, Uttaradhyayan Sutra, Tatvarth Sutra, and Aagam literature, we find many such similar concepts that stand in line to Chakras. The six Leshyas or rather mental tendencies as described in Jainism can well be equated with chakras. These Leshyas are Krishna Leshya, Neel Leshya, Kapot Leshya, Tejo Leshya, Padma Leshya and Shukla Leshya. Lehsya is related to two internal powers: Kashya and Yoga. The Yoga Leshya forms the mental Aura and the Kashya Leshya forms the emotional aura.

Just below the 'Centre of Tranquillity' is another important centre called Jyoti Kendra, the 'Centre of Enlightenment'. This is located in the pineal gland. The physiologists have not been able to gather much information about it. Recently, some research work has been conducted about it on the basis of which its importance is being assessed. As a matter of fact this Jyoti Kendra, the Centre of Enlightenment, is called the 'third eye'.

Some people recognise Darshan-Kendra (The Centre of Intuition) or Ajna-Chakra (The Centre of Command) to be the third eye. From another point of view, Darshan Kendra (The Centre of Intuition) and Jyoti Kendra (The Centre of Enlightenment) may both be called the third eye, but the latter, because of its usefulness has a greater importance. Jyoti Kendra (The Centre of Enlightenment) is the centre which annihilates anger. By meditating on this centre, wrath dissolves very soon. From the point of view of brahmacharya too, this centre has great utility. It has been recognized as the controlling or master-gland. It controls the secretions of all the lower glands. The purification of this centre resolves many of our physical and psychological problems.

According to **Guru Granth Sahib**, the most sacred book in **Sikhism**, the experience of total ecstasy of love of the Guru that is "Wahe Guru." Wahe Guru is the ecstasy of experience of total selfless love of the Guru and this experience manifests on all levels of existence: physical, mental and spiritual. In this perfect ecstasy of Wahe Guru, a being glows and his Kundalini rises from the base of his spine to the top of his head to the **pineal gland**. The pineal gland radiates, and the pituitary gland secretes. The pineal gland is the "Dasam Duar" or the Tenth Gate. This experience is the real yoga and without this yoga, without this experience, there is no Sikh Dharma because the Dharma is based upon experience of this occurrence. By whatever name you call it, this stage of awareness, this state of consciousness is the ultimate goal of every spiritual path, of every yogi, and of every religion. Whether one starts by practicing Kundalini Yoga and then meditates on *'Naam'*, his personality becomes lost in Gurbani; or whether he first develops a love for Gurbani, does not matter. No matter how it is accomplished, it all must be achieved: meditation on Naam, rising Kundalini and personality lost in Gurbani. Raj Jog (Yoga) means this very experience. Guru Ram Das was given the throne of Raj Yog forever. So in the Siri Guru Granth Sahib, in the praises of Guru

Ram Das, it is written: *"Kundalini surjhi sat sangat Parmanand Guru much macha."* "Associating with the saints their Kundalini radiates and through the Supreme Guru they enjoy the Supreme Bliss."

Sikhism scripture (973-8, Ramkali, Namdeo Ji) says:

Khechar Bhuchar Tulsi Mala Gur Parsadi Paeia.

Meaning: Control of the breath and positioning of the tongue, focusing at the **third eye** and wearing malas of tulsi beads, are all obtained through Guru's Grace.

The Eye of Horus is an ancient Egyptian symbol of protection, royal power and good health. Horus was the ancient Egyptian sky god who was usually depicted as a falcon, most likely a lanner or peregrine falcon. His right eye was associated with the sun god, Ra. The eye symbol represents the marking around the eye of the falcon, including the "teardrop" marking, sometimes found below the eye. The eye is personified in the goddess Wadjet (also written as Wedjat, or "Udjat", Uadjet, Wedjoyet, Edjo or Uto). It is also known as the "Eye of Ra".

Figure 1.8: The Eye of Horus

The name **Wadjet** is derived from "wadj" meaning "green", hence "the green one", and was known to the Greeks and Romans as "uraeus" from the Egyptian "iaret" meaning "risen one" from the image of a cobra rising up in protection. Wadjet was one of the earliest of Egyptian deities who later became associated with other goddesses such as Bast, Sekhmet, Mut, and Hathor. She was the tutelary deity of Lower Egypt and the major Delta shrine the "per-nu" was under her protection. Hathor is also depicted with this eye.

In one myth, when Set and Horus were fighting for the throne after Osiris's death, Set gouged out one of Horus's eyes. The majority of the eye was restored by either Hathor or Thoth (with the last portion possibly being supplied magically). When Horus's eye was recovered, he offered it to his father, Osiris, in the hope of restoring his life. Hence, **the eye of Horus** was often used to symbolize sacrifice, healing, restoration, and protection.

Figure 1.9: Third Eye depicted on U.S. one-dollar bill

The Egyptian connection with the 'third eye' does not stop there. Some people feel that the great **pyramid of Giza** was not only built to stimulate Pineal activity, it was built with the initiation chamber in the shape/location of the pineal gland. This pyramid/third eye connection was not lost on the Founding Fathers of the U.S.A., who were mostly Free Masons; they used it as part of the country's seal, which can be seen on the back of the American dollar bill to this day.

According to the **neo-Gnostic teachings** of Samael Aun Woer, the third eye is referenced symbolically and functionally several times in the Book of Revelation 3:7-13, a work which, as a whole. Kundalini is quite often represented as a sleeping serpent, coiled three-and-a-half times around the central axis, located at the base of the spine (muladhara chakra). According to neo-Gnosticism it describes Kundalini and its progression upwards through the seven chakras. This interpretation equates the third eye with the sixth of the seven churches of Asia detailed therein, the Church of Philadelphia.

Many portrayals of **Sumerian gods** depict a pine cone extended in one hand. These gods are believed to be a representation of the Annunaki, or an ancient extraterrestrial visitor race and their ability to access their pineal gland for its consciousness-expanding abilities. Pine cones can be found in ancient Greek mythology on the staff of Dionysus, or his Roman iteration Bacchus. A pine cone staff with snakes wrapped around it is also carried by Osiris in Egyptian lore. Cambodian temples in Angkor Wat bear a striking resemblance to pine cones. These ancient ancestors clearly had a healthy awareness of our pineal gland and the mysticism surrounding its purpose and connection to a higher level of consciousness. This pine cone shape adds to the mysterious symbolism seen across cultures. It comes as no surprise that the pine cone also forms in a sacred geometric pattern from Fibonacci golden ratio.

According to **Max Heindel's** Rosicrucian writings, called Western Wisdom Teachings, the **third eye** is localized in the pituitary body and the pineal gland. It was said that in the distant past, when man was in touch with the inner worlds, these organs were his means of ingress thereto.

An important point to keep in mind is that the **third eye is not physical.** The grossest part of the third eye is a structure of energy belonging to the etheric body or layer of life force. The etheric body has many connections with the physical body and therefore the third eye, being the 'main switch' of the etheric body, is also closely connected to certain structures of the physical body, for instance **the pituitary and pineal glands**. However **it would be over-simplified to say that the third eye is the pineal gland or the pituitary gland**, as stated by certain books. It would be far too simplistic and limiting to pick one of these physical structures and label it 'third eye'. Asserting once more, the third eye is not physical; it is an organ of energy. It may have some privileged connections with certain physical structures, but it cannot be limited to any of them. Third eye is not just having one more eye on the forehead; it means your vision is in tune with the cosmic vision.

So in this book, whenever we talk about 'the third eye', we mean a certain location in the head, like the area between the eyebrows. That does not mean the area between the eyebrows is the whole third eye, of course. We shall consider this as the main switch, the place to remain aware of permanently. If you get sensations in other areas of the head, don't try to suppress them, but don't pay attention to them either. Third eye is the portal of higher vision.

One aspect about the third eye needs to be clarified in the first chapter itself. The ajna chakra or the 'third eye' is not in your physical body, though one may focus for it in between the two eyebrows of in the location of pineal gland to get the desired effects. But if you were to dissect a dead body, you would not find any 'third eye' in it physically. The third eye is located in your subtle body.

The third eye is just like a crystal to graze the past, present and future. It is believed that the one, whose third eye has opened even a little bit, is capable of showing super natural powers. Thus a suitable crystal for the third eye confers clairvoyance upon the seeker. Third Eye is not just used for seeing alone. It can be used even to hear, touch, feel, and work. So the third eye is a powerful new possibility. It is called Third Eye because the moment it is activated, the first thing that happens is you will be able to see, hear beyond the physical organs. You start seeing, perceiving the whole life in higher dimension, with higher possibility. Your *Kundalini Shakti* starts staying in higher planes, so it always keeps you in the highest levels of completion, in the highest health, and all your peak possibilities open up. All the extraordinary spiritual, mystical traditions continuously work on awakening the third eye. It is the easiest and yet the most powerful way of awakening oneself to higher dimensions. The awakened third eye creates the psychic power for psychic vision, the ability to destroy evil energy blockages and create the kindness and empathy within you. Third Eye is an important power which is stored in every human being. We need to awaken it. We need to make it a reality.

There are innumerable benefits of the awakened third eye. These include: (i) greater wisdom as you tap into the source of all wisdoms; (ii) greater confidence as you discover your true purpose; (iii) access to inner counsellors who will guide you on your path; (iv) the ability to make correct decisions effortlessly, with commitment, certainty and assurance; (v) clarity of mind in all the endeavours; (vi) development of psychic and intuitive abilities; (vii) spiritual development of higher consciousness; (viii) direct communication with Higher beings; (ix) greater inner peace, fulfilment, contentment, and joy; (x) ability to see through illusions to perceive reality and truth; (xi) spiritual gifts of certain sensory perception, prophesy, and direct voice; and (xii) robust physical health, well-being, longevity, and youthfulness, etc.

In other words, here are the potential gifts you can open up to when you learn how to open your third eye:

- Clairvoyance (clear seeing),
- Claircognizance (clear knowing),
- Clairaudience (clear hearing),
- Clairempathy (clear feeling),
- Clairtangency (clear knowing through touch),
- Clairsentience (clear knowing through feeling),
- Clairgustance (regarding taste), and
- Clairsalience (regarding smell).

This eye of wisdom is literally your inner teacher. In Hinduism, the planet Jupiter, which is associated with the 'third eye', is called *'Guru'*, which can *be* translated as 'spiritual teacher'. Therefore, by awakening and developing your third eye, you are opening the lines of communication between your ego self and the higher self, between *Jivatma* and *Atma*. The third eye is the eye of illumination, which shines the light of wisdom on your spiritual pathway. Our third eye is the invisible spiritual tool within our head, which acts as a bridge to connect between our individual soul and the Supreme Soul. It is the spiritual laser for stimulating your inner awakening; it is the beacon that guides you to your true destination – the long-awaited home you have been so passionately longing for. It is the lighthouse of consciousness, which the truth-seekers wish to rely upon. With the awakened third eye, you come home to the abode of perfect peace, divine understanding, inner joy, fulfilment, and the deepest contentment.

The Third Eye is not an endocrine gland, not the pineal or the pituitary. The Third Eye is a chakra or force centre as this term implies it. The Third Eye is a vortex of energy, positive and negative, receptive or donative, formed out of the joint interplay of the radiant energies produced through the simultaneous arousal of the thousand petalled lotuses, the brow centre, and the Alta major centre. It is wise, during the perusal and application of the techniques outlined next, to re-examine this definition of the Third Eye. The third eye is where the truth lies, and where all untrue dies and disappears. The third eye is the seat discernment and discrimination. With the awakened third eye, the falsehood will be engulfed into darkness in the light of pure wisdom. You will be enveloped in the divine light. You will be able to distinguish between real and unreal, like a swan (*humsa*) who drinks only the pure milk and leaves behind the water, in the milk-water mixture.

These aspects will be discussed in details in the chapters to follow.

Chapter - 2

Chakras (Energy Centres), Nadis (Channels) and Kundalini in Human Body

In the subsequent chapters of this book we shall be discussing about the effect of inner awakening on various chakras (centres of energy) in the human body. It is therefore advisable to learn about them, in details, in this chapter itself.

Chakras are the crux of the human system. These are also called the energy centres or energy organs in the human body.

2.1 Seven chakras in human body

There are seven chakras in the human body. The Chakras are represented as energy centres aligned along the spinal cord, which forms the integrating channel. Chakras serve as the collection and transmission centres for both subtle, and metaphysical, energy and concrete, or biophysical, energy. "Chakra" is a Sanskrit word literally meaning "wheel." Blocked energy in our seven chakras can often lead to physical and mental illness. So it is important for us to understand our chakra system and try to keep these clean so that the energy flow is blocked. These seven chakras are connected with different glands and organs and responsible to uniform life energy in our body.

Figure 2.1: Location of Seven Chakras in the Human Body

(i) Root Chakra: This is a Base Chakra and also called the '***Muladhara Chakra'***. It sits at the base of our spine. Its sense is smell. This chakra holds the basic needs for survival, security and safety. Root body parts include the hips, legs, lower back and sexual organs. Its normal positive function is as the foundation of life energy which feeds the whole human mechanism and connects us with the Earth, keeping our feet on the ground and in tune with our basic needs. A balanced root chakra keeps us rooted in our life. It is what keeps us humble and grounded. It makes us feel safe and emotionally secure.

The Base Chakra (Muladhara Chakra) is located in the coccyx (a small triangular bone at the base of the spinal column). The trigger point in the perineum where resides a muscle which stops us from urinating and ejaculating semen in men. The trigger point is in the vulva (the female external genitals) in women. It controls the fight or flight reaction through the adrenal gland. (The adrenal glands, also known as suprarenal glands, are the endocrine glands that produce a variety of hormones including adrenaline and the steroids aldosterone and cortisol. They are found above the kidneys).

In case of imbalance of this chakra, a person may feel fearful, anxious, insecure and frustrated. Problems like obesity, knee troubles and anorexia nervosa (Anorexia nervosa is an eating disorder characterized by weight loss, or lack of appropriate weight gain in growing children; difficulties in maintaining an appropriate body weight for height, age, and stature; and, in many individuals, distorted body image). With the imbalanced root chakra, one may develop problems with the smooth legs movements, weak knees or sciata problems (pain affecting the back hip).

Each gland has an outer cortex which produces steroid hormones and an inner medulla). The energetic blockages of fear in the base chakra cause stiffness, pain and illnesses in the vulva, prostate, hips and legs. Base Chakra blockages cause problems with the emotion, fear, and problems with sex, problems with money or being a miser, and problems with security. The fear of losing our job, our house, our security creates a great deal of general stress. This fear, held in the base chakra, relates to many health problems in the legs, knees hips, lower spine and head. Any stress of a mental kind eventually exhibits as emotion and then physical problems in the body as eventually stress held over the years becomes greater in an additive way. Eventually the last straw breaks the camel's back. We become physically ill and die.

(ii) Sacral Chakra: This Chakra is also called ***'Swadhisthana Chakra'***. It sits at the lower part of your belly button. Its sense is taste. This Chakra holds the basic needs for sexuality, creativity, intuition, friendliness, emotions and self-worth. In case of imbalance of this chakra a person may feel emotionally explosive, obsessed with thoughts of sex or may lack energy. This area is believed to be the seat of all desires, and the storehouse of the collective unconscious, holding all the darker energies in the deep subconscious. Physical problems may include kidney weakness, lower backache, constipation, and muscle cramps. Belly body parts include sexual organs (women), kidneys, bladder, and large intestine. You may also find it difficult to have passion for hobbies and other interests you once had. Energy imbalance may also manifest itself with the urinary tract infections or infertility.

Its blockages are associated with selfish, uncontrolled sexual desire and attachment. Its function is the creation of children and the energetic feeding of children through energetic connections. It controls the sex glands: ovaries and testes. When we are in the womb of our mother, we are fed physically through the umbilical cord into the abdomen, the seat of the Second Chakra. When we are born the chord is cut into the very same spot (the second chakra), we are already getting the energies of the father and mother along with psychic, energetic, connections. The child and then the adult think that the energy, transferred to the child along this lower emotional connection is love. This addiction to the energies of the second chakra is one of the major causes of the failure of the integration of the emotional body. The emotional body tries to become integrated between the ages of 15 and 24 months. The child tries hard to understand that its parents have interests other than him. Their child is not the sole focus of the world. The problem is that of disappointment. Physical illness is caused by blockages in this area. Its normal function is blocked by the fear of being hurt by relationships. By people or things which we are strongly attached to - like parents, children or spouse being taken away from us by death or disagreement. The result of this pain, which is stored in the second chakra, is the inability to breathe into the abdomen.

When this deep unconscious material is cleared out with a balanced sacral chakra, the person is said to be free from lust, anger and greed, to feel integrated, calm and fearless, and is able to have a strong will and dedication to their spiritual life.

(iii) Solar Plexus Chakra: This Chakra is also called '***Manipura Chakra***'. It sits just above your naval. Its sense is vision. It is the major energetic reservoir of the body. It releases its energy through the pancreas which synthesizes insulin which burns sugar. This Chakra holds personal power, the place of ego, of passions, impulses, anger, strength, astral travel and astral influences, willingness of spirit guides and for psychic development.

In case of imbalance of this chakra a person may feel lack of confidence, confusion, worry about what others think, feeling of controlling by others, depression, liver problems, diabetes, nervous exhaustion, and food allergies. When blocked, it results into misplaced personal ambition, anger and jealousy. When used too much or thwarted by personal power, it leads to a lack of energy in this area - anaemia, etc. Some people in a spiritual awakening or spiritual crisis report chronic fatigue, listlessness, and even being bedridden for a long period. This indicates that their spiritual energy has either burnt out or become depleted in this area. Some of the things that might trigger this depletion are because the *sadhakas* may be working with intense energy, breathing or meditation practices that concentrate all energy in the upper chakras; paying little attention to the basic physical needs of the body either because of a belief that it is unimportant or because of being too busy; or psychological issues that lead to one of the two extremes identified above.

(iv) Heart Chakra: This Chakra is also called '***Anahata Chakra***'. It sits in the centre of your chest. Its sense is touch and its energy emanates through the hands as in Reiki as well as in the centre of the chest. It controls the immune system through the Thymus gland (a ductless, butterfly-shaped gland lying at the base of the neck, formed mostly of lymphatic tissue and aiding in the production of T-cells of the immune system: after puberty, the lymphatic tissue gradually degenerates). This Chakra holds personal power, the place of ego, of passions, impulses, anger, strength, astral travel and astral influences, willingness of spirit guides and for psychic development.

In case of imbalance of this chakra a person may feel sorry for oneself, paranoid, indecisive, afraid of separation, afraid of getting hurt, or unworthy of love. Physical illnesses include heart attack, high blood pressure, insomnia, and difficulty in breathing. Any problems with the giving and receiving of love will cause toxins to reside there and the immune system thus to suffer. Heart disease, AIDS, Cancer are physical expressions of this problem. Its normal function is blocked by the fear of being hurt by relationships or by the people or things which we are strongly attached to - like parents, children or spouse being taken away from us by death or disagreement. The result of this pain, which is stored in the second chakra, is the inability to breathe into the abdomen.

During the opening of this chakra one may hear voices or sounds from other realms, hear buzzing or humming sounds and the music of a flute, and feel great sensitivity to the feelings of others. One may temporarily have clairvoyant or psychokinetic experiences, or even a capacity to heal. One may become detached from worldly things, and find old pleasures meaningless. One can feel unusual sensations in the heart, or have a sudden rising of unconditional love or compassion. It can be like an emotional roller coaster for a while, but as one settles out, there is a deep peace and internal happiness. It is important to think positively, some yogis report, because one is likely to manifest what one thinks as this chakra transforms itself. Some people begin to feel that all that exists in the world is 'love'.

(v) Throat Chakra: This Chakra is also called ***'Vishuddha Chakra'.*** It sits in centre of 'V' in the collarbone. Its senses are speech, singing, chanting and hearing both normal and psychic. This Chakra holds the communication power, voice tone/sound, creative thought, speech, and writing. In case of imbalance of this chakra a person may feel physical illnesses like hyperthyroid, skin irritations, ear infections, throat, inflammations, and back pain etc.

When vishuddhi is out of balance or blocked, the thyroid can be damaged, and ears, throat and hearing may be challenged. It can be difficult to express thoughts and feelings. Sometimes there are random movements or periodic shaking of the neck and head. If for some reason the person has become attracted to psychic powers, their energy can become stuck, and it is applicable when one has learned to suppress their feelings and self-expression.

This chakra is emphasized in therapies that use sound, that is, Shabd and nada yoga, and can be opened through mantras, music, and chanting, especially if the person is very devotional. It is believed that people with remarkable speaking skills, or beautiful singing voices were born with vishuddhi chakra open and active.

(vi) Third Eye Chakra: This Chakra is also called ***'Ajna Chakra'.*** Ajna means to know or to follow. It sits in centre of forehead above the eyes. This Chakra holds psychic ability, higher intuition, the energies of spirit and light. It also assists in the purification of negative tendencies and in the elimination of selfishness. This chakra gives guidance and help in creating channel, and tune into one's Higher Self. In case of imbalance of this chakra a person may feel non-assertive, afraid of success, or go the opposite way and become egotistic, headaches, with blurred vision, blindness, and eyestrain.

The Ajna or Brow Centre is the seat of personality power. The Ajna centre has strong links with Hypothalamus, which governs the autonomic system. Ajna is ruled by the Monadic plane. It is an organ of idealism. Ajna controls the expression of the personality and "grounds" and distributes the spiritual energy of the Soul. When the Ajna centre is active, it has a two-fold flow, inward and outward. The outward flow enables a healer to have inner vision and perception concerning the person's underlying condition and then to creatively work to correct it. The inward flow of the Ajna is utilised when the healer is balancing the centres. Linked to Alta major centre, the Ajna centre controls Cerebellum (muscular action) and the central nervous system.

Ajna centre has 3 sections:

(i) **Upper Ajna** (related to front pituitary lobe > 7 hormones) governing all centres in the body, their endocrine glands and expression through the circulatory system and heart. Has power to visualise.

(ii) **Middle Ajna** (related to pituitary's stalk) has 5 points related to major centres of spine (see diagnosis).

(iii) **Lower Ajna** (related to back pituitary lobe) governing central nervous system with a special relation to Alta major centre and Throat centre. In the back pituitary lobe the reasoning mind has its seat and through it we express the desire in its highest form.

The Ajna is the most important centre in magnetic healing. Its powerful energy is always transferred to the etheric body of the patient via the hand minors of the healer. Ajna embodies the idea of lying behind the act of creativity. The organ of creativity itself is the Throat centre. Ajna fuses the creative energies of the throat and the sublimated energies of desire or true Love of the Heart. In the Higher healer system working according to the Inner Plan, the Ajna centre becomes the directing agent or the distributor of the blended energies of the Divine Man.

A blocked third-eye chakra will increase the problem of insomnia and fatigue. It may also result in headaches and depression. Ajna, is translated from Sanskrit as "perceive," "command" or "beyond wisdom" intuition, insight, self-realization, inspiration and imagination. The energy of the Ajna chakra allows us to not only see but also to understand the inner and outer worlds. See things as they truly are. ***Third eye chakra is the central theme of this book.***

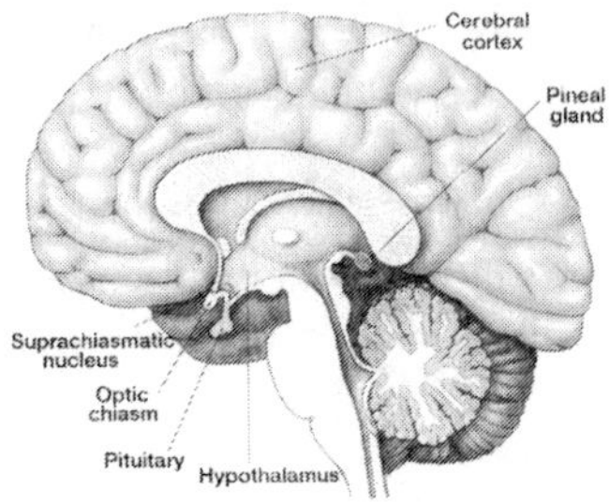

Figure 2.2: Location of Pineal Gland

There are many esoteric and meditation practices that emphasize putting attention on this third eye, with the belief that this will purify the mind and prepare one to awaken their entire energy system with fewer problems. A series of spiritual events have been attributed to this chakra, especially flashes of great light, falling into light or bliss, visions, profound stillness, and psychic revelations. It is at this transformational opening that one glimpses the false reality of the personal identity, and consequently he may feel detached from the senses. As energy moves upward from here (to the seventh chakra), the subtle body may rise or sink into states of *samadhi*, and one may feel merged with the universe, or lose all consciousness of separation from the cosmos.

Nowadays there are very few people with the completely opened third eye that always accompanies an advanced state of consciousness. However, in spite of the incomplete development, the sixth Chakra can function far more harmoniously than any of the other chakras. This expresses itself in an active mind and advanced intellectual skills. The holistic pursuit of scientific research or the recognition of far-reaching philosophical truths may be a sign of a partly opened and harmoniously functioning third eye chakra. We possess a well-developed capacity for visualization and the ability to comprehend many things intuitively. The more our third eye chakra develops, the more our thoughts are based on a direct inner awareness of reality. Increasing number of people are beginning to develop sixth chakra skills, such as clairvoyance or sharpened sensitivity at particular levels of being; others achieve temporary insight into other dimensions of reality, for instance during sleep or meditation.

Ajna chakra sometimes cuts off energy blockages from the soul and provides the main battleground of the human spirit. These methods are the ways in which the power possessing people on this planet still control everyone. Ajna Chakra without the soul conscience connection can result into the "Final Solution" of Hitler, which involved the mass murder of six million human beings in concentration camps. Ajna chakra supported the excesses of Stalin who killed tens of millions. The excesses of the "Cultural Revolution" of Mao Tse Tung who set brother against brother, killing yet more millions of people in the name of making sure that Stalin and Mao could get rid of their rivals for power, using and distorting the philosophy of Karl Marx to support their position. Ajna chakra, without the soul consciousness, resulted into the killing fields of Cambodia; when the Bourgeois middle classes, "The enemies of the masses", as were understood incorrectly from the writings of Karl Marx. Four million middle and upper class human beings were exterminated by Pol Pot.

(vii) Crown Chakra: This Chakra is also called '***Sahasrara Chakra'***. Sahasrara chakra is likened to a thousand-petal lotus. It is thus alternatively called "The Thousand Petalled Lotus" or the "Golden Flower". It controls the Seventh Sense of Connection with higher Energies, and is associated with the Pituitary Gland. It sits in the top of one's head. This Chakra holds spirituality, enlightenment, dynamic thought and energy. It allows inward flow of wisdom, and brings cosmic consciousness. It is like silver cord that connects the aura bodies extending from the crown. The soul comes into the body through the crown at birth and leaves from the crown at death. Tantra sees this as symbolizing unlimited possibilities and the full realization of Truth -a vast knowledge of nothing and everything, or merging with the wholeness of all. The *samadhi* experience here is the death one's ego (merging of individual self to Supreme Self); a movement forever out of the mundane and limited human awareness. Perspectives of life and one's role in it are profoundly altered.

The mental consciousness of the indwelling Soul is focused in the Head centre, which itself is controlled by the Logic plane. The

Crown centre controls the will and destiny of the Soul in incarnation, directs all the other centres and links one to one's Higher Self. It is developed chiefly through meditation. The energy of the Crown centre flows in from the top of the head via the fontanel and precipitates in the pineal gland, producing melatonin. Melatonin has an influence over the circadian biorhythms of our lives. The gland is affected by light, possibly because it has a pigment similar to that in the retina of the eye.

The usefulness of the Crown centre only becomes apparent when the person has develops a certain degree of wisdom, discrimination and spiritual integrity. The Crown centre anchors the consciousness stream from the causal lotus on the Soul level. The Crown centre governs the cerebrum (main part of thinking brain matter) and the right eye. If this centre should be over stimulated, epilepsy, headaches, migraines, and growths in the brain tissue could form or neurosis become apparent. The Crown centre only comes into conscious function when the Kundalini fires have risen significantly and the person is highly developed spiritually, morally and philosophically.

Figure 2.3: Crown Chakra (Sahasrara Chakra): The Chakra of A Thousand Petals

When the Kundalini ascends, the body of the Yogi is maintained by the nectar which flow, from the union of Shiva and Shakti in Sahasrara. Glory to Mother Kundalini who, through Her Infinite Grace and Power, kindly leads the Sadhaka from Chakra to Chakra and illumines him and makes him realise his identity with the Supreme Brahman! The Yoga-Kundalini Upanishad attaches great importance to the search for and finding of right Guru. It insists upon revering the illumined Guru, as God. Guru is one who has full Self-illumination. He removes the veil of ignorance in the deluded individuals.

The Sahasrara chakra is symbolized by a lotus with a thousand different coloured petals, arranged in twenty layers of 50 petals. It encompasses the crown of the head, where all chakras are integrated, while it passes into infinity from the top of the head.

According to Yoga-shikha Upanishad (verse 6):

At the top of the head (the Brahman Gate), or at Mahabatin, there are one thousand petals (the Sahasrara chakra).

By the whole process of the Kundalini Yoga Sadhana, the body of the Yogi attains very subtle state of the spiritual consciousness. The Yogi who has attained to Samadhi experiences everything as consciousness. The Yogi realises the oneness of the macrocosm and the microcosm. Because, the Kundalini Shakti has reached the Sahasrara Kamala or the thousand-petalled lotus and has become united with Shiva, the Yogi enjoys the highest avastha. This is the final beatitude. In the human body the potential pole of Energy which is the Supreme Power is stirred to action. The Shakti is moved upward to unite with the Shiva, the quiescent Consciousness in the Sahasrara.

A wise Yogi should take the Kundalini from the Muladhara to the Sahasrara or the thousand-petalled Lotus in the crown of the head. This process is called Shakti-Chalana. Heated by Agni and stirred up by Vayu, Kundalini stretches its body in the interior of the mouth of the Sushumna. The Kundalini Reaches The Sahasrara By Piercing Through The Three Knots.

We ascend the Sahasrara chakra from which all chakras emanate. We have achieved the last milestone of human awareness, the pinnacle of the human spiritual condition. Here, sacred energy is infinite and wisdom is pure and eternal. Before, things were merely relative. Now, things are absolute. We have obtained a state of Nirvikalpa Samadhi, a state of non-duality where we realize we are one with the cosmos and everything in the cosmos is one with us. A singularity of self has been reached. The cosmos has emptied its energy into us, as we have emptied our energy into it.

According to Shat-chakra-nirupana (verse 40):

> Above all these, in the vacant space wherein the Shankhini Nadi is, and below the Brahman gate is the Lotus of a thousand petals. This lotus, lustrous and whiter than the full moon, has its head turned downward. It charms. Its clustered filaments are tinged with the colour of the young sun. Its body is luminous with letters beginning with A, and it is the absolute bliss.

According to Gorakshashtakam (verse 83):

> With the gaze fixed on the tip of the nose (and) meditating on the sky (the Sahasrara), on the absolute and peaceful Shiva, whose face is turned in all directions, one is freed from suffering.

In case of imbalance of this chakra a person may feel frustration, no spark of joy, and destructive feelings. Illnesses may include migraine headaches and depression. Blockages and Implants above the crown chakra cause a lack of conscience along with heart blockages which cause a lack of empathy.

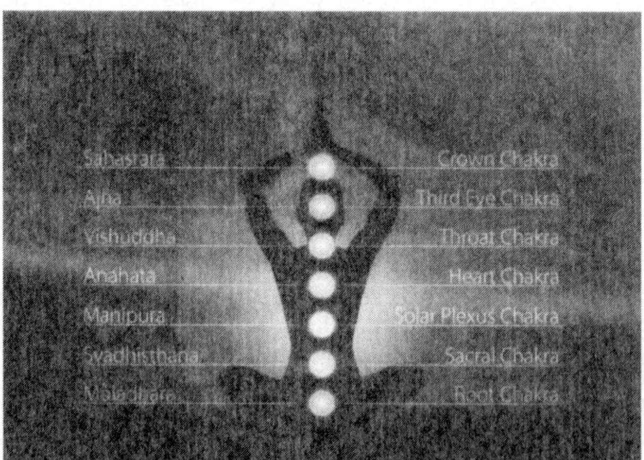

Figure 2.4: Display of location of seven chakras

The Integration of all the Chakras ends in complete freedom, Kaivalya or Enlightenment. We can use this meditational formula to ground all negativity and remove all negative energy blockages.

2.2 Introducing Aura of a Human

What is an 'Aura'? The aura is supposed to be a field of energy that surrounds the human and other animate and inanimate objects. Aura is the name given to the 'halo' of subtle, luminous light (many times invisible to the naked eyes) that is said to surround all the people and living beings, according to several spiritual traditions. It is linked with some yogic philosophies and beliefs because the aura is believed to be connected with the nadis (channels or pathways) of the prana and chakra system. Aura is the invisible etheric / electromagnetic / energy field which surrounds the human body or an object. Aura is made up of Prana (energy). Some people link the perception of auras to the degree of opened 'third eye' of people.

The aura has long been described as an electromagnetic energy field that surrounds people—like an egg-shaped ball of energy that encompasses the body. The aura consists of seven levels/layers/auric bodies, also known as the physical, astral, lower, higher, spiritual, intuitional, and absolute planes. Each one of these subtle bodies that exists around the physical body has its own unique frequency. They are interrelated, and each body affects the others. They also affect a person's feelings, emotions, thought patterns, behaviour, and overall health. Just like with chakras, a state of imbalance in one of the bodies leads to a state of imbalance in the others.

Auras are often worked with as part of an energy or spiritual healing process. This is said to be a powerful way to release energy blocks and allow prana to flow freely through the body. Often, aura healings will focus on the chakras and energy channels of the body. Healers may tackle what is seen as the root causes of energy blockages rather than physical problems since such problems are often perceived as only the symptoms of deeper energetic, spiritual and/or emotional issues.

Here is a breakdown of each layer and what our body seeks and gains from that layer.

(i) The Physical Aura Plane

This layer is closest to us and is diminished through our waking hours but increased while we sleep or take rest. For this layer to be in balance, we need physical comfort, pleasure, and good health. If our auras are in poor health, we shall have smudges in this layer. Also, people who are harbouring negative emotions or who are dwelling in a negative space will have a darker physical aura plane.

(ii) The Astral Aura Plane

This plane is also called the "emotional layer" as it stores our emotional history and experiences with colleagues, friends and family. It is easy to tell when your astral aura is out of whack because you feel sensitive, unstable, and often irrational. Your astral aura will respond best when you amplify what it interacts with your surroundings. For example, to heal negative emotions, try visualizing green. Lie on grass or spend some time under a tree. Or go out alone for a walk in the open and in the green surroundings. This will help to add the colour to your auric space.

(iii) The Lower Mental Aura Plane

This plane relates to reason, thought patterns, and how we construct our own individual reality. Most people spend their waking hours in this plane. This plane expands when our minds are at work, when we are studying, or when we are focused on something particularly hard. This is also where a person's belief systems are stored, as well as their values and ideas. When someone's lower mental aura plane is twisted and out of alignment, they will become judgmental, down, and agitated.

(iv) The Higher Mental Aura Plane

This plane connects with our lower mental aura plane but adds a deeper spiritual element as well. This is where we store our higher-mind beliefs such as self-love, gratitude, selflessness, and unconditional love. Your self-talk can be affecting your whole vibe—not only your confidence but also the energy you project into the world.

So, regardless of what that little voice in your head is telling you, make sure that your higher plane is all about how beautiful, kind, and loving you are; because even though you might think that it is just an internal conversation with yourself, everyone around you can sense the conversation you are having inside.

(v) The Spiritual Aura Plane

This plane has solely to do with our spirituality and connects us to both our immediate surroundings and to the wider universe. When we are aware of this layer and are connected to other people's spiritual planes, we can better sense the like-minded souls. When you have a clear spiritual aura you will find yourself connecting with other people who are walking on the same path as yours, discovering the same things.

(vi) The Intuitional Aura Plane

This plane, also known as the celestial plane, is where we store our dreams, intuition, and overall spiritual awareness. This is where we store forgiveness and acceptance as well. When you think of an enlightened person, you tend to go to peacefulness, calmness, kindness, and patience.

You can sense a healthy intuitional aura plane in complete nirvana. When you are near the people like this—you also start to feel more centred in their presence. Enlightened souls live in their intuitional aura plane—sensitive, often eccentric, profound souls who are creative, intuitive, and gifted. When you have one of those ah-ha moments or a massive brainwave after you have felt blocked for ages, your intuitional aura plane is clearing the runway for major spiritual growth.

(vii) The Absolute Aura Plane

The absolute aura plane works to balance and harmonize the other layers. It houses all the experiences of a soul's journey and is the blueprint of a person's spiritual destiny. This is the finishing touch on top of your energy field.

2.2.1 Opening and Closing the Aura

When one is not working as a medium one can allow the aura to rest in what many mediums call a closed state. The terms "opening the aura" and "closing the aura" are commonly used and frequently misunderstood. In reality, the aura cannot close completely. If it did, we would be dead, as we would have no life force. The aura is not a solid object that opens wide or slams shut to close. When we talk of opening, it is an energizing and expanding of the aura.

Closing is a quieting of the aura, as in normal day-to-day awareness. During these times of inactivity, the energy is recharging so that when the time comes to meditate or practice the medium ship, one can draw on considerable amounts of renewed prana energy.

If you are a sincere medium and working with the prana light for the benefit of others, your psychic powers will be active and you will be receptive to vibrations, but you cannot be harmed by other people's negative energy or by intruding entities.

2.2.2 Can Aura Energy be Measured?

Discovered by Semyon and Valentina Kirlian in 1939, Kirlian photography is a technique of photographing the aura around an object. Kirlian photography is a contact photography, with the object being photographed being in contact with the film. A high voltage, high frequency, ultra low current electric discharge is introduced around the object being photographed, to produce the Kirlian photograph of the aura. In its original form, Kirlian photography does not work for the whole body, but for small areas like the thumb or fingers.

The aura is supposed to be many hued and in constant motion, but the original Kirlian photographs were black and white. Today's Kirlian cameras (also called gas discharge visualization or GDV cameras) are capable of producing colour photos as well as videos that are directly recordable onto a PC. The GDV digital video station also contains a CCD colour video camera and connects to a PC through the USB port.

2.3 Twelve-Chakra System

You are familiar with the 7 major chakras of the human body. But did you know that some chakra systems count 12 or more chakras? In order to enhance your understanding of the energy body, it is essential to know your 12 chakras. Familiarity with the 12-chakra system adds depth, context, and appreciation for your understanding of how chakras work and how to best balance energies in your life.

There are two main types of configurations presented in modern healing schools of thoughts: The 12 chakras are located either both inside and simply outside of the body or all inside:

The first type locates 5 additional chakras outside of the human body in addition to the 7 primary chakras located from the base of the spine up to the crown. This is the most common way to represent the 12-chakra system, including one chakra below the root chakra and the remaining ones above the crown.

Type-Two system includes all 12 chakras inside the human body, positioning 5 additional energy centres in-between the commonly known 7 chakras.

2.3.1 The 12-Chakra System: First Type

The idea of a 12-chakra system is considered as relatively new. As much as one may appreciate simplicity in learning about the chakras, there is no unique or unified understanding of the 12-chakra system to this day. The knowledge about the 12 chakras mostly comes from modern perspectives expressed by contemporary healers and energy workers.

There are 5 additional chakras outside of the human body in addition to the 7 primary chakras located from the base of the spine up to the crown. This is the most common way to represent the 12-chakra system, including one chakra below the root chakra and the remaining ones above the crown. The 12-chakra system brings forth the vision of our connection to the entire universe.

Besides the basic seven energy centres, let us focus on the remaining five chakras introduced in the 12-chakra system. Similar to the format of standard spiritual chakra charts, each one of the five additional chakras possess their own location, colour, and function.

The traditional chakra colours follow the spectrum of the rainbow, while the extended system may add colours associated with metals or other elements. Among them are gold, platinum, and a combination of colours that are sometimes referred to as "opalescence" or "iridescence" for the highest frequencies.

(i) 8th chakra

It is located slightly above the crown chakra, about 1 inch above it. With the 8th chakra, we enter realms transcending space and time. This energy centre is said to open access to parallel universes and lives; it gives access to the realm of the Akashic records and the sphere of potentialities in the making. It is a useful centre for shamanic healing and communication with spirit guides.

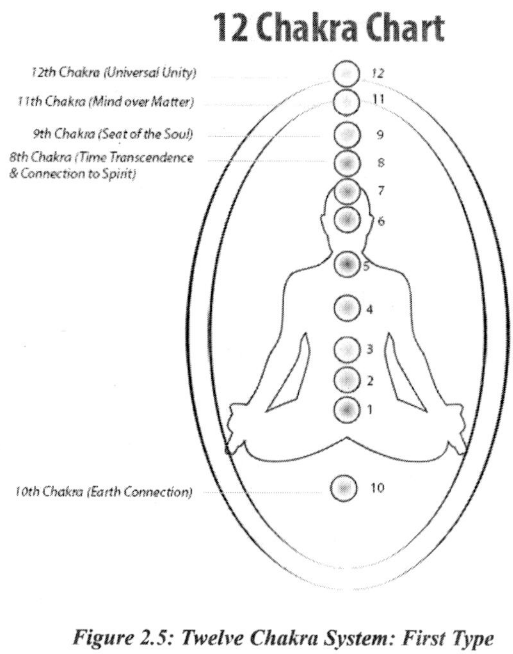

Figure 2.5: Twelve Chakra System: First Type

(ii) 9th chakra

It is located further above the crown chakra. The 9th chakra is said to be the "seat of the soul." It allows access to your soul's code or higher purpose. It can be seen as the door to archetypal energies or patterns that play an important role in shaping our destiny.

(iii) 10th chakra

It is located about a foot and a half below the surface of the ground.

It ensures our connection with the earth. Because it works primarily with the energies of the earth, it is very physical in nature. It participates to our physical well-being and connects us to the grounding energies of the earth and our environment. Just like the first chakra (root chakra or base chakra), it is useful to heal any bone and bone marrow-related issues. It can also play a role in any DNA-related or hereditary issues.

(iv) 11th chakra

It is located outside of the human body, it is said to be accessible through the hands and feet. It makes up an energy field that connects the human sphere of influence to the supernatural. Shamans can use this chakra's dimension to produce magic and influence the physical with supernatural powers. The 11th chakra emphasizes the mind as a powerful tool to shape matter.

(v) 12th chakra

It is on the outskirts of the 12-chakra system; it allows us to stretch beyond our common sphere of understanding into Universal unity with all that is. It is said that it is the chakra of mastery of the soul's purpose through our human existence.

2.3.2 The 13-Chakra System (0-12): Second Type

The second 13-chakra (0-12) system follows the following scheme. The energetic body actually consists of thirteen chakras (numbered 0-12, where 0 stands for Earth Star Chakra). This is a fairly new piece of information developed by energy workers following recent universal shifts.

(i) Earth Star Chakra (0th Chakra)

As the name suggests, this 0th chakra connects our physical bodies and our souls to the Mother Earth and her energies. We become one with the Mother Earth, the Womb, which is the very core of the Universe and Goddesses. Essentially, it enables you to create the feeling of oneness with the Nature, all living things and the Universal force or chi. The grid that connects it, looks like a perfectly designed geometrical net spanning between oneself and the rest of the world; objects, plants, and people. When your Earth Star chakra is accessed, you can feel this grid. The boundary between the nature and the human becomes unclear (blurred) and you seek constant exposure to the outdoors. Also, as the connection grows deeper, the wounds that we inflict on the Mother Earth can also be felt by your psyche, resulting in increased environmentalist attitude on your behalf.

After the 0th chakra, there are seven chakras located at different points in the human body: starting from the Base chakra and ascending up to the Crown Chakra. These seven chakras have already been described, in details, in the current chapter. We now discuss here below about the remaining five chakras (8-12) in the ascending order above the seventh charka.

(ii) Soul Star Chakra (8th Chakra)

Our 8th chakra, also known as the 'seat of the soul' is located above the Crown Chakra, around 6 inches (15 cm) above the top of the head. Soul Star Chakra is where the Divine love, Universal and spiritual energy is purified and sent through the Stellar Gateway to the Crown Chakra from which it enters the body. It is also the home of our Higher Selves, which can make the opening of this chakra tricky, as we are forced to face (sometimes undesired) reality about our souls and ourselves. However, once we have faced the truth we consequently gain an immense power to change the beliefs and habits that have been holding us back. Once our Soul Star Chakra is opened we are able to access our soul's Akashic records (all the information about the soul's Hamsa Protection journey) and learn from our past life lessons to reach our full potential in this life. Essentially, we step on the path of self-realisation that leads us closer to our Higher Selves.

(iii) Spirit Chakra (9th Chakra)

Our 9th chakra is located around 12-18 inches (30-45 cm) above our head and is associated with our spiritual connection and communication with the Universe, angels, spirit guides and other light beings. Do you remember that time when you listened to yourself closely and received a message or just simply followed your intuition without knowing where or why? This was your Spirit Chakra speaking. When your communication with the spiritual realm around you has opened, you can be sure to experience regular synchronicities which are there to remind you that all is connected in the Universe and all you have to do is trust the flow of the Spirit by surrendering to these signs and see where they take you. Having too many expectations and over-planning your life can hinder your ability to hear your Spirit's guidance. Sometimes the Universe wants to take you somewhere that might not make any sense or seem aligned with your goals, but it is always important to remember that your Spirit is working for you and not against you that will always lead you towards your highest purpose.

(iv) Universal Chakra (10th Chakra)

Our 10th chakra is located above the Spirit chakra and is associated with the Universe and our perception of it. When we start listening and following the messages that our Spirit Chakra provides us with, we are inevitably aligning ourselves with the Universal flow to which we have gained access through our Universal Chakra. Opening this chakra enables us to create and manifest a life that is in accordance with our Higher Selves. This is where we become one with the Universe and surrender to the flow, which aligns your physical and spiritual bodies. You are closely linked to your spirit guides, angels and other light beings and follow Cosmic rules rather than rules made up by humans.

(v) Galactic Chakra (11th Chakra)

Ascending up the spiritual ladder we have our 11th chakra, located above the Universal Chakra. While everyone has the potential to activate this chakra, not many people actually reach such an advanced level of spirituality. This chakra enables our souls to ascend even higher in the spiritual realm and communicate with the highest ascended Masters and light beings. Time and space have no meaning and things such as teleportation and instant manifestation can be applied. Accessing your Galactic chakra allows you to not only connect with the higher realms but to explore them and use their laws for your own healing and balancing. The information that you gain can be brought back into this dimension to enlighten and heal others, as well as the world itself. You become a channel for such messages and a great force for improving Earth's vibration. An opened Galactic Chakra is a powerful thing, and once you have experienced such a spiritual ascension, there is no way back to the old way of thinking and perceiving – you see our world for what it really is, stripped of all illusions.

(vi) Divine Gateway Chakra (12th Chakra):

Our 12th and final chakra is located above the Galactic Chakra. The clue lies in the name itself – an activated Divine Gateway Chakra concludes our spiritual ascension and connects us to the Divine Source. We have reached All that is, and are one with the Cosmos and the Source, which enables our soul to travel to different worlds, dimensions and whatever else lies beyond. It acts as a gateway for the Divine Light to flow down our chakras through the spinal column to the Earth Star Chakra and into the Earth, all the way down to the core, from where it returns all the way up again, forming an endless loop of oneness. With an opened Divine Gateway Chakra, all is possible. We become a part of the Divine and bring a substantial level of peace and love to Earth and to its inhabitants.

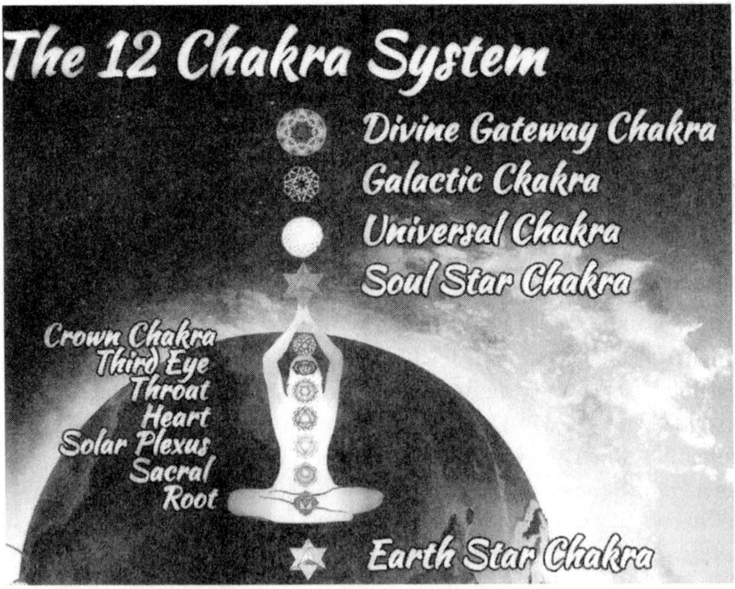

Figure 2.6: 12-Chakra system: second type

2.4 Kundalini

Kundalini is the name of a sleeping dormant potential force in the human organism and it is situated at the root of the spinal column. In the masculine body it is in the perineum, between the urinary and excretory organs. In the female body its location is at the root of the uterus, in the cervix. This centre is known as muladhara chakra and it is actually a physical structure.

The word kundalini actually comes from the word kunda (कुंड), meaning "a deeper place, pit or cavity". The fire used in the ceremony of initiation is kindled in a pit called 'kunda'. Similarly, the place where a dead body is burnt is kunda. If you dig a ditch or a hole, it is called kunda. Kunda refers to the concave cavity and kundalini, resembling a coiled and sleeping serpent, nestled in the muladhara chakra. Kundalini is illustrated as a sleeping serpent coiled three and a half times. Of course there is no serpent residing in muladhara, sahasrara or any other chakra, but the serpent has always been a symbol for efficient consciousness.

The Chakras interface with other energy bodies to assist in the awakening of Kundalini, a type of life energy that invites union with the Divine. Through Yoga, one reawakens the Kundalini energy; so that it could rise through the higher chakras and eventually transform oneself back into the highest state. In other words, the chakras provide the path of returning to enlightenment. Spiritual emergence or Kundalini awakening brings many shifts in energy and consciousness, working through the chakra system.

At the base of the spine is the foundational chakra, muladhara, which holds you into a sense of having a body, of being a separate person, a connection and agreement that spirit is making with the existence. Three qualities are rooted here: the tendency to lethargy (tamas), activity (rajas) or harmonious balance (sattva). Each of us has a mix of these. Our life force is rooted here and active, because we feel we are alive and pranic energy is moving throughout our body. Kundalini is said to be the residual energy that is stored here, holding us in stasis, unless or until it is jolted into awakening and winding upward through our chakras in the body.

In Muladhara chakra, Shakti, the static unmanifested Kundalini, is symbolized by a serpent coiled into three and a half circles around the central axis, Svayambhu-linga at the base of the spine. The serpent lies blocking the entrance to Sushumna, the central channel with his mouth. Sushumna remains closed at its lower end so long as Kundalini is not awakened.

Although kundalini arises from this point, this does not mean the chakra has awakened and transformed at the time of awakening. This does not happen until the rest of the transformation is done and the system is ready to embody the spiritual sense of spacious presence that a full awakening offers. Then there may be a profound letting go into living a life of internal freedom.

Although kundalini is said to reside in the muladhara chakra, we are all at different stages of evolution, and in some of us kundalini may have already reached swadhisthana, manipura or anahata chakras. If this is so, whatever sadhana you do now, might start an awakening in anahata or some other chakra. However, awakening of kundalini in muladhara chakra is one thing, and awakening in sahasrara, the highest centre of the brain, is another.

In Scandinavian, European, Latin American and Middle Eastern countries and many different civilizations of the world, the concept of the serpent power is represented in monuments and ancient artefacts. This means kundalini was known to people from all parts of the world in the past. However, we can conceive kundalini in any manner we like because actually, prana has no form or dimension, it is infinite.

Whatever happens in spiritual life, it is related to the awakening of kundalini. And the goal of every form of spiritual life, whether you call it samadhi, nirvana, moksha, communion, union, kaivalya, liberation or whatever, is in fact awakening of kundalini.

Kundalini is often depicted as a serpent. Why a serpent? Snakes has been revered (and feared) for millennia as a powerful representation of life force or universal energy. Historic and modern day symbolism of Kundalini energy shows a coiled serpent resting at the base of the human spine. Kundalini is also illustrated as two serpents intertwined around one another as they climb the spine. Interestingly enough, the shape of the serpent coupling is nearly identical to the design of double helix DNA. A widely-recognized, mainstream depiction of serpent coupling is associated with medicine. Originating in Greek mythology, the caduceus is two serpents coiled around Hermes' walking stick, which is crowned with wings.

Whether it is consuming its own tail, it is draped over a cross, worn as a charm, or is wrapped around a mountain, spiritual practices around the world recognize and acknowledge the snake as a symbol of Kundalini, or life force, energy. For millennia, humans have strived to awaken the dormant, static Kundalini energy to achieve their version of Enlightenment, whether they call it nirvana, union with the divine, communion, etc. Awakening the power of Kundalini is a journey. Arousing this vital energy can take a few days, weeks, months, or a lifetime depending on the individual. Once the root chakra (the muladhara), the home of Kundalini, opens, the static energy housed there flows freely through the entire system provided there are no serious blockages in one's energy centres. As it flows up the spine, Kundalini boosts the remaining chakras along the way before igniting the crown, or the seventh chakra. Physical, emotional, and psychological symptoms are common during the process of Kundalini awakening, like sweating, nausea, and increased energy.

When energy flows uninterrupted, like a snake winding up the spine, the chakra circuit is complete. Only then there is potential for transcending the physical plane to reach the Enlightenment. The imbalance of awakened shakti energy is known as Kundalini Syndrome. When Kundalini power, also known as Kundalini Shakti, falls out of balance, a range of sensory, cognitive, and physical symptoms can arise. The most common symptoms of Kundalini Syndrome are: tingling throughout the body, headaches, intense emotions, limb weakness, fatigue, and hallucinations. If such symptoms arise, relaxation, a healthy diet, and making a conscious effort to spend time in nature are recommended.

The meaning of the three-and-a-half coils of the serpent is as follows: The 3 coils represent the 3 matras of Om (as depicted below), which relate to the past, present and future; to the 3 gunas: tamas, rajas and sattva; to the 3 states of consciousness: waking, dreaming, and sleeping; and to the 3 types of experience: subjective experience, sensual experience and absence of experience. The remaining half coil represents the state of transcendence, where there is neither waking, nor sleeping nor dreaming. So, the three-and-a-half coils signify the total experience of the universe and the experience of transcendence.

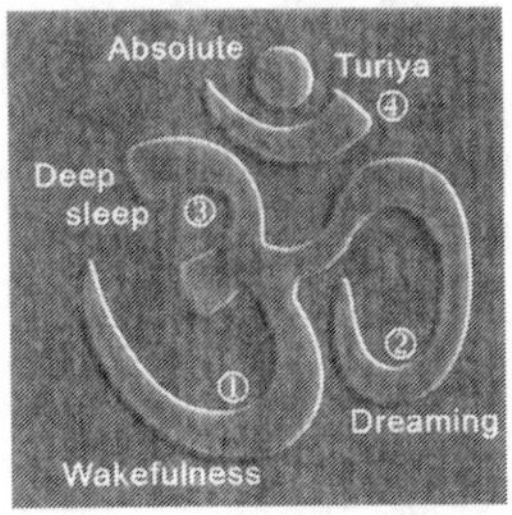

Figure 2.7: Symbol of 'Om'

Figure 2.8: Symbol of static kundalini as 'a serpent'

2.5 Channels (नाड़ी) in Human Body

In addition to the seven chakras of the subtle body, there is a network of subtle channels known as nadis through which the life force (prana) circulates. Nadi means "stream or channel". Nadis are the astral tubes made up of astral matter that carry psychic currents. The Sanskrit term 'Nadi' is derived from the root 'Nad', which means 'motion'. It is through these Nadis (Sukshma, subtle passages), that the vital force or Pranic current moves or flows. Since they are made up of subtle matter they cannot be seen by the naked physical eyes and you cannot make any test-tube experiments in the physical plane. These Yoga Nadis are not the ordinary nerves, arteries and veins that are known to the Vaidya Shastra (Anatomy and Physiology). Yoga Nadis are quite different from these. Nadis play a vital part in this Yoga.

Kundalini, when awakened, will pass through Sushumna Nadi and this is possible only when the Nadis are pure. Therefore, the first step in Kundalini Yoga is the purification of Nadis. A detailed knowledge of the Nadis and Chakras is absolutely essential.

According to the tantric treatise Shiva Samhita, out of the innumerable Nadis (72000, according to one estimate), fourteen nadis are said to be important. They are: (i) Sushumna, (ii) Ida, (iii) Pingala, (iv) Gandhari, (v) Hastajihva, (vi) Kuhu, (vii) Saraswati, (viii) Pusha, (ix) Sankhini, (x) Payasvini, (xi) Varuni, (xii) Alambusha, (xiii) Vishvodhara, and (xiv) Yasasvini.

Out of these 14 nadis, Ida (ईड़ा), Pingla (पिंगला) and Sushmna (सुषुम्ना) are the most important ones. and Sushumna is the chief. It is the highest and most sought nadi by the Yogis. Other Nadis are subordinate to this. These nadis run along the spinal column in a curved path and cross one another several times. These nadis are the subtle energy channels of the body and they conduit Prana (life energy) throughout the whole body. At the points of intersection, nadis form strong energy centres, known as Chakras. A Chakra is a centre of activity that receives, assimilates, and expresses Prana. Each Chakra can be seen as a pair of conical vortices emanating from the front and the back of the body. Various esoteric systems see chakras in different colours, with varied symbols, and ascribe various characteristics and attributes to each.

(i) Sushumna Nadi

The Spinal Cord was called Sushumna Nadi by the Yogis of yore. The modern anatomy deals with the gross form and functions of the spinal cord, while the Yogis of ancient times dealt with all about the subtle (Sukshma) nature. Sushumna nadi extends from the Muladhara Chakra to Brahmarandhra. Spinal Cord is dropped or suspended in the hollow of the spinal column. In the same way, Sushumna is dropped within the spinal canal and has subtle sections.

Sushumna is the central channel and is associated with the river Saraswati. Within the Sushumna nadi there are three more subtle channels: Vajra, Chitrini and Brahma nadi (or Saraswati nadi) through which Kundalini moves upwards running up the body from just below Muladhara chakra to Sahasrara chakra at the crown of the head.

This canal through which Kundalini, when awakened, passes from Muladhara to Sahasrara Chakra. In this central column, exist all the six chakras (lotuses, viz., Muladhara, Svadhisthana, Manipura, Anahata, Vishuddha and Ajna). The canal within the Chakra is called Sushumna, because the canal is within the Sushumna. Ida and Pingala Nadis are on the left and right sides of the spine.

(ii) Ida And Pingala Nadis

From Muladhara chakra, Ida and Pingala alternate from the right to left sides at each chakra until they reach Ajna chakra where they meet again with Sushumna. These are the subtle Nadis that carry the Sukshma Prana. In the physical body these tentatively correspond to the right and left sympathetic chains. The stream to the right of the central column is the male side controlling the sympathetic nervous

Figure 2.9 : Illustration of Sushumna, Ida and Pingala Nadis in the Human Body

system, the fight or flight reaction, the energy of action. The stream to the left is the female side controlling the Parasympathetic nervous system which, through the vagus nerve, controls the speed of the pulse beat from the heart. When the vagus nerve is activated the heart slows down and the body is relaxed.

Ida starts from the right testicle and Pingala from the left testicle. They meet with Sushumna Nadi at the Muladhara Chakra and make a knot there. This junction of three Nadis at the Muladhara Chakra is known as Mukta Triveni. Ganga, Yamuna and Sarasvati dwell in Pingala, Ida and Sushumna Nadis respectively. This meeting place is called Brahma Granthi. Again these meet at the Anahata and Ajna Chakra. In the macrocosm also you have a Triveni at Prayag where the three rivers Ganga, Yamuna and Sarasvati meet.

Ida flows through the left nostril and Pingala through the right nostril. Ida is also called Chandra Nadi (moon) and Pingala as Surya Nadi (sun). Ida is cooling and Pingala is heating. Pingala digests the food. It is the great nourisher of the world. Ida and Pingala indicate Kala (time) and Sushumna swallows time. The Yogi knows the time of his death; takes his Prana into Sushumna; keeps it in Brahmarandhra, and defies the time (Kala—death).

As sushumna flows inside the central canal of the spinal cord, ida and pingala simultaneously flow on the outer surface of the spinal cord, still within the bony vertebral column. Ida, pingala and sushumna nadis begin in muladhara in the pelvic floor. From there, sushumna flows directly upwards within the central canal, while ida passes to the left and pingala to the right. At swadhisthana chakra, or the sacral plexus, the three nadis come together again and ida and pingala cross over one another. Ida passes up to the right, pingala to the left, and sushumna continues to flow directly upwards in the central canal. The three nadis come together again at manipura chakra, the solar plexus, and so on. Finally, ida, pingala and sushumna meet in the pineal gland - ajna chakra.

Ida and pingala function in the body alternately and not simultaneously. If you observe your nostrils, you will find that generally one is flowing freely and the other is blocked. When the left nostril is open, it is the lunar energy or ida nadi which is flowing.

When the right nostril is free, the solar energy or pingala nadi is flowing. Investigations have shown that when the right nostril is flowing, the left hemisphere of the brain is activated. When the left nostril is flowing, the right hemisphere is activated. This is how the nadis or energy channels control the brain and the events of life and consciousness.

Now, if these two energies - prana and chitta, pingala and ida, life and consciousness, can be made to function simultaneously, then both hemispheres of the brain can be made to function simultaneously and to participate together in the thinking, living, intuitive and regulating processes.

Manic depression is common and occurs when the right and left energies are uncontrolled through the presence in their Aura of an Entity or energy blockage. When a person is stuck on the right, the male manic side, then the body becomes wiry and thin and heart attacks become prevalent. When stuck on the left, the female depressive side the person becomes lethargic and fat and easily depressed.

The technique of Kundalini Yoga consists in using Prana (the vital air), guiding its circulatory movement through Ida and Pingala down to the base of the spine into the space where Kundalini lies coiled. The vital energies of the opposite forces circulating in Ida and Pingala will be unified and Shakti Kundalini will then awaken and rise up Sushumna, energizing the seven chakras.

Kundalini activation of the Left channel activates the side of the brain and awakens prophesy, intuition and prediction. Kundalini awakening of the Right channel awakens the side of the brain controlling healing and the giving of energy, control over nature, matter and the mind. However, Kundalini awakening of either the right or left channels alone is an unbalanced awakening and can lead to madness. The balanced Kundalini awakening of the central channel means liberation from the dream of life and death. When the right and left energies are balanced, the central column can become activated and the person can then choose whether he wants to be active or relaxed.

(iii) Importance of awakening sushumna:

Sushumna nadi is regarded as a hollow tube in which there are three more concentric tubes, each being progressively more subtle than the previous one. The tubes or nadis are as follows: sushumna - signifying tamas, vajrini - signifying rajas, chitrini – signifying sattva and Brahma - signifying consciousness. The higher consciousness created by kundalini passes through Brahma nadi. When kundalini shakti awakens it passes through sushumna nadi. The moment the awakening takes place in muladhara chakra, the energy makes headway through sushumna up to ajna chakra.

Muladhara chakra is just like a powerful generator. In order to start this generator, you need some sort of pranic energy. This pranic energy is generated through pranayama. When you practice pranayama you generate energy and this energy is forced down by a positive pressure which starts the generator in muladhara. Then this generated energy is pushed upward by a negative pressure and forced up to ajna chakra. Therefore, awakening of sushumna is just as important as awakening of kundalini.

Supposing you have started your generator but you have not plugged the cable, the generator will keep running but distribution will not take place. You have to connect the plug into the generator so the generated energy can pass through the cable to the different areas of your house.

When only ida and pingala are active and not sushumna, it is like having the positive and negative lines in your electrical cable, but no earth. When the mind receives the three currents of energy all the lights start working, but if you remove the earth wire, the lights will go down. Energy flows through ida and pingala all the time, but its effulgence is very low. When there is a current flowing in ida, pingala and sushumna, the enlightenment takes place. This is how you have to understand the awakening of kundalini, awakening of sushumna and the union of the three in ajna chakra.

The whole science of kundalini yoga concerns the awakening of sushumna, for once sushumna comes to life, a means of communication between the higher and lower dimensions of consciousness is established and the awakening of kundalini occurs. Shakti travels up sushumna to become one with Shiva in sahasrara.

2.6 Brain Waves Frequencies: Gamma, Beta, Alpha, Theta, Delta

All humans display five different types of electrical patterns or "brain waves" across the cortex. The brain waves can be observed with an EEG (or an "electroencephalograph") – a tool that allows researchers to note brain wave patterns. Each brain wave has a purpose and helps serve us in optimal mental functioning.

Our brain's ability to become flexible and/or transition through various brain wave frequencies plays a large role in how successful we are in managing stress, focusing on tasks, and getting a good night's sleep. If one of the five types of brain waves is either over-produced and/or under-produced in our brain, it can cause problems. For this reason, it is important to understand that there is no single brain wave that is "better" or more "optimal" than the others. Each brainwave frequency serves a purpose to help us cope with various situations – whether it is to help us process and learn new information or help us calm down after a long stressful day. The five brain waves in the order of highest frequency to lowest are as follows: **gamma, beta, alpha, theta, and delta.**

It is important to realize that when a certain brain wave is referred to, it is implied that a particular brain wave is "dominant." Throughout the day in your waking state, your EEG will display all 5 types of brain waves at the same time. However, one particular brain wave will be dominant depending on the state of consciousness that you are in.

A description of each of these five brainwaves is given here below:

(i) Gamma Waves

These are involved in higher processing tasks as well as cognitive functioning. Gamma waves are important for learning, memory and information processing. It is thought that the 40 Hz gamma wave is important for the binding of our senses with regards to perception and is involved in learning new material. It has been found that individuals who are mentally challenged and have learning disabilities tend to have lower gamma activity than average.

- Frequency range: 40 Hz to 100 Hz (Highest);

- Too much of intensity and frequency of Gamma waves results in: Anxiety, high arousal, stress;
- Too little of intensity and frequency of Gamma waves results in: ADHD (Attention Deficit Hyperactivity Disorder), depression, learning disabilities;
- Optimal intensity and frequency of Gamma waves results in: Binding senses, cognition, information processing, learning, perception, REM sleep

(ii) Beta Waves

Beta waves are known as high frequency low amplitude brain waves that are commonly observed while we are awake. They are involved in conscious thought, logical thinking, and tend to have a stimulating affect. Having the right amount of beta waves allows us to focus and complete work-based tasks easily. Having too much beta may lead to us experiencing excessive stress and/or anxiety. The higher beta frequencies are associated with high levels of arousal. When you drink caffeine or have another stimulant, your beta activity will naturally increase. Think of these as being very fast brain waves that most people exhibit throughout the day in order to complete conscious tasks such as: critical thinking, writing, reading, and socialization.

- Frequency range of Beta waves: 12 Hz to 40 Hz (High)
- Too much of Beta waves: Adrenaline, anxiety, high arousal, inability to relax, stress
- Too little of Beta waves: ADHD, daydreaming, depression, poor cognition
- Optimal of Beta waves: Conscious focus, memory, problem solving

(iii) Alpha Waves

Alpha wave frequency range bridges the gap between our conscious thinking and subconscious mind. In other words, alpha is the frequency range between beta and theta. It helps us calm down when necessary and promotes feelings of deep relaxation. If we become stressed, a phenomenon called "alpha blocking" may occur which involves excessive beta activity and very little alpha. Essentially the beta waves "block" out the production of alpha because we become too aroused.

- Frequency range: 8 Hz to 12 Hz (Moderate)
- Too much: Daydreaming, inability to focus, too relaxed
- Too little: Anxiety, high stress, insomnia, OCD (Obsessive Compulsive Disorder)
- Optimal: Relaxation

(iv) Theta Waves

Theta waves frequency range is involved in daydreaming and sleep. Theta waves are connected to us experiencing and feeling deep and raw emotions. Too much theta activity may make people prone to bouts of depression and may make them "highly suggestible" based on the fact that they are in a deeply relaxed, semi-hypnotic state. Theta has its benefits of helping improve our intuition, creativity, and makes us feel more natural. It is also involved in restorative sleep. As long as theta is not produced in excess during our waking hours, it is a very helpful brain wave range.

- Frequency range: 4 Hz to 8 Hz (Slow)
- Too much: ADHD, depression, hyperactivity, impulsivity, inattentiveness
- Too little: Anxiety, poor emotional awareness, stress
- Optimal: Creativity, emotional connection, intuition, relaxation

(v) Delta Waves

Delta waves are the slowest recorded brain waves in human beings. They are found most often in infants as well as young children. As we age, we tend to produce fewer amounts of delta waves even during deep sleep. They are associated with the deepest levels of relaxation and restorative, healing sleep. They have also been found to be involved in unconscious bodily functions such as regulating heart beat and digestion. Adequate production of delta waves helps us feel completely rejuvenated after we wake up from a good night's sleep. If there is abnormal delta activity, an individual may experience learning disabilities or have difficulties maintaining conscious awareness (such as in cases of brain injuries).

- Frequency range: 0 Hz to 4 Hz (Slowest)
- Too much: Brain injuries, learning problems, inability to think, severe ADHD
- Too little: Inability to rejuvenate body, inability to revitalize the brain, poor sleep
- Optimal: Immune system, natural healing, restorative / deep sleep

2.7 Bija Mantras (बीज मंत्र) as Spiritual Diet to Seven Chakras

We have discussed earlier about the seven chakras in human body. Each chakra has its own significance. There is a specific mantra (called the 'Bija mantra') for each chakra. It is illustrated and described here below:

Figure 2.10: Seven Chakras and their Bija Mantras

Seven Chakras and their Bija Mantras

Muladhara (मूलाधार) Chakra: Base or Root Chakra: Cervix/ Perineum Bija Mantra: ***Lam***

Frequency in Hz: 261.6, 523.3, 1046.5, 2093, 4186
It keeps you grounded. Connects your feet, to the earth.

Swadhisthana (स्वाधिष्ठान) Chakra:
Sacral Chakra: last bone in spinal cord
Bija Mantra: ***Vam***
Frequency in Hz: 293.7, 587.3, 1174.7, 2349.3, 4698.7
Helps in Emotions, Passion, intuition and creativity.

Manipura (मणिपूर)
Solar Plexus Chakra : Navel area
Mantra: ***Ram***
Frequency in Hz: 329.6, 659.3, 1318.5, 2637.1, 5274.1
Confidence, Assertiveness, ability to be a stand and say 'No'. Enhances Will Power.

Anahata (अनाहत) Chakra:
Heart Chakra: Heart area
Mantra: ***Yam***
Frequency in Hz: 349.2, 698.5, 1396.9, 2793.9, 5587.7
Love, Kindness, Compassion, Harmonious relationships

Visuddha (विशुद्ध) Chakra:
Throat Chakra (throat and neck area)
Mantra: ***Ham***
Frequency in Hz: 196, 392, 784, 1568, 3136
Self-Expression and Open communication.

Ajna (आज्ञा) Or Brow Chakra:
Third Eye Chakra (pineal gland or ***third eye***)
Mantra: ***OM***
Frequency in Hz: 110, 220, 440, 880, 1760, 3520.
Insight and visualization.
Opens up your perceptive physic ability.

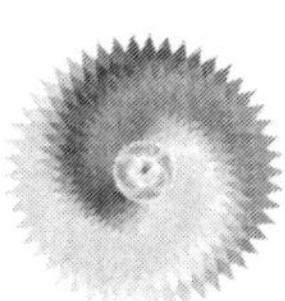

Sahasrara (सहस्रार) Chakra:
Crown Chakra (Top of the head; 'Soft spot' of a newborn)
Mantra: ***No Sound***
Frequency in Hz: 123.5, 246.9, 493.9, 987.8, 1975.5, 3951.1
Wisdom. Connecting you to your higher self and spirituality.

2.8 Pranayama (प्राणायाम)

Pranayama (prana = energy + yama = control) is a type of meditation technique that involves various ways of controlling the breathing, with the goal being to withdraw ones senses from the outside world. This helps one to raise one's prana (or Kundalini energy in this case) up the deep spine to the spiritual eye or sixth chakra, which brings one to enlightenment. It is also the fourth limb of spiritual advancement as laid out in Patanjali's Yoga Sutras. According to Maharishi Patanjali, there are eight stages of Yoga, called 'Ashtanga Yoga'. These are (i) Yama (personal discipline), (ii) Niyama (social discipline), (iii) Asana (discipline of body posture), ***(iv) Pranayama*** (rhythmic breathing exercises), (v) Pratyahara (inward withdrawal of the senses), (vi) Dharana (concentration), (vii) Dhyana (meditation), and Samadhi (total awareness and evenness "Sama" of one's true self without conflicts)

तस्मिन् सति श्वासप्रश्वास्योर्गतिविच्छेदः प्राणायामः ।।
– (दर्शन शास्त्रः योग दर्शन, 2.49)

tasmin sati svasta-prasvasyor-gati-vicchedah praṇayamah ||
– (Darshan Shastra: Yoga Darshana, 2.49)

Meaning: Regulation of breath or the control of Prana is the stoppage of inhalation and exhalation, which follows after securing that steadiness of posture or seat, Asana.

By exercising control over this breathing one can control the subtle Prana inside. Control of Prana means control of mind. Mind cannot operate without the help of Prana. The vibrations of Prana only produce thoughts in the mind. It is the Prana that moves the mind. It is Prana that sets the mind in motion. It is the Sukshma Prana or Psychic Prana that is intimately connected with the mind.

चले वाते चलं चित्तं निश्चले निश्चलं भवेत् ।
योगी स्थाणुत्वम् आप्नोति ततो वायुं निरोधयेत् ।।
– हठयोगप्रदीपिका–2

chale vate chalam chittam nischale nischalam bhavet.
yogi sthanutvam apnoti tato vayum nirodhayet.
– Hathayogapradipika-2

Meaning: When prana moves, chitta (the mental force) moves. When prana is without movement, chitta is without movement. By this (steadiness of prana) the yogi attains steadiness and should thus restrain the vayu (air).

The yogis practicing the complete mastery over mind and body came to a conclusion that when the breath moves, the mind moves and when the breath stops, the mind stops. So, whosoever wants to still the mind should bring his/her breath under complete voluntary control.

Further, it is said that:

यावद्वायुः स्थितो देहे तावज्जीवनमुच्यते।
मरणं तस्य निष्क्रान्तिः ततो वायुं निरोधयेत्।।
— (गोरक्षशतकम् 2, 91)

Yavadvayuh sthito dehe tavajjivanamuchyate.
Maranam tasya nishkrantih tato vayum nirodhyet.
(Gorakshashatakram 2, 91)

Meaning: As long as there is air in the body, there is life, out of the air (death) is death, so air should be regulated.

In Patanjali's Yoga Sutras, it says:

बाह्याभ्यन्तरस्थम्भ वृत्तिः देशकालसन्ख्याभिः परिदृष्टो दीर्घसूक्ष्मः।
— पातञ्जल योगदर्शन, 2.50

bāhya-ābhyantara-sthambha vṛttiḥ deśa-kāla-sankhyābhiḥ
paridṛṣṭo dīrgha-sūkṣmaḥ .
-Yoga Sutras. 2.50

Meaning: Exhalation, inhalation, retention, technique, time and number must be very precisely regulated over a lengthy duration.

बाह्याभ्यन्तर विषयाक्षेपी चतुर्थः।।
— पातञ्जल योगदर्शन, 2.51

bāhya-ābhyantara viṣaya-akṣepī caturthaḥ.
– Yoga Sutras. 2.51

Meaning: The fourth pranayama technique ultimately transcends breath retention after exhaling or inhaling. ||51||

When the breath is expired, it is *Rechaka*, the first kind of Pranayama. When the breath is drawn in, it is the second, termed *Puraka*. When it is suspended, it is the third kind, called *Kumbhaka*. Kumbhaka is retention of breath. Kumbhaka increases the period of life. It augments the inner spiritual force, vigour and vitality. If you retain the breath for one minute, this one minute is added to your span of life.

2.9 Types of Prana Vayus (प्राण वायु)

As stated earlier, *Prana* means life. The word *vayu* translates as 'wind', connoting (means conveying in addition to exact explicit meaning) the all-pervading movement. The root 'va' means "that which flows" – and so a vayu is a vehicle for activities and experiences within the body, or a "force" that moves throughout the system controlling functions such as digestion, respiration, nerve impulses act. *Prana Vayu* is the life force. Without this there will be no life, it will simply be a dead body. This cohesive force is also known as "*Maha Prana*" or great prana. In the human body, this universal prana has been observed to move in specific ways in specific regions in the body, regulating and controlling physical and mental function. Though there are 49 distinct prana vayus or types of vayus in the body, five principle vayus or "***pancha pranas***" are important for the yogi to recognize.

These pancha (five) pranas are categorized as: (i) Prana vayu (प्राण वायु, inhalation), (ii) Apana vayu (अपान वायु, exhalation), (iii) Samana vayu (समान वायु), (iv) Udana vayu (उदान वायु), and (v) Vyana vayu (व्यानु वायु). Though they function in unison together, each is governing a specific area of the body, they can be thought of as elemental forces that are not just the physical, but govern emotional qualities and mental energies, fundamental to physical, mental and emotional well- being.

(i) Prana Vayu: While "Prana" is the general name of the life force, the prana vayu is one of its specific functions. Prana vayu literally means "forward moving air" and moves inward toward the centre of the body. Prana vayu is the energy that receives things coming into the body in the form of food (eating), liquids (drinking) and air (breathing) as well as all sensory perceptions and mental experiences. Prana is propulsive by nature and is the driving force for all the other vayus. The energy known as prana vayu governs the region from the abdomen or diaphragm to the base of the throat. The "seat" of the prana vayu is the heart, and this vayu ensures that the heart goes on beating. It is associated with the element of air. It works to maintain the proper temperature of the body relative to one's environment, and sustains one's vital organs, particularly the heart. Though its seat is in the heart, it moves through the centre of the body in a downward direction from the base of the throat to the navel, as well as from the navel back up to the throat.

(ii) Apana Vayu: Apana vayu translates as "the air that moves away". The dominant energy of Apana vayu is a downward and outward movement. Its energy moves primarily in the lower abdomen from the navel to the floor of the pelvis. Apana is the aspect of the prana that governs the ability to eject or eliminate what is not needed to the system. Just as with the breath we exhale what is not needed after assimilating the in-breath, the apana vayu is the force behind the elimination of waste in general, working in the kidneys, colon, rectum, bladder and genitals. It is also the moving force in the process of reproduction – which essentially moves new life 'out' into the world – from insemination to childbirth. The healthy functioning of the apana vayu is as vital as that of the prana vayu. Without the healthy functioning of apana vayu, one lacks motivation and determination; one feels lazy, dull and even confused, indecisive and befuddled.

Apana vayu is associated with the element of earth, which is concerned with having a strong, sure and reliable foundation, especially in fundamental matters of survival. The seat of the apana vayu is in the core of the pelvis, and it governs from the navel to the perineum. As with Prana vayu can have both a downward movement in the body as well as an upward movement within its primary region.

Prana vayu and Apana vayu move in complimentary opposite directions during inhale and exhale. As you inhale, Prana vayu moves upward from the navel to the chest, while Apana vayu moves downward from the navel toward the floor of the pelvis. On exhaling, both move in the reverse direction; Prana moving from the base of the throat down to the navel and Apana moving from the perineum back up the navel. Both oscillate from the centre of the abdomen.

अपाने जुह्वति प्राण प्राणेऽपानं तथाऽपरे।
प्राणापानगती रुद्ध्वा प्राणायामपरायणाः।।

– श्रीमद् भगवद्गीता, 4.29

Apane juhvati pranam pranepanam tathapare;
Pranapanagatee ruddhva pranayamaparayanah.

– Srimad Bhagavad Gita, 4.29

Meaning: Some offer Prana (outgoing breath) in Apana (incoming breath) and Apana in Prana, restraining the passage of Prana and Apana, absorbed in Pranayama. Pranayama is a precious Yajna (sacrifice).

Some practise the kind of Pranayama called Puraka (filling in). Some practise the kind of Pranayama called Rechaka (emptying). Some are engaged in the practice of Pranayama called Kumbhaka, by impeding the outward passage of air, through the nostrils and the mouth, and by impeding the inward passage of the air, in the opposite direction.

The chief aim of Pranayama is to unite the Prana with the Apana and take the united Pranapana slowly towards the head. The effect or fruit of Pranayama is Udghata or awakening of the sleeping Kundalini.

(iii) Samana Vayu: It is literally "the balancing air" Moves primarily in the region between the navel and the heart and its seat is said to be in the navel. It is the controlling power of the metabolism or "digestive fire" and the functioning of the digestive organs and glands. It also governs the assimilation of oxygen from the air we breathe. It is also the vayu that unifies the two opposite forces of prana vayu and apana.

Samana vayu is associated with the element of fire. When unbalanced, its fiery energy can be used to assert one's will or to dominate, especially through anger. In the yoga tradition, anger is the direct result of a combination of desire, delusion and lack of discrimination.

(iv) Udana Vayu: Udana is "that which carries upward." It rules the region of the throat and head and is seated specifically in the throat. It also rules muscle function and strength in the extremities as well as the sensory function of the eyes, ears and nose. It is said to be the force behind all growth, our ability to stand erect, speech, effort, enthusiasm and will. While apana vayu is concerned with elimination or outward moving energy in general, udana vayu is the specific force that expels air with the exhalation in a way that is particularly concerned with speech and the production of sound. In the region of the head, its function is mental and expressive in the form of ideas and speech. When udana is unbalanced, speech is disjointed and one cannot speak or articulate ideas properly. Imbalances can also cause shortness of breath and other respiratory problems particularly associated with the throat, which can have their root in obstacles to self-expression, or emotional repression.

Ether or space is the element associated with this vayu. This upward moving energy continues through the upper chakra, the Ajna chakra, to the Sahasrara, and is purified during the upward journey.

(v) Vyana Vayu: It literally means "outward moving air" and moves from the centre of the body out to the periphery. This vayu pervades the whole body, and is a coordinating, connecting force. It has no specific seat, but rather coordinates all the powers such as sensory awareness, and runs through the whole network of the 72,000 nadis (glands) or passageways of prana in the body, connecting the functions of the nerves, veins, muscles and joints and circulates nutrients and energy. Its function is cohesive and is associated with the element of water. Vyana vayu is fundamental to making one feel and function as an integrated whole. Though it governs and coordinates all of the senses as well as the functioning of all muscles, both voluntary and involuntary, it is felt especially in the skin. Goosebumps and perspiration, and all of the various actions and reactions of the skin to the environment are manifestations of vyana vayu.

Within the body, Vyana vayu governs our internal sense of coordination, balance and physical integrity or cohesiveness. When unbalanced, one feels uncoordinated and clumsy. Coordination between mind and body suffers, and one's own thoughts can be disjointed, fluctuating and rambling. Dysfunctions in Vyana vayu can also lessen our power of sensation.

"Gheranda Samhita," was written in Sanskrit in the late 17th century. The seven chapters of "Gheranda Samhita" follow the sevenfold path of yoga, which was taught by the sage Gheranda to his student, Chanda Kapali. It is focused on the shatkarmas and differs in a few respects from the path of yoga that is described by Patanjali in the Yoga Sutras. The fifth chapter of Gheranda Samhita deals with the lightness through Pranayama.

According to Gheranda Samhita (घेरण्ड संहिता, 5.61-62):

हृदि प्राणो वहेन्नित्यमपानो गुदमण्डले।
समानो नाभिदेशे तु उदानः कण्ठमध्यगः ।।61।।

Hridiprano vahennityam apano gudamandale.
Samano naabhideshetu udanah kanthamadhyamah. (5.61)

व्योनो व्याप्य शरीरे तु प्रधानाः पञ्च वायवः।
प्राणाद्याः पञ्च विख्याता नागाद्याः पञ्च वायवः।।62।।

Vyano vyapya shatire tu pradhanh panchavayavah.
Pranadyah pancha vikhyata nagadyah panchavayavah. (5.62)

Meaning (61-62): The Prana moves always in the heart; the Apana in the sphere of anus; the Samana in the naval region; the Udana in the throat; and the vyana pervades the whole body. These are the five principal Vayus, known as Pranadi. They belong to the Inner body. The Nagadi five Vayus belong to the Outer body.

Srimad Bhagavad Gita (श्रीमद्भगवद्गीता) also mentions about Prana, Apana vayu, as given here below:

अपाने जुह्वति प्राणं प्राणेऽपानं तथापरे।
प्राणापानगती रुद्ध्वा प्राणायामपरायणाः।। 4–29।।

apāne juhvati prāṇaṃ prāṇe'pānaṃ tathāpare ||
prāṇāpānagatī ruddhvā prāṇāyāmaparāyaṇāḥ || 4-29 ||

Meaning: Still others, who are inclined to the process of breath restraint to remain in trance, practice by offering the movement of the outgoing breath into the incoming, and the incoming breath into the outgoing, and thus at last remain in trance, stopping all breathing. Others, curtailing the eating process, offer the outgoing breath into itself as a sacrifice.

स्पर्शान्कृत्वा बहिर्बाह्यांश्चक्षुश्चौवान्तरे भ्रुवोः।
प्राणापानौ समौ कृत्वा नासाभ्यन्तरचारिणौ ।। 5–27।।

sparśānkṛtvā bahirbāhyāṃścakṣuścaivāntare bhruvoḥ |
prāṇāpānau samau kṛtvā nāsābhyantaracāriṇau || 5-27 ||

Meaning: Having external contacts excluded, and with gaze fixed between the eye-brows; having made equal the outgoing and incoming breaths moving within the nostrils.

अहं वैश्वानरो भूत्वा प्राणिनां देहमाश्रितः।
प्राणापानसमायुक्तः पचाम्यन्नं चतुर्विधम्।। 15–14।।

ahaṃ vaiśvānaro bhūtvā prāṇināṃ dehamāśritaḥ |
prāṇāpānasamāyuktaḥ pacāmyannaṃ caturvidham || 15-14 ||

Meaning: I, having become the Fire of Life, take possession of the bodies of breathing things, and united with the life-breaths I digest the four kinds of food.

The phase of breathing in during a Pranayama (प्राणायाम) is called a Pooraka (पूरक, inhaling) and that of breathing out is called a Rechaka (रेचक, exhaling); the intermediate phase of holding the breath in and out are called the Antah Kumbhaka and Bahya Kumbhaka

Direction of Pranic movement (vayus) in the Physical body

- Prana moves down from the base of the throat to the navel (the pranic centre) and energizes and all the vayus. It also moves up from the navel to the throat.
- Udana moves primarily up from the throat up to the head
- Apana moves from the navel down to the floor of the pelvis.
- Samana moves from the periphery of the body into the core.
- Vyana moves from the core out to the periphery.

The whole universe is nothing but the vibrations of sound. The fire (Agni) creates sound while burning, the flowing water creates sound, the air creates sound when it strikes with leaves or other objects, and the earth creates sound when it rotates around the sun or about its own axis.

'Pranayam (breathing exercise)' is for the very purpose of re-establishing the interface between the Supreme Soul (God) and the individual soul (Human being). Through Pranayama, the individual is reminded of that eternal relationship with the Creator.

Chapter - 3

Ajna Chakra and the Third Eye

According to Srimad Bhagavad Gita:

प्रयाणकाले मनसाऽचलेन
भक्त्या युक्तो योगबलेन चौव।
भ्रुवोर्मध्ये प्राणमावेश्य सम्यक्
स तं परं पुरुषमुपैति दिव्यम्।।
– भगवद् गीता अध्याय 8, श्लोक 10

Prayaanakaale manasaa chalena
bhaktyaa yukto yogabalena chaiva .
Bhruvormadhye praanamaaveshya samyak
sa tam param purushhamupaiti divyam.
– Srimad Bhagavad Gita 8.10

Meaning: At the time of death with steadfast mind and devotion; making the flow of Pranic impulse rise up (to the middle of two eye brows) by the power of yoga and holding there; attains the Supreme divine spirit.

3.1 Ajna Chakra

Our reflection on the psychic centres begins from ajna chakra. According to tradition, muladhara is generally designated as the first chakra since it is the seat of kundalini shakti. However, there is another system in which the consideration and the study of the chakras commence from ajna. Ajna chakra is the point of confluence where the three main nadis or forces – Ida, pingala and sushumna merge into one stream of consciousness and flow up to sahasrara, the crown centre.

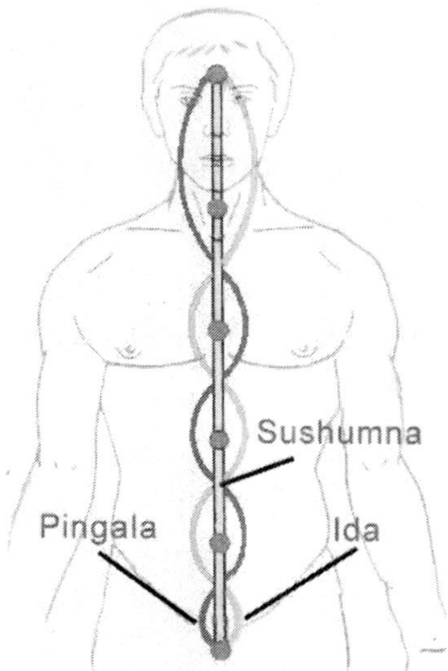

Figure 3.1: Sushumna, Ida and Pingala nadis start at muladhara chakra and again meet at Ajna Chakra (the location of Third Eye)

In mythology, these three nadis are represented by three great rivers - Ganga (Ida), Yamuna (Pingala) and Saraswati (a subterranean current which represents Sushumna). They converge at a place called Prayag or Triveni, which is in present-day Allahabad. Hindus believe that every twelve years, when the sun is in Aquarius, if one takes a dip at the point of confluence, he or she will be purified. This place of confluence in the human body corresponds symbolically to ajna chakra. When the mind is concentrated at this conjunction, the transformation of individual consciousness is brought about by the merging of the three great forces. Individual consciousness is mainly comprised of ego, and it is on account of ego that we are aware of dualities. As long as there is duality there cannot be samadhi; as long as you remember yourself you cannot get out of yourself.

Although there are experiences of trance in other chakras, there is no merger of the individual ego with the cosmic ego. All throughout, you find that you are trying to assert yourself behind all the experiences you are having, but when Ida and pingala unite with sushumna in ajna chakra, you lose yourself completely. It does not mean that you become unconscious. Your awareness expands and becomes homogeneous. Then the individual awareness falls flat and you completely transcend the realm of duality. Thus ajna chakra is a very important centre, which one must experience in order to bring about purification of the mind. Once the mind is purified, the experience and awakening of the other chakras can proceed.

There is a certain problem with the awakening of the other chakras. Each one contains a store of karmas or samskara, good and bad, positive and negative, painful and pleasant. The awakening of any chakra will definitely bring to the surface an explosion or expression of these karmas, and of course, not everybody is prepared or ready to face them. Only those who have reason and understanding are able to cope. Therefore it is said that before you start awakening and manifesting the great force, it is best to purify the mind at the point of confluence. Then, with a purified mind, you can awaken the other chakras. For this reason we begin our exposition of the chakras with the ajna chakra.

3.2 The Centre of Command

The word ajna comes from the Sanskrit root which means 'to know, to obey or to follow'. Literally, ajna means 'command' or 'the monitoring centre'. In astrology ajna is the centre of Jupiter, which symbolizes the Guru or preceptor. Amongst the deities, Jupiter is represented by Brihaspati, the Guru of the Devas and preceptor of the gods. Therefore, this centre is also known as 'the Guru Chakra'. Ajna is the bridge which links the Guru with his disciples. It represents the level at which it is possible for direct mind-to-mind communication to take place between two people. It is in this chakra that in communication with the external guru, the teacher or preceptor takes place. And it is here that the directions of the inner guru are heard in the deepest state of meditation, when all the sense modalities are withdrawn and one enters the state of shoonya or void.

This is a state of absolute nothingness, where the empirical experiences of name and form, subject and object, do not penetrate. In this completely static state, the light of the mind is extinguished; the consciousness ceases to function and no ego awareness remains. This void state is the same as the death experience, and in order to traverse it, the voice or command of the guru must be heard in ajna chakra. At the moment your problems may be just mental - dispersion of mind, worries, anxiety, restlessness, etc., but when the night is dark and you have gone very deep in meditation, losing your individual awareness, the only thing that can guide you at this point is the instructions or command of your guru (external or internal Guru) heard through ajna chakra.

The Ajna chakra has also been called 'the eye of intuition', and it is the doorway through which the individual enters the astral and psychic dimension of consciousness. The most common name for this chakra is 'the third eye', and the mystical traditions of every age and culture make abundant references to it. It is portrayed as a psychic eye located midway between the two physical eyes and it looks inward instead of outward. In Hinduism, ajna chakra is called divya chakshu (the divine eye), gyana chakshu or gyana netra (the eye of knowledge) because it is the channel through which the spiritual aspirant receives revelation and insight into the underlying nature of existence. It is also called 'the eye of Shiva', for Shiva is the epitome of meditation, which is directly associated with the awakening of ajna chakra.

It is interesting to note that ajna chakra is generally more active in females than it is in males. Women are more sensitive, psychic and perceptive and they are often able to predict the coming events. However, in most people this inner eye remains closed, and though they see the events of the outside world, knowledge and understanding of the truth cannot be gained. In this sense, we are blind to the real possibilities of the world, unable to view the deeper levels of human existence.

3.2.1 The Location of Ajna Chakra

The location point of Ajna chakra is in the brain directly behind the eyebrow centre. It is at the very top of the spinal cord, at the medulla oblongata. Initially it is very hard to feel the exact location point of ajna, so we concentrate on ajna kshetram, at the mid-eyebrow centre, bhrumadhya. These two centres are directly connected. That is why it has always been an Indian custom to place tilaka, chandan, sindur or kumkum on the mid-eyebrow centre. Sindur contains mercury, and when it is applied to the eyebrow centre, a constant pressure is exerted on the nerve which runs from bhrumadhya to the medulla oblongata. May be the original purpose for applying these substances has been forgotten by most of the people these days, but it is not a religious mark or even a beauty spot. It is a means by which you can maintain constant conscious and unconscious awareness of ajna chakra. It should also be mentioned here that ajna chakra and the pineal gland are located at the same place. The pituitary gland is sahasrara, and just as the pituitary and pineal glands are intimately connected, so are ajna and sahasrara. We could say that ajna is the gateway to sahasrara chakra. If ajna is awakened and functioning properly, all the experiences happening in sahasrara can be managed well.

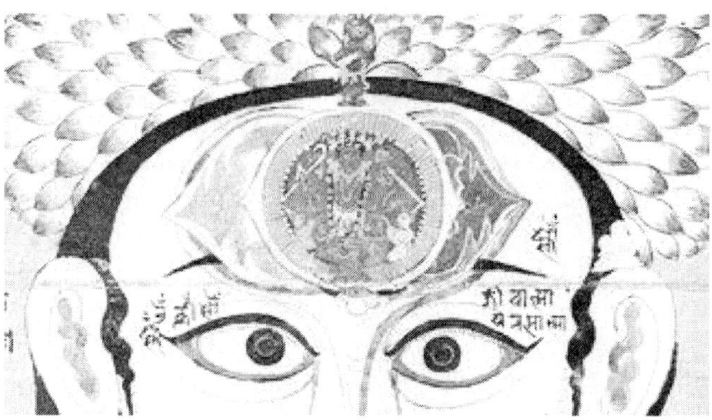

Figure 3.2: Location of Ajna Chakra (Brow Chakra)

Each chakra is considered to possess a tanmatra, or specific sense of modality, a gyanendriya or organ of sense perception, and a karmendriya or organ of action. The tanmatra, gyanendriya and karmendriya of ajna chakra are all considered to be the mind. The mind is able to gain knowledge by subtle means rather than by the input of sense data from the various sense organs, which are the gyanendriyas of the other chakras. The mind perceives knowledge directly via a sixth or intuitive sense, which comes into operation as ajna chakra awakens. This sense is the gyanendriya of the mind. Similarly, the mind can manifest actively without the aid of the physical body. This is the faculty of astral projection, which manifests with the awakening of ajna chakra. Therefore, mind is considered to be the karmendriya of ajna. The mode of operation of this centre is purely mental and so the tanmatra is also the mind. The plane is tapa loka, where vestiges of imperfection are purified and the karmas are burned away. Along with vishuddhi chakra, ajna forms the basis for vigyanamaya kosha, which initiates psychic development.

He who meditates on this awakened chakra sees a flaming lamp shining as the morning sun and he dwells within the regions of fire, sun and moon. He is able to enter another's body at will, and becomes the most excellent amongst munis, being all-knowing and all-seeing. He becomes the benefactor of all and is versed in all the shastras. He realizes his unity with the Brahman and acquires siddhis. Different results accruing out of meditation on the various centres are collectively realized by meditating on this centre alone.

3.3 More on Third Eye and Ajna Chakra

As mentioned earlier, the sixth centre of force, Ajna Chakra is located on the physical level in the space in between the eyebrows, at the middle distance. It is also named "the third eye" or "Shiva's eye". Ajna Chakra represents the superior mental consciousness, which allows the direct perception of the invisible worlds and the direct perception of the subtler aspects of the manifested universe. On the physical level, it coordinates the activity of the pituitary gland (hypophisis) and of the cerebellum. The hypophysis has a vital role in the sense that together with the hypothalamus it constitutes the command system of the rest of endocrine glands. On a psychic level, it controls the superior intuition, clairvoyance, the capacity to anticipate certain events, the instantaneous capacity of perceiving all the qualities of any human being, the extra-sensorial perceptions. The mental centre of command, the centre of brilliant intuitive, spiritual knowledge, Ajna Chakra is one of the three superior centres of force. Ajna Chakra represents for us the third eye oriented both towards our inner universe, and towards the subtle aspects and mental of the world, to the direct perception of the parallel universes.

Ajna Chakra is considered the centre of the spiritual perception. Just as the physical eyes help us establish certain rapports with the exterior things and phenomena analogically Ajna Chakra facilitates and puts our rapports with things, entities and phenomena characteristic to mental and astral subtle manifestations. This Chakra is a focal point of emission-reception of energies, ideas, thoughts, mental structure through which we can conceive and understand coherently the subtle mental universe exterior to our being, its characteristic energies, helping us govern "our inner universe". The person who knows how to focus on Ajna Chakra, the space located in the middle of the forehead, gains through this focus a new perspective on the principles and concepts of time, space and causality. The gradual awakening and the opening of the inner vision on this level means in fact the access to certain superior levels of consciousness that we each have potentially, latently, but which we cannot even imagine. The harmonious activation of Ajna Chakra grants mental insight, telepathic capacities, self-control, mental understanding through intellectual identification, creative intelligence. Ajna Chakra harmoniously activated grants the state of unity, of communion with the cosmic laws, of non-identity with the physical body and identification with its spiritual nature. The person who focuses intensely and meditates deeply on Ajna charka will destroy gradually the negative effects of his or her previous bad actions, from this life and from the previous lives. It thus leads the human being to the most refined and elevated inner perceptions, through the awakening, enhancement and control of the mental energies. This means evading from the limited concepts of the consciousness that is mainly focused on experiences and phenomena in which we realize, we are one with the Infinite. All these mean also surpassing the barrier of time, space and causality, which are apparently inexorable. The adept becomes a great yogi and a jivanmukta, a liberated person while still alive. He or she will obtain the 8 great paranormal powers (siddhis) and the 32 minor paranormal powers.

The real opening of the third eye equals the combination of analysis and discrimination, characterizing the right hemisphere with the opening and direct access to the intuitive world, characterizing the left hemisphere. This means ending both the sterile intellectualization and the superstition of fantasist "premonitions". The awakening of Ajna Chakra is the harmonious union of these two ways of knowledge into one. On the path of spiritual evolution, the devotee who aspires to the supreme perfection will gradually go through various mental levels, identified by the great yogis as follows: ordinary mental, superior mental, illuminated mental, intuitive mental and supra-mental. These different levels correspond to deeper and deeper awakenings of the consciousness and to the access to increasingly elevated levels. From a fragmented vision of reality, one can reach gradually a sublime overall view. On this superior level, there is an inflaming state of enthusiasm and happiness, accompanied by a spontaneous blossoming of the creative capacities. In this respect, it is known the fact that the awakening and harmony of Ajna Chakra leads to the control of the sexual energies corresponding to the second centre of force, Svadhishthana Chakra. When person reaches the level of consciousness of Ajna Chakra, focusing there, then this person has the direct knowledge of the Supreme Self Atman. For this person, there is only a transparent veil, like silk.

3.4 Ajna and the Mind

Ajna is essentially the chakra of the mind, representing a higher level of awareness. Whenever you concentrate on something, whether it is muladhara, swadhisthana or manipura chakra, or you concentrate on an external object or an idea, ajna is affected, sometimes mildly, sometimes powerfully, depending on the degree of your concentration. When we visualize or when we dream at night, the inner vision that occurs is through ajna chakra. If you are eating, sleeping or talking and you are not aware of it, then ajna chakra is not operating. But if you are talking and one area of your awareness knows it, this knowing, this awareness is the faculty of ajna chakra.

When you develop ajna chakra, you can have knowledge without the aid of the senses. Normally, all knowledge comes to us by means of information the senses conduct to the brain, and a process of classification, logic and intellect that takes place in the frontal brain. However, the smaller brain, where ajna chakra is situated, has the capacity to acquire knowledge directly without the aid of the indriyas or senses. Supposing it is a very cloudy day, you can know, through logic that it will rain. But if there are no clouds in the sky and still you know beyond a doubt that it will rain, this means your intuition and perception are very acute and ajna chakra is functioning.

When ajna chakra is awakened, fickleness of the individual mind disperses and the purified buddhi (subtle intelligence or higher perception) manifests. Attachment, which is the cause of ignorance and lack of discrimination drops away, and sankalpa shakti (will power) becomes very strong. Mental resolves are almost immediately converted into fruits, provided they are in accordance with individual dharma.

Ajna chakra is the witnessing centre where one becomes the detached observer of all events, including those within the body and mind. Here the level of awareness is developed whereby one begins to 'see' the hidden essence underlying all visible appearances. When ajna chakra is awakened, the meaning and significance of symbols flashes into one's conscious perception and intuitive knowledge arises effortlessly.

Ajna chakra is the centre of extrasensory perception where various siddhis (accomplishments) manifest according to one's samskaras or mental tendencies. For this reason, ajna chakra is said to resemble a knot directly on top of the spinal cord. According to tantra this knot is called rudra granthi, the knot of Shiva. This knot is symbolic of the aspirant's attachment to the newly developed siddhis which accompany the awakening of ajna chakra. The knot effectively blocks the spiritual evolution until attachment to psychic phenomena is overcome and the knot in consciousness is freed.

3.5 Understanding Cause and Effect

Until ajna chakra awakens, we are under delusions; we view things incorrectly and we have many great misconceptions, about love and attachment, hatred and jealousy, tragedy and comedy, victory and defeat, and so many things. Our fears are unfounded, so are our jealousies and attachments. Our mind is functioning within a limited sphere and we can't transcend it. Just as we dream at night and our dream experiences are relative, we are also dreaming in our waking state and our experiences are relative. In the same way that we wake from a dream, when ajna awakens, there is also a process of waking up from this present dream we are living, and we can fully understand the relationship between cause and effect.

It is necessary for us to understand the law of cause and effect in relation to our lives otherwise we shall remain depressed and sorrowful about certain events in life. Supposing you give birth to a child and shortly after it dies. Why did it happen? This is what everybody would ask, isn't it? If a child was meant to die straight after birth, why was it born at all? You can only understand the reason if you understand the laws of cause and effect.

Cause and effect are not immediate events. Each and every action is both a cause and an effect. This life we have is an effect, but what was the cause? You have to discover it. Then you can understand the relationship between cause and effect. It is only after awakening of ajna chakra that these laws can be known. Thereafter your whole philosophical attitude and approach to life changes. No events of life will affect you adversely, and the various objects and experiences that come into your life and fade out of your life do not disturb you at all. You participate in all the affairs of life and you live fully, but as a detached witness. Life flows like a fast current and you surrender and move with it.

3.6 Ascending from Ajna Chakra to Sahasrara Chakra

It requires sadhana, discipline, firm belief and persistent effort to reach ajna chakra. With our present state of mind it is not possible to know how to reach sahasrara, but once ajna chakra becomes active, you develop superior perception and you realize how sahasrara can be reached. It is like setting out on a journey from Delhi to Somnath temple via Rajkot. Once you reach Rajkot, reaching Somnath temple in a taxi is no problem. So it is not important for us to know how to reach sahasrara from ajna chakra, but it is essential for us to know how to awaken ajna chakra.

Chapter - 4

Pineal Gland and the Third Eye

4.1 Location and Significance of the Pineal Gland

A region of the head perceived between the two eyebrows is called the 'third eye', which consists of the pineal gland. Its shape resembles a tiny pinecone (hence its name in Latin, pinea, which means "pinecone"). The Hebrew word *Penial* translates as the 'face of God'. The pineal gland is a photosensitive organ. It is also called the epiphysis cerebri, epiphysis or conarium. It is a small endocrine gland in the vertebrate brain. It produces serotonin and melatonin, hormones that affect the mood and modulate our wake/sleep patterns and seasonal functions. Some people (depending on their faith and background) also term it as the 'mind's eye' or the 'third eye' or 'divine eye' or 'all seeing eye' or 'eye of the soul' or 'inner eye' or 'eye of illumination' or 'eye of wisdom' or 'eye of Horus', or 'eye of providence' or 'brow chakra' or 'sixth sense' etc.

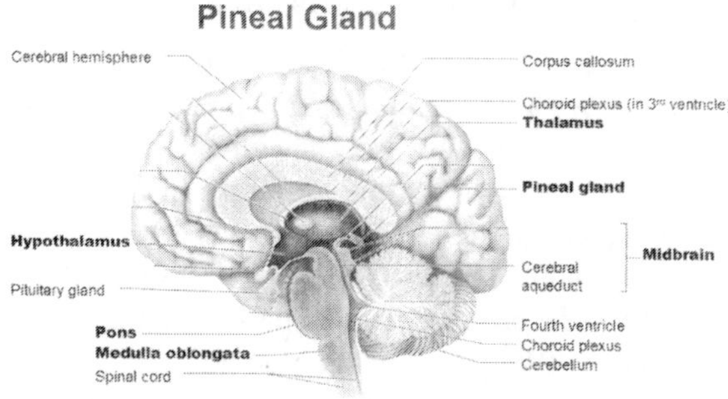

Figure 4.1: Display of location of Pineal Gland in the brain

The mechanism of inner sight (insight or intuition) uses an inner third eye, seated in the pineal gland. This gland, somewhat a mystery to the modern allopathic medicine, has been well known to Ayurvedic medicine practioners in India, to Chinese medicine, to Druidic, Judaic, Sufism, Taoists, Mayan, Tibetan monks, Aboriginal, many other countries; and to the ancient Egypt, Sumeria, Assyria, Babylonia, Greece, Rome and Mesoamerica.

There are eighty-four meridian points on the upper palate of a human mouth. One can feel that upper palate with the tongue and experience its different surfaces. There are two rows of meridian points on the upper palate and on the gum behind the upper teeth. The tongue stimulates those meridian points, and they in turn stimulate the hypothalamus, which makes the pineal gland radiate. When the pineal gland radiates, it creates an imposition in the pituitary gland. When the pituitary gland gives impulsation, the entire glandular system secretes, and a human being feels himself in a blissful state.

Pineal gland is activated by Light, and it controls the various biorhythms of the human body. It works in harmony with the hypothalamus gland, which directs the bodies thirst, hunger, sexual desire and the biological clock that determines our aging process.

When the pineal gland awakens, one feels a pressure at the base of the brain. This pressure will often be experienced, when connecting to higher frequency. It is also known that sometimes a head injury can also Activation of the Pineal Gland: the opening of the Third Eye.

While the physiological functions of the Pineal Gland has been unknown until recent times, mystical traditions and esoteric schools have long known this area in the middle of the brain to be the connecting link between the physical and spiritual worlds.

As we create and change the electromagnetic energy fields and react to these energy stimuli around us, the pineal gland also changes, expanding its possibilities and its connections with different realms and vibrations, helping us to decode different frequencies and codes of Light. A magnetic field is created around the pineal gland by focusing the mind on the midway point, between the pineal gland and the pituitary body. The creative imagination visualizes something and the thought energy of the mind gives life and direction to this form.

When activated, the pineal gland becomes the line of communication with the higher planes. The crown chakra reaches down until its vortex touches the pineal gland.

4.2 Relationship of Pineal Gland with other Organs

There is an occult relationship between the pineal gland and other organs of the body. For example, its activity has an effect on the heart, as an organ of the spiritual consciousness. The aura of the Pineal Gland vibrates during the activity of the Consciousness in the Brain, and shows the play of the seven colours. This septenary disturbance and play of light around the Pineal Gland are reflected in the Heart, or rather in the aura of the Heart, which is negative to the brain in the ordinary man. This aura then vibrates and illumines the seven brains of the Heart, as that of the Pineal Gland illumines the seven centres in the Brain. If the Heart could, in its turn, become positive and impress the Brain, the spiritual Consciousness would reach the lower Consciousness. This is the "memory of the Heart"; and the capacity to impress it on the Brain, so that it becomes part of its Consciousness, which is the "opening of the Third Eye."

The activity of the pineal gland, in its turn, is affected by that of the brain as a whole, and in particular by the medulla oblongata. Of course, the normal and abnormal state of the brain, and the degree of active work in the medulla oblongata, reacts powerfully on the pineal gland, for, owing to the number of "centres" in that region, which controls by far the greater majority of the physiological actions of the animal economy, and also owing to the close and intimate neighbourhood of the two, there must be exerted a very powerful "inductive" action by the medulla on the pineal gland.

The medulla oblongata is among the oldest evolutionary parts of the brain. Anatomically, it connects the higher levels of the brain to the spinal cord. It is responsible for regulating several basic functions of the autonomic nervous system which include respiration, the cardiac centre (sympathetic and parasympathetic system), the vasomotor centre, and the reflex centres of vomiting, coughing, sneezing, and swallowing. People who experience brain damage can still have functioning bodies, as long as the medulla oblongata is working. Damage to the medulla oblongata can be fatal. A variety of drugs and medications can cause changes in the function of the medulla oblongata, which can sometimes result in physical states which resemble death. Opiates and alcohol can both cause dysfunction until the body is able to express these substances, and in cases of overdose, it may lead to death because this area of the brain is not able to function normally. Sedatives can cause similar effects, as can hypothermia and coma.

Other occult connections of Pineal Gland are the following:

The Pineal Gland is the focus of the spiritual, hence inorganic, sensorium. Its action has nothing to do with the circulation of the Blood, but it is concerned with the spiritual fiery emanation that proceeds from the Blood. The Pineal Gland, at the upper pole of the human body, corresponds with the Uterus (in the female and its analogue in the male) at the lower pole; the peduncles of the Pineal Gland corresponding with the Fallopian Tubes of the Uterus. The Pituitary Body is only the servant of the Pineal Gland, its torch-bearer, like the servants carrying torches that run before the carriage of a princess.

The right eye is the "Eye of Wisdom," i.e., it corresponds magnetically with that occult centre in the brain which we call the "Third Eye" while the left corresponds with the intellectual brain, or those cells which are the organ on the physical plane of the thinking faculty.

4.3 Greek Accounts of the Pineal Gland

The earliest surviving description of the pineal in the Greek tradition was in the 8th book of Galen's 'On the usefulness of the parts of the body', in which he gave it the name "pineal" because of its resemblance to pine nuts (Greek κωναριου, Latin glandula pinealis). Galen commented that the gland was known before him and considered it a 'gland' partly because of its appearance and partly because it appeared to support local blood vessels, which he believed to be the function of all glands. He worked to refute an opinion, apparently current at that time but of unknown origin, that the pineal gland regulated the flow of psychic pneuma between the middle and posterior brain ventricles, similar to the way in which the pylorus regulates the movement of food from the esophagus to the stomach. Galen regarded the lateral ventricles of the brain as a single paired anterior ventricle, so he dubbed the third ventricle 'middle' and the fourth 'posterior'. Although he accepted that the ventricles contained the intangible pneuma, Galen disputed the valve function of the pineal gland because (i) it is attached to the outside of the brain and (ii) it cannot move on its own. Galen argued that the 'worm-like appendage' of the cerebellum was better suited to act as the valve that regulated psychic pneuma flow.

Subsequent ideas were built upon Galen's. According to the 5th century compiler Aetios, in the late 4th century CE, Poisonous of Byzantium and Nemesius of Emesa attributed imagination to the anterior ventricle, reason to the middle ventricle, and memory to the hind part of the brain. This view persisted, with variants, until the mid 16th century CE, when Niccolò Massa (1536) found that the ventricles were filled with fluid instead of psychic pneuma, and Vesalius (1543) dismissed the notions of ventricular localization and the flow of spirits being controlled by valves.

In many medieval writings on the subject, there seems to have been confusion between the pineal gland and the vermiform structure in the cerebellum. Galen believed that the vermiform structure was the true regulator of psychic pneuma flow between the middle and posterior ventricles, which was then combined with the ventricular localization doctrine of Nemesius and Posidonius. It was stated that people who wanted to remember should look up in order to raise the 'worm-like appendage (pineal gland)' and allow for memory retrieval from the posterior ventricle. However, the vermiform structure was termed pinea by Vincent Beauvais in the 13th century CE and Publicius in 1492, thus causing continued confusion between the pineal gland and the vermiform structure. Moreover, Mondino dei Luzzi (1306) described the choroid plexus as a worm that opens and closes the canal between the anterior and middle ventricles. Therefore, by the late Middle Ages in Europe, three 'worms' were described in the brain: (i) the vermis of the cerebellum, (ii) the choroid plexus, and (iii) the pineal gland.

4.4 Contribution of Rene Descartes to Pineal Gland

René Descartes (1596-1650) was a French philosopher, mathematician, and scientist. His best known philosophical statement is "I think, therefore I am". Rene Descartes termed the pineal gland as the 'principal seat of the soul'. In 'The Passions of the Soul' written between 1645 and 1646 by Rene Descartes, he discussed that the common contemporary belief that the human body contained animal spirits. These animal spirits were believed to be light and roaming fluids circulating rapidly around the nervous system between the brain and the muscles, and served as a metaphor for feelings, like being in high or bad spirit. These animal spirits were believed to affect the human soul, or passions of the soul. Descartes distinguished six basic passions: (i) wonder, (ii) love, (iii) hatred, (iv) desire, (v) joy and (vi) sadness. All of these passions, he argued, represented different combinations of the original spirit, and influenced the soul to will or want certain actions. He argued, for example, that fear is a passion that moves the soul to generate a response in the body. In line with his dualist teachings on the separation between the soul and the body, Descartes hypothesized that some part of the brain served as a connector between the soul and the body and singled out **the pineal gland as connector**. He argued that the signals passed from the ear and the eye to the pineal gland, through animal spirits. Thus different motions in the gland cause various animal spirits. He argued that these motions in the pineal gland are based on God's will and that humans are supposed to want and like things that are useful to them. But he also argued that the animal spirits that moved around the body could distort the commands from the pineal gland, thus humans had to learn how to control their passions.

Descartes attached significance to the pineal gland because he believed that this gland is the only section of the brain to exist as a standalone single part rather than any other part of the brain which exists as one-half part of its pair. He argued that, because a person can never have 'more than one thought at a time', the external stimuli must be united within the brain before being considered by the soul and he considered the pineal gland to be situated in 'the most appropriate location for this purpose'. Pineal gland is located centrally in the brain and surrounded by the branches of carotid arteries.

In view of the discoveries by Massa and Vesalius a century earlier, and indeed of the more accurate observations by Galen, Descartes' remarks about the pineal gland were in many ways ill-informed. He said it was suspended in the middle of the ventricles, a point on which

Galen would have corrected him. Remarks about the pineal gland were found in his La Dioptrique (Dioptrics) (1637) where he described certain small gland in the middle of the ventricles as the seat of the sensus communis. He maintained the view that it was full of psychic pneuma and ascribed this to the arteries that supplied the structure; but Galen had recognized that the main vasculature to the gland is venous.

4.5 Recent Observations about the Pineal Gland

There was little or no progress towards a modern scientific understanding of the pineal gland until the later part of the 19th century. In this period, the notion that the pineal is an evolutionary relic of a dorsal third eye was proposed. Additionally, the hypothesis that the pineal is an endocrine gland was also proposed. In 1958, it was determined that the pineal gland secretes melatonin, which regulates the circadian rhythm. While a modified theory of the pineal as a vestige of a third eye is still accepted today, the hypothesis that it is an endocrine organ was fully established in the 20th century in the wake of the isolation of melatonin as a pineal secretory product in 1958 by Lerner and colleagues.

Recent scientific research has shown that there are substantial, biological similarities between the retina and the pineal gland. Piezoelectric microcrystals may be transmitting photons that can be picked up by the retina-like tissue in the pineal gland—where they are then sent to the brain and descrambled into visual images. This may be responsible for what we call the "mind's eye"—such as when we suddenly see a mental image of our friend right before he or she calls us. DNA itself seems to accumulate light and in the process transmit light to other cells as a form of communication. Can we watch this process in our mind's eye? Clearly, more research is necessary to fully understand how the Pineal Gland actually works, but we already have some intriguing research available.

Dr. Rick Strassman has hypothesized that the pineal gland, which maintains light sensitivity, is responsible for the production and release of DMT (dimethyltryptamine), an entheogen which he believes possibly could be excreted in large quantities at the moments of birth and death. DMT is released during sleep and causes dreams.

DMT in large amounts causes the mind to slip like trans-loke state and illusive imagery. This type of drug has been used for centuries in Native American and South American cultures for spiritual practice and the so-called communication with gods.

4.6 Brain, Pineal Gland in Human Body and the 'Third Eye'

How does the pineal gland impact the awakening of the third eye? In the human body, this energy centre is traditionally associated with the pituitary gland, as well as the pineal gland.

Digging science behind the third eye, the pineal gland is the source of Melatonin. This hormone is a potent agent in reducing stress by encouraging restful sleep, enhance the immune system & prevent premature aging. Darkness triggers increased production and release of melatonin and eventually of pinoline and DMT (Dimethyltryptamine) as a result of its effect of activating the pineal gland and helping to stimulate function of and open the third eye. So it is also found to have some amount of light sensitivity, indicating that it might be the remnant of an organ of sight. However, pineal gland function still remains much of a mystery in man. One of the profound ways to awaken Ajna Chakra (6th Chakra) is through Sadhana, Yoga & Meditation. Meditation on Ajna chakra is said to become possible after one has substantially mastered the practice of regular meditation. Stressing the importance of Meditation, Ajna is the access which allows one to learn from their internal/gut feelings and hunches. It is through the 6th Chakra that almost all thoughts & messages one sends & receives are decoded. It just bridges our intuition & the conscious awareness. Commonly, we do get some insights as 'aura' before an attack of epilepsy, some horrific dreams and weird feelings of mishappenings that would occur later. Third eye is the portal through which we invite that Auric-insight, Clairvoyance & extrasensory perception – from telepathy to psycho kinesis and occult powers. These are regarded as supernormal faculties and are awakened in some people to a certain degree.

Glands and chakras are intimately related as they represent different levels of bodily functions, the first one being focused on the physical, the other on the subtle energetic level. The pituitary gland is considered to be the "master gland" in the human body because it controls most of the other glands and their hormone production.

Pineal Gland's connection with the third eye chakra or Ajna in the Hindu system has long been investigated by yogic traditions and modern metaphysics alike. They view this gland as a possible seat of the soul and its development, a source for mystical experiences and extrasensory perception or psychic abilities. The ways it functions is closely connected to the cycles of light and darkness.

It is said that when the pineal gland or 'third eye' is awakened, one is able to see beyond space time into time space. It raises the frequency on which one operates and moves one into a higher consciousness. With more research it is being realized that it is essentially a spiritual antenna of 'lord Shiva'. For many, the third eye has been seen as a way to reach higher levels of consciousness while still being present in a physical body. This concept of the pineal gland is the "seat of the soul" or the "spiritual gateway to all realms and all dimensions". This notion of the third eye is a scientific fact. The third eye opens the door to the metaphysical interpretations that ancient wisdom talks about.

4.7 Calcification of Pineal Gland and its Harmful Effects

The word 'calcification' implies that the calcium itself is the cause to affect the pineal gland and other organs of the body. Calcium is one of the most abundant minerals in our bodies, making up the structure of bones, creating muscle contraction; and many people are actually defiant of calcium. Taking a calcium supplement is very common but if not take in the prescribed amount, it could cause calcification of the pineal gland. Calcium requires Vitamin D to be absorbed and utilized in the body. Lack of Vitamin D means that calcium will float around in the blood until it deposits somewhere in the body. The result is 'calcification' of the important glands or deposits of the calcium, wreaking havoc in the kidneys.

Two of the biggest causes of pineal calcification are 'chloride' and 'fluoride'. Chlorine is the chemical used to kill bacteria in the swimming pools and fluoride is added to water to prevent dental caries in the general population. While small amounts of these chemicals are actually necessary for the body, it is very easy to get overdose of the same.

When the pineal gland is not making melatonin, one's sleep remains disturbed, the production of happy hormones, like serotonin, does not occur. One feels tired, sluggish and depressed. It means that the calcification of pineal gland has occurred. Calcification is the process of mineral build-up. This can occur anywhere in the body as a result of too much of minerals in the environment. This may manifest itself as kidney and gallstones. These minerals disrupt the flow of energy and nutrients from the blood entering the pineal gland.

Environmental toxins also play a big role in the calcification process. Whenever the body comes into contact with a substance that is foreign to it, like pesticides and pollution, these chemicals circulate in the blood and deposit around the pineal gland. Further, high levels of mercury and lead end up in hair follicles and other strange places and the toxic levels can shut down the systems altogether. The choices we make with our food every day affect the functioning of our pineal gland. Processed foods are harmful for the pineal gland. Preservatives and compounds not normally found in the nature are now regularly added to foods to improve their texture and enhance their shelf life. If consumed in large amounts, these chemicals harm the pineal gland by settling around it.

Pineal gland calcifications upon dissection resemble gravel, and are composed of calcite (calcium carbonate) and/or calcium hydroxyl apatite, the latter of which is not unlike dentin or bone. Pineal gland calcification is associated with a number of diseases in the medical literature: (i) Alzheimer Disease, (ii) Bipolar Disease, (iii) Circadian Dysregulation, (iv) Hormone Imbalances: Low Melatonin, (v) Insomnia, (vi) Low Back Pain, (vii) Parkinson Disease, (viii) Schizophrenia, (ix) Sleep Disorders, and (x) Stroke.

In the late 1990's, a scientist by the name of Jennifer Luke carried out the first study about the effects of sodium fluoride on the pineal gland. She determined that the pineal gland, located in the middle of the brain, was a target for fluoride. The pineal gland simply absorbed more fluoride than any other physical matter in the body, even bones. Pineal gland is like a magnet to sodium fluoride. This calcifies the gland and makes it no longer effective in balancing the entire hormonal processes through the body. Various Researches ever since have proved Sodium Fluoride goes to the most important gland in the brain? It is the only thing that attacks the most important centre of our gland in the brain. It is prevalent in foods, beverages and in our bath and drinking water. Sodium Fluoride is put in 90% of the United States water supply. Water filters you buy in supermarkets do not take the fluoride out. Only reverse osmosis or water distillation. The cheapest way is to buy a water distiller. Sodium Fluoride is in our water supply, food, pepsi, tooth paste, mouthwashes, and coke, to dumb down the masses, literally! The fluoride was introduced into the water by the Nazis and the Russians in their concentration camps to make the camp population docile and do not question authority.

The accumulation of fluoride in the pineal gland causes it to harden which makes it produce less melatonin, disturbs its wake-sleep regulation and halts its ability to enable psychic perception. Therefore, it is essential to clear your third eye chakra of blockages and decalcify your pineal gland if you plan to awaken your third eye. If you force your third eye to awaken prematurely, you are very likely to attract negative entities and become very vulnerable to psychic attacks. Research published in 2001 shows that fluoride consumption is associated with the rapid calcification of the pineal gland in the brain. (http://enlightenment-meditation.org/category/astrology/). Eleven corpses were dissected and their pineal glands studied. There was a positive correlation between pineal Fluoride and pineal Calcium ($r = 0.73$, $p<0.02$).

Now that it has been established that fluoride exposure contributes to the calcification of the pineal gland, the question remains: what are the subjective affects of these tissue changes to those who undergo them?

Prozac may represent an archetypal example of how fluoride affects the personality/soul. This drug (chemical name fluoxetine) is approximately 30% fluoride by weight and marketed as an "antidepressant," even while a major side effect of its use and/or withdrawal is suicidal depression. Modern psychiatry often treats depressive disorders – the "dark night of the soul" – as an organic disorder of the brain, targeting serotonin reuptake by any chemical means necessary. Fluoride and fluoxetine, in fact, may accomplish their intended "therapeutic effects" by poisoning the pineal gland. Animal studies confirm that when mice have their pineal glands removed they no longer respond to fluoxetine.

Perhaps the primary reason why Prozac causes a favourable reaction in those who are treated (poisoned) with it, is that it disassociates that person from the psycho spiritual conflicts that they must normally suppress in order to maintain the appearance of sanity and functionality in society, i.e. it is control and not health that is the goal of such "treatment. If Prozac and other sources of fluoride in our environment deposits within the pineal gland, accelerating the transformation of functional pineal tissüe into calcification, is it possible that it works by dehumanizing and flattening the affect of those who are under its influence?

4.8 Decalcification of Pineal Gland

The Pineal gland or the "seat of the soul" is where high consciousness can be developed. This means that by detoxification and decalcification of the body, it will make us reach our consciousness to a higher level to perceive other dimensions. If you take away the seat of the soul, this disconnects our oneness with our God and power of our source, our spirituality and turns us into a mundane slave of secret societies, shadow organizations and the control freak corporate world.

There are a number of things one can do every day to reduce the amount of foreign substances that enter our body. We can add smaller than the usual amounts of fluoride in water. People with public water that is treated with fluoride, have an option of using filters that will eliminate or reduce the fluoride content. Fluoride is also found in some amounts in the products like toothpastes to prevent tooth decay. Small children should avoid swallowing the toothpastes.

Pesticide exposure increase fluoride as well. The common fluoride-based pesticide, cryolite, is used on many fresh fruits and vegetables to prevent bugs. Buying organic fruits and vegetables can be a good option. Otherwise peels should be taken off from such fruits and vegetables before eating. Avoid eating non-organic fruits like strawberries where there is no peel. The same goes with grapes, resins etc. Any pesticide residue will be directly on the skin of the fruits, and therefore, will make it into your body. Green and black tea leaves and wines contain concentrated levels of fluoride. Moderate levels of consumption are advisable to limit this exposure.

Like fluoride, chlorine can also be found in public drinking water. It is used as an anti-bacterial remedy to reduce the risk of food-based illness from water. Drinking filtered water is not enough. If you are still using unfiltered water for showers, cleaning dishes and brushing your teeth, you are still exposed. The ideal solution is that the whole-house water filter should be used to avoid chlorine from the public water supply. Chlorine is also a major component of household products like laundry detergent. It is the main component of the bleach. One can consider to an all-natural chlorine-free version of the detergents.

To help the pineal gland function healthier, sleeping in a dark bed room is highly recommended. It is not too late to change your diet for you to be able to detoxify and to decalcify your pineal gland. Healthy eating like practicing vegetarianism helps cleans the pineal gland which makes it function accordingly. The sunlight or sun ray is very friendly for the pineal gland. Making a way to expose your face towards the sun is a good exercise to decalcify the gland. Sun-dried seaweeds are also friendly for the pineal gland because of the vitamin D contained in the sea plant. Consuming green salad leafs and organic raw vegetables and fruits like water melon, rather than meat is the best way to clean your pineal gland.

In general, we should eat a diet that contains a good amount of protein. We should also add starchy food and carbohydrates for immediate energy supply. Brown rice, whole grain bread and fruits fall in this category. Non-starchy vegetables like green salads, cucumbers, tomatoes etc should be added in your food. Foods that support melatonin production for stimulating our pineal gland should also be consumed. Beans and foods with Vitamin D are advised for this purpose. Antioxidant fruits with Vitamin C and E are also advisable. Citrus fruits, lemon juice, spinach and broccoli should be a part of your food. Garlic is great for fighting off infection and for boosting your immune system.

4.9 Pineal Gland in Infants

The pineal gland is active in the infants, as it is said that the infants directly receive the cosmic energy for their survival. Thereafter pineal gland gets inactive / calcified and it can be witnessed as early as 2-yrs of age and the calcification rate tends to increase with age. The calcification occurs due to our environment and our lifestyle habits. Children are seen as the most spiritual beings as they do not have any of the fears or concerns of adults when they are born. They are born free and full of unconditional love. It is the society that places these fears and conditioning on our children. It would be interesting to know what would happen if a child's pineal gland wasn't affected by its environment and was allowed to develop, grow and be activated. It is part of epithalamiums. It produces melatonin, a hormone that affects the modulation of wake/sleep patterns. It is this vigilance of light and dark that allows us to fall asleep and wake up in a normal pattern and daily routine. Disruptions in melatonin cause sleep disruption, insomnia, narcolepsy and general fatigue.

To support your pineal gland and to awaken of your third eye, here is what you can do:

- Go outside and get lots of natural light.
- Eat foods or supplements that support a healthy activity of the pineal gland (and counter its calcification), such as iodine, chlorella, apple cider, Tamarind fruit (as it helps remove excess of fluoride involved in decreased pineal activity).
- Meditate; meditation balances the activity of the nervous system and stimulates parts of the brain that help the pineal gland.
- Spend time in complete darkness, as it stimulates a healthy activity in the gland and production of its associated hormones.

4.10 How to Activate the Pineal Gland

We shall review seven pineal gland activation methods. They include:

- Meditation
- Sun Gazing
- Qigong
- Psychedelics
- Brainwave Entrainment
- Third Eye Acupressure Technique
- Third Eye Mudra

- Visualization
- The Projective Technique

4.10.1 Pineal Gland Activation Method #1: Meditation

Perhaps the most traditional method of opening one's third eye is through formal sitting meditation. Meditation is an important topic for anyone interested in accessing their higher potential. But for our purposes here, through various meditative techniques, you can stimulate and activate your pineal gland.

How? The pineal gland is sensitive to the bioelectrical signals of light and dark in its environment. Meditation can activate this bioelectric energy. And, with practice, you can direct this energy to the pineal gland, stimulating it and helping it open. For your meditation to be effective, your mind must become still so the scattered energy in your body can consolidate. We can't, however, quiet our minds through force. Instead, we just observe or watch our mind and allow it to become still without effort.

Third Eye Meditation

- Sit in a comfortable, relaxed posture.
- Close your eyes or just lower your eyelids.
- Allow your breath to become deep and slow. (Meaning don't force it to become deep and slow, but simply watch the breath. Detached observation will naturally cause your breathing to slow down.)
- Rest your attention on the third eye region just above and between your two eyes.
- That's it. You can also imagine that you are breathing a golden white light through the centre of your third eye.

The key is to remain relaxed and avoid trying to force the exercise. Let go of wanting or expecting any result as this will create tension that will block the flow of energy in this process.

Why This Meditation Works?

By placing your attention on the pineal gland, you are focusing your internal energy in this region. This relaxed focus releases neuropeptides and nitric oxide, which trigger the relaxation response. These chemicals will allow you to move into deeper meditation while stimulating the third eye region.

Recall that melatonin is the main chemical produced and circulated by the pineal gland. Not surprisingly, in the brains of meditators, they find an increase in melatonin secretion.

You'll know your third eye meditation is working when you begin to feel either a slight pressure in this region or a pulsating sensation. It can feel as though there is a mini heart beating in your forehead—an unusual sensation for certain.

4.10.2 Pineal Gland Activation Method #2: Sun Gazing

We've all been told not that staring directly at te sun will damage our eyes. One thing I will say with fair certainty: for those of us committed to actualizing our higher potential, we must be willing to challenge everything we think we know. Sun gazing is a powerful, ancient technique with tremendous benefits. The theory behind sun gazing is that you are absorbing the energy of the sun directly through your eyes and skin.

The Man Who Eats the Sun

Hira Ratan Manek (known as HRM) is the person who brought this method to the mainstream. Through sun gazing, HRM and many others have been able to go long periods of time (years!) without eating and remain physically healthy. A team of physicians from the University of Pennsylvania examined HRM 24/7 for 130 days. They confirmed his claims that he survives largely on sunlight with a minimal amount of water. Neuroscientist Andrew Newberg and pineal gland authority George Bernard studied HRM's brain during this 130 day period. They found that the gray cells in HRM's brain were regenerating. Further, the pineal gland shrank in individuals after their mid-fifties. In HRM's case, this 64-year-old man's pineal gland was expanding! (His pineal was measured at 8 x 11 mm compared to the maximum average size of 6 x 6 mm.) The research cited in that guide supports the idea that sunlight reduces the harmful effects of artificial blue light. Here, we're learning that the sun's support goes further: the sun can help us restore the original size and function of this all-important gland.

Figure 4.2: Sun-gazing Hira Ratan Manek

Note: More recently, HRM started eating. Apparently, the documentary "Eat the Sun" exposes him as a fraud, but this is more likely a consequence of an archetype possessing him. Like many so-called "gurus," he became inflated and now he can't regulate his behaviour. Sun gazing, like all such techniques, should be used responsibly and with great care.

The Benefits of Fasting

While stopping eating isn't the goal of pineal gland activation, many who sun gaze report that hunger is reduced. Eating becomes a choice, but there's no longer hunger or a physical need to eat. This 2011 study by the Intermountain Medical Centre found that periodic fasting:

- Lowers your risk of heart disease and diabetes
- Causes changes to your blood cholesterol levels
- Increases human growth hormone (HGH). HGH is a metabolic protein that protects lean muscle and metabolic balance. HGH increased an average of 1,300 percent in women and 2,000 percent in men during a 24-hour fasting period

Most foods block the flow of energy or chi in the body. The less you eat the more energy you can experience. Finally, fasting also supports detoxification, which might be the greatest benefit to your pineal gland.

How to use Sun Gazing to Activate the Pineal Gland

Why are we told that it's dangerous to look at the sun? Ultraviolet (UV) radiation can damage the retina. But did you know that the UV index is usually zero during sunrise and sunset? When sun gazing, it's important to only look at the sun within the first hour in the morning and the last hour in the evening when the sun still has an orange glow. You don't sun gaze during the day when the UV index is high. Sun gazing is reportedly safe whenever the UV index is less than 2%. In fact, using HRM's method, you start within the first 15 minutes of sunlight in the morning and the last 15 minutes at the end of the day.

You only gaze into the sun for a couple of seconds at first, building up to 45 minutes per day over the course of nine months. Sun gazing is also done barefoot, so you get the added benefits of grounding too. But even if you're not interested in following this particular protocol, occasional sun gazing in the early morning or late evening will support your efforts to activate your pineal gland. Finally, ditch your sunglasses. Direct and indirect sunlight stimulates the pineal, prompting it to produce serotonin. This neurotransmitter will elevate your mood and your level of energy. Direct sunlight will also make you more resilient to blue light.

4.10.3 Pineal Gland Activation Method #3: Qigong

Qigong translates to "life energy cultivation" or "energy skill." Qigong exercises are designed to increase the practitioner's sensitivity to the flow of energy within the body, called chi (or qi). One learns how to move this energy with gentle physical motions and breathing. Finally, the practitioner learns how to move this chi with one's mind, or intent.

Most of us have many blocked energy meridians and centres that keep the body's chi from reaching vital glands in the endocrine system. Circulating the body's energy using qigong helps open these pathways, allowing this energy to reach these areas and activate the pineal gland. In truth, the meditation practice described above is a form of qigong as you're focusing your intention on the pineal gland to increase the energy flow in this region. If you first develop sensitivity to your body's energy through qigong before doing a meditative practice like this, it will be far more effective. In fact, if you practice Zhan Zhang daily and your body opens up, you'll experience an increased flow of energy throughout your body and brain.

Pineal Gland Qigong Using the Sun

"When the sun starts to rise over the horizon, extend one of your arms toward the sun, and point your index finger at the sun. "Look at the sun from your index finger to the sun. While the sun is still red in colour, focus on the sun as it rises completely above the horizon. It is said that with this training, one will open the Heavenly Eye."

4.10.4 Pineal Gland Activation Method #4: Brainwave Entrainment

Our brains operate on a range of brainwave patterns. Each pattern establishes a particular state of consciousness. From high to low, here are the most commonly cited brainwave frequencies and their associated state of consciousness:

Brainwave Frequency	:	State of Consciousness:
Gamma (40 – 100 Hertz)	:	Ecstatic peak experiences / Oneness
High Beta (22 – 40 Hertz)	:	Anxiety / Nervousness
Low Beta (14 – 22 Hertz)	:	Alertness / Focus
Alpha (8 – 14 Hertz)	:	Physically relaxed / Meditative
Theta waves (4 to 8 Hertz)	:	Deeply relaxed / REM sleep
Delta (0.5 – 4 Hertz)	:	Dreamless sleep / deepest meditation

These programs are usually a combination of binaural beats and isochronic tones. When you simultaneously hear one pure-tone sine wave in the left ear and another sine wave in the right ear, it creates an auditory illusion called a binaural beat. An isochronic tone is simply a pure tone that's turned on and off rapidly. Sound engineers calibrate these tones to specific frequencies. The goal of these programs is to induce a particular state of consciousness by entraining the brain to the frequencies of the sounds. Although there's a lack of controlled research studies, preliminary research suggests brainwave entrainment does facilitate a change in brainwave patterns and has a therapeutic effect. The effects of these changes, however, are likely only temporary.

Brainwave Frequencies for the Pineal Gland Activation

While there's no clear answer, research does point us in several directions. This study of two individuals during an ayahuasca (DMT) experience found that they produced an increase in "global EEG coherence in the 36-44 Hz and 50-64 Hz frequency bands for both subjects." These frequency bands are known as gamma waves. Some people term DMT as the 'spirit molecule'.

Then, we need to consider what brainwave frequencies are consistent with the production of the pineal gland's main chemical: melatonin. The answer is delta waves—the brain waves we experience during deep, dreamless sleep.

Finally, what frequency is active during the REM stage of sleep? Theta waves; And theta and gamma waves work together during REM sleep.

Put the above together, and to use brainwave entrainment for pineal gland activation, use binaural beats and isochronic tones that activate delta, theta, and gamma frequencies.

4.10.5 Pineal Gland Activation Method #5: DMT

Your Pineal Gland, we learned that the pineal synthesizes and secretes a hormone called melatonin. But the pineal is also responsible for another chemical we didn't discuss, that is, DMT (N,N-dimethyltryptamine). Psychiatrist and researcher Rick Strassman theorized that the pineal gland produces another important chemical called or DMT. And, in 2013, Strassman along with other researchers did indeed find DMT in the pineal gland of rats. (It seems science is still unclear whether the pineal produces DMT or just regulates it.)

Dubbed the "Spirit Molecule," DMT is a natural hallucinogen capable of producing extraordinary visions and mystical states of consciousness. DMT is similar to the properties of lysergic acid diethylamide (known as LSD or acid) but is naturally occurring in our bodies whereas LSD is a synthetic drug. In DMT, Strassman explains: "DMT exists in all of our bodies and occurs throughout the plant and animal kingdoms. It is a part of the normal makeup of humans and other mammals; marine animals; grasses and peas; toads and frogs; mushrooms and molds; and barks, flowers, and roots." In the 1970s, Japanese scientists discovered that the brain transports DMT across the blood-brain barrier into its tissues.

Strassman continues: "I know of no other psychedelic drug that the brain treats with such eagerness … If DMT were only an insignificant, irrelevant by-product of our metabolism, why does the brain go out of its way to draw it into its confines?" Researcher Graham Hancock theorizes that DMT is the lens of the pineal gland that allows us to see wider areas of our reality than are usually inaccessible to us.

DMT is present in the Amazonian botanical tea called ayahuasca. Ayahuasca is a sacred tea made from the vine of the Ayahuasca plant combined with the leaves of either chacruna or chagropanga bush. A very small amount of DMT is reportedly produced by the pineal gland every night while we dream. But when you take Ayahuasca, you're getting a massive DMT boost that may be able to break up any existing calcification in your pineal. This "herbal medicine" is taken as part of a South American shamanic ritual that leads participants through profound experiences—both "positive" and "negative"—as content from their unconscious comes into conscious awareness. When used with the proper mindset and environment, ayahuasca and other substances like iboga and psilocybin ("magic mushrooms") have the potential to heal our minds and activate our pineal glands. (Too bad they are classified as illegal substances.)

4.10.6 Method #6: Third Eye Acupressure Technique

Acupressure, a method of traditional Chinese medicine, is massage based upon the same concepts as acupuncture. You can stimulate your

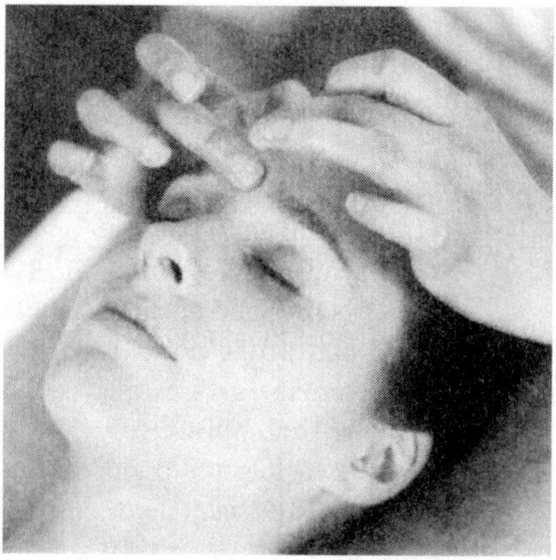

Figure 4.3: Third-Eye Acupressure

own third eye yintang point using controlled finger massage and pressure to adjust the flow of energy to your pineal gland/third eye point. The yintang is located on the midline of your face, directly between and just above your eyebrows. Feel for a slight depression just beneath the skin. By using the end of your fingernail on this acupressure point, you will quickly feel the effects of this mild stimulation.

Some tips:

- Breathe deeply and slowly when performing acupressure on yourself or another person.
- Focus your mind on your third eye acupressure point as you apply this stimulation.
- Acupressure stimulation should feel strong, but should not create a sense of an uncomfortable level of pressure. Be gentle with this point! The preferred choice is to end this with gentle and extremely light "circle massage" on the entire area.

4.10.7 Method #7: Third Eye Mudra

You can use an ancient East Indian yoga mudra method to open your third eye chakra. Mudras are special hand positions believed by yogis to have the power to direct more energy to specific chakras. To enhance the effect for third eye activation, simultaneously chant the Aum or Om sound as you hold the mudra position.

Using the Third Eye Mudra

Here's how to use a traditional yogic third eye mudra for pineal gland/third eye activation:

- Position your hands in front of the lower part of your breast.
- Your middle fingers should remain straight and touch at the tops while pointing forward.
- Your other fingers are bent and touch at the upper portions of the fingers.
- Your thumbs should point toward you and touch at their tops.
- Close your physical eyes and mentally focus your inner vision on the position of your third eye chakra on your forehead –

in between and just above the eyebrows. Do not strain your physical eyes.

Chant Om or Aum while remaining relaxed and contemplative.

Figure 4.4: Third-Eye Mudra

4.10.8 Visualization

Visualization is always a very powerful way to activate your pineal gland and encourage your third eye to open. This method may seem much more comfortable to you if you are not a meditator, or do not practice yoga.

Third Eye Visualization Technique:

Figure 4.5: Third-Eye Visualization

- To prepare for third eye visualization, begin by settling into a comfortable position, either sitting up or lying down. If you fall asleep easily when lying down, sit upright instead.
- Take steps to relax your body.
- Once your whole body feels relaxed, shift your focus to your breathing.
- Visualize feeling lighter and lighter with each inhale, and letting go of any tension or worry with each exhale.
- To begin your third eye visualization, shift your attention to the place between your eyes on your forehead.
- Imagine your head surrounded by a glowing indigo or violet light.
- Visualize your pineal gland as a glowing area directly in the centre of your head.
- Envision a bright fluorescent light streaming out of your pineal gland.
- Picture the light becoming brighter and brighter until you can feel it tingling and heating your forehead, and especially the area above and between your eyebrows.
- When you feel ready to finish your third eye meditation, slowly move or wiggle your fingers and toes then open your eyes and take a few deep breaths.

4.10.9 The Projective Technique

(i) First sit comfortably with your eyes closed.

(ii) Calm your mind of intrusive thoughts and with your mind's eyes, imagine your Ajna Chakra (third eye chakra) being intensely bright. Imagine a ball of light with a blue-whitish tone pulsing in your forehead. It is like a little Sun which obeys the volition of your Will, pulsating, dilating continuously. Keep your attention to this point for about 3 minutes.

(iii) Now, lie down and with a very serene mind, visualize two small spheres with white light that are now pulsating near your ears. Using your Will, make them pulsate and irradiate their light and energy inside your ears, and feel with all your senses the vibrational energy of their presence. Keep this image and situation alive in your mind for at least two minutes.

(iv) Now, slowly, with a steady pace to your breathing (if you lose your rhythmic pace, go back to the cyclical breathing 4x4), try to visualize both spheres inserting into both sides of your head at the same time. This part of the exercise has to be performed with the upmost care, attention and seriousness.

(v) With care, visualize both of the spheres inside of your ears. Slowly merge the two spheres into one sphere inside of the Cranium box, in a straight line from both ears. This is the place where the Pineal Gland is located.

(vi) Carefully make this new merged sphere of light start pulsing as an energetic valve, projecting its light from inside. Breathe slowly as you are starting to get acquaintance with this new source of energy.

(vii) From this point of light, make a straight line from there to your Anahata, the Heart Chakra. Fill your heart cavity with this brand new light.

(viii) With your mind's eye draw another line connecting your pineal gland with your Ajna Chakra, or Third Eye, and another line connecting to the base of the head. This point is called "The Mouth of God".

We would advise the practitioner to practice this Activation when it is time for bed, and to allow you to fall asleep if necessary. It is important to allow the Theta waves of the brain to permeate all this process. In the "theta" state, we are resting deeply and still conscious, at the threshold of drifting away from or back into conscious awareness. As the brain enters deeper states our consciousness is less concerned with the physical state, and the Pineal is gradually activated and the walls of separation from the Divine start to disappear.

This Meditation activation must be practiced every night for an extended period of time, as there is much energy detritus accumulated by the ages to be cleansed. Be persistent and keep yourself motivated, as this is an extraordinary tool for improvement and to expand your spiritual, cosmic and galactic connections. You may feel some energetic side effects from this exercise, such as pressure in your Cranium, but all of these are transitory and they will diminish and disappear with practice.

4.11 Achieving Total Brain Coherence

Ultimately, all of the pineal gland activation methods discussed above, work to bring the entire brain online—not just the pineal. So again, when we speak of pineal gland activation, we're talking about bringing the whole brain online, integrating all the various brain regions.

While psychedelics appear to accomplish this goal temporarily, methods like meditation, sun gazing, and qigong give us the ability to change the physical structure of our consciousness over time. As the pineal activates and the brain becomes more integrated, one's reality is perceived differently. You'll begin to notice more of your unconscious behaviour, which helps you get to know your shadow. You may wake up to many new realities about your life, the universe, and existence itself that were unavailable to you before.

Chapter - 5

Alta Major and the Third Eye

5.1 What is Alta Major Chakra and where is it located?

Alta major chakra was earlier known as the four-and-a-half chakra. It is now more common to hear it called the Alta major chakra. The Alta major chakra is a relatively unknown chakra in the typical "traffic light" chakra system, with which we have become most familiar. It is also known by some as 'The Breath of God' or the 'Mouth of the Goddess', allowing shakti to ignite and flow down the spine.

The back of the neck is an important sacred vortex of energy in our body. Alta major centre is the counterpart of the forehead. It is located at the back of head at the base of the skull where the skull and the spine meet. It has roots reaching down the spine into the root chakra where is disperses throughout the body and branches up to the crown chakra. It is also connected to the third eye and crown chakras. Alta major chakra serves like a computer monitor for the visual and the data interpretation aspects of the third eye. Just as hind brain processes signals for the two physical eyes, the Alta major chakra process information for the third eye. Thus some people term this centre as the brain of the third eye. Alta Major has powerful link with cerebellum (voluntary muscle movements), medulla oblongata (breathing, heart rate and blood pressure. The Alta major is also known as the portal or galactic doorway to higher forces. This energy centre has been visualized as the bright light at the rear of the heads of saints and sages.

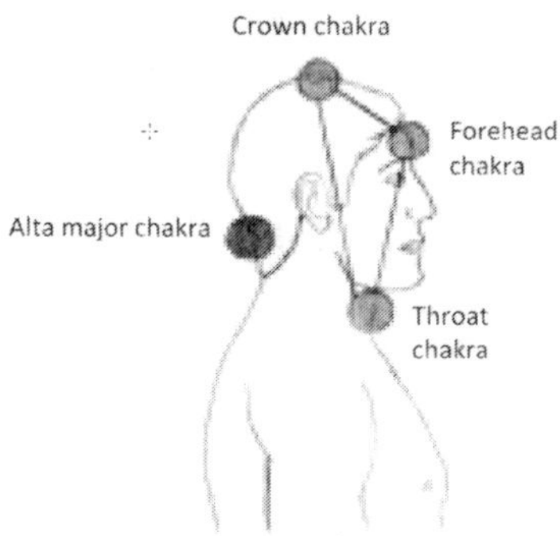

Figure 5.1: Picture displaying (i) Alta Major Chakra, (ii) Throat Chakra, (iii) Forehead Chakra (Ajna Chakra), and (iv) Crown Chakra

The Alta major chakra is the last to become activated. The reason for this involves the waking of Consciousness -- antaskarana, sutratma and the antahkarana (energetic channels or threads). 'Antaskarana' is a thread or channel between the personality (lower worlds) and the higher worlds of Consciousness. The 'sutratma' is the energetic life aspect; it anchors at the heart, runs with the spinal column (energetically), to the head (at the crown) and moves up through the crown to the Soul. The 'antahkarana' is the major pathway for connecting to our lower, everyday consciousness with our highest and the spiritual consciousness. It is also known as the 'Rainbow Bridge' or the 'Bridge of Light' and is a frequency consisting of three main components of energy fields. Although everyone has all three components (antaskarana, sutratma and the antahkarana), one of the three requires additional work to be built upward from the individual back to the Soul. When the Alta major chakra is activated, human consciousness expands to merge with Consciousness.

It is apparent here that we are talking about building a bridge from the lower ego mind to higher mental planes. There is an etheric channel, which we must cross, at the Alta major centre. Bridging this etheric gap involves creating an ephemeral thread, which is called the antaskarana. Once constructed, this bridge becomes the thread of the antaskarana, which is the path of communication between the human personality and its Soul. Part of the work of the human who is developing thought-power has to do, is build a temporary channel in the etheric matter to bridge the gap, this channel is the antaskarana.

The throat chakra connects with the Alta major chakra where the Antahkarana is beginning to be built. Alta Major is connected with the Carotid body, which monitors oxygen content in the blood and controls respiration. In fact some people assert that the Alta major chakra is located at site of the Catotid Gland, as illustrated in the following picture:

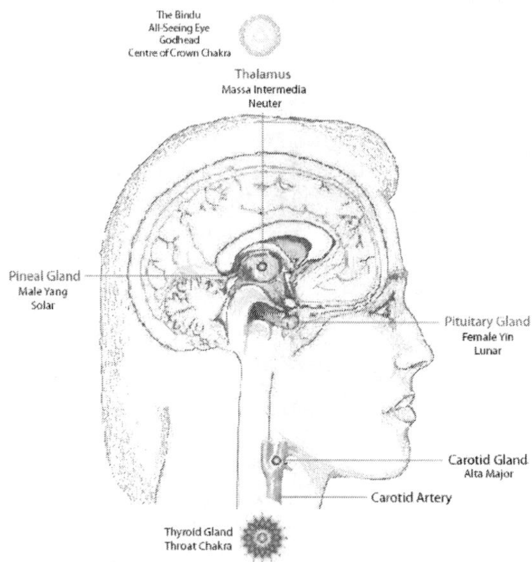

Figure 5.2: Picture showing the location of Alta Major Chakra, Pineal and Pituitary Glands

This chakra point acts as an energetic doorway through which we communicate spiritually with other dimensions. It has been known the 'Atlas' bone by the ancient Egyptian cultures as the energy centre, which the gateway through which you can access higher dimensions of consciousness. The ancient Atlantis civilization may have actually existed (and still does) as a high-level spiritual dimension that is accessed via the energy centre over the 'Atlas Bone' - the spiritual gateway - rather than a physical place.

When we open up and activate our heart chakra with daily love-based meditation, this directly accesses the soul. When our soul is free to rise in the body, this then leads to the opening of our mouth - via the throat (the voice). This activates the back of the neck - what is called 'the spiritual gateway chakra', or the 'Alta major chakra, or the 'Breath of God', or the 'Mouth of the Goddess'. Once this chakra is activated, it then sends an energetic signal to our pineal gland and pituitary gland - forming a pyramid or light within the brain that joins up with the back of the neck. This pyramid (in 3-D) or a triangle (in 2-D) is reflected in the following picture:

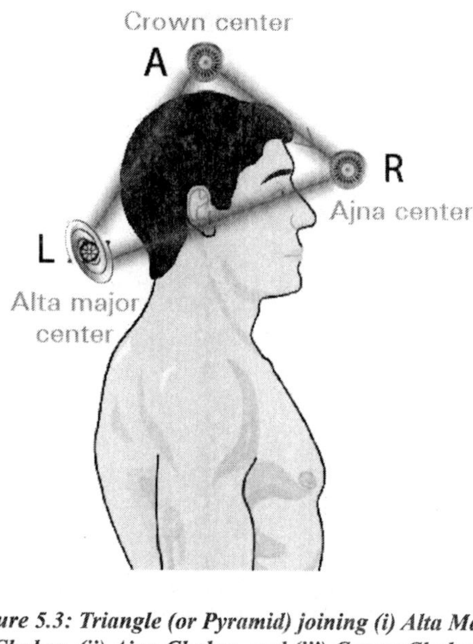

Figure 5.3: Triangle (or Pyramid) joining (i) Alta Major Chakra, (ii) Ajna Chakra, and (iii) Crown Chakra

In the above image, the base of the skull points to the Alta major chakra, in the etheric field, which aligns with the location of the cerebellum, medulla oblongata and the RAS (Reticular Activating System). On the right is the ajna chakra in the etheric field. When Alta Major is fully developed, it forms a communication centre between vital energy of the spinal column (Kundalini) and the energy of the two head centres (Crown and Ajna). Based on the experience of some mystics, the 'third eye' is located at the point of centroid of the above-mentioned pyramid formed by joining the three chakras, viz., Alta Major, Ajna, and the Crown.

It is a highly sensitive portal of energy with heightened awareness. It is a clever little antenna alerting one to the disturbed energies, untruths and toxic influences. It is also considered an entry point for psychic attacks. So there is stronger reason to keep it clear, strong and healthy. It is also worth mentioning that many of us have a sensitive Alta major chakra. Through the Alta Major chakra the Spiritual Will of the Crown centre is balanced. This chakra is particularly related to sleep and to the working out of past experiences in sleep. It is helpful to go to sleep with the consciousness gently focused in the Ajna centre.

If you are journeying on your spiritual path and regularly experiencing either a stiff neck and/or a sore throat (particularly when there are powerful cosmic alignments occurring), it could be that your 'spiritual gateway chakra' or 'Alta major chakra' is activating. That means you are connecting with other dimensions.

Tune into your Alta major chakra by placing your left hand gently over the base of your skull, upper neck area. And your right palm over your third eye. Feel into it, sense, listen, and witness its existence.

5.2 Activation of Alta Major Chakra

Though there are several explanations from Eastern and Western views of how the Alta Major works and what it does, a point where they all meet in regards to the essence of this Chakra. They see that this area as auspicious; points to the systems and Glands it is connected to; and the amplifying of one's inherent vibration through the activity of these systems. According to Vedic teachings it is necessary to activate and balance the Alta-major chakra in order to achieve ascension in the next phase of human development. There are twenty-four books in the Alice Bailey collection of esoteric teachings, and a majority of them have references to the Alta major centre and its operative power. Esoterically speaking, the Alta major centre or chakra is believed to be in the etheric body. In Esoteric/Spiritual communities, the vibrating and opening of this area was a step for the more advanced student who had gone through an extensive spiritual practice. And in some ways they had gone through trials and tribulations, of intense purification, perhaps akin to the seven levels of transformation of alchemy. From decalcification, washing away, shedding, brewing, fermenting, distilling, all sense of hindering emotions and ego-self, to coming into a true essence of where one is. Arriving at this pure essence of being was a major step that would render one ready for opening and receiving that higher vibration and/or cosmic waves.

In ancient Egypt, it is said, this was a centre where initiation was transmitted to the "ready" adept, by priests pointing to the back or top of the head, with a rod. These rods were known to generate a sound, a frequency that would resonate and assist further in carrying out the vibratory-pulse of this activation, throughout the nervous system, spine, brain and the subtle bodies. What it looks like is that this vibratory-pulse aligns the body to become more like a Tuning Rod itself - to be able to receive and/or withstand higher vibratory frequencies, ultimately connecting one with source while bringing this vibration and light into being and into higher Consciousness. This is equivalent to 'Shaktipat' in Hinduism, where the advanced spiritual master (the Guru) or the God Himself would transmit the spiritual energy to the deserving disciple or devotee.

On a biological note, when vibrating, and activating this triangular connection, it is said, there are bio-chemical reactions that happen between the Pineal, Pituitary, and the Carotid Glands. This activity happens throughout the brain, nervous system, down the spine to the heart and throughout the body. That means, through the body's bioelectric, biosonic and bioluminescence functions, in essence, these reactions amplify the vibratory frequencies at the cellular level, thus becoming more electrical and magnetic. And this brings about the amplification - that higher vibratory level needed, to withstand and hold, at the physical level of being, that higher vibration/higher frequency cosmic rays coming in. The vibration and activation of this triangular set, transforms this area known as the ancient "Reptilian" part of the brain, transcending one to further become a more realized human being. Basically, when one is ready, opening the Alta Major is one step further to take to activate the light body to enter into physical body. Light body may be also known as: Diamond Body, Rainbow Body and/or Ascension. Therefore, by bringing this activation, purification and transformation results into the opening to higher chakras.

The development of the Alta major chakra leads to an acquired and conscious control of one's dharma or soul work on earth, a realization of what one is to do in life as opposed to being tossed about like a leaf in the wind (a reference to the creative thread of the pingala). It therefore has powerful connections with ancient memory. The Alta major chakra's correspondence in the physical body makes it the distributor of energy by way of the vagus nerve in the consciously underdeveloped person. In the consciously developed person the sutratma assumes this function in harmony with the vagus nerve. When activated, the Alta major chakra has the power to bring intuitive vision into consciousness. This chakra can be said to be the healer's conscious link with the higher mind, because through the Alta major chakra our higher intelligence is activated through thought. And energy follows the thought. In the interest of clarity, "activation" is a natural evolutionary step in the spiritual development of one who is journeying on the spiritual path.

5.3 RAS-Vagus Nerve-Alta Major 'Spiritual Axis'

The RAS-Vagus-Alta Major Chakra Axis describes the communication hub of the human being -- body, mind and Soul. Until there is fusion between the personality consciousness and Spirit consciousness, the vagus nerve is commanding the rhythm of the entire body. The RAS-Vagus-Alta Major Chakra Axis communicates with the anatomy of spirit in the self.

Dedication to the Path of Consciousness means that the activated Alta major chakra will become the distribution centre of life-force energy. This life-force energy moves down and up the antahkarana, the energetic spinal column, radiating magnetically to open the chakra centres. The RAS is the network hub of the physical nervous system, sending and receiving signals, creating connections using the endogenous hormones, neurotransmitters and neuropeptides that move throughout the body. The vagus nerve carries the signals that coordinate these collective movements and activations, creating a homeodynamically balanced nervous system within the body. The reticular formation is the area of the body that arouses the cortex of the brain. This RAS-Vagus Nerve-Alta Major Chakra connection is an axis, which acts as a communication nexus between the physical systems and Consciousness, which when activated consciously can arouse a profound Spiritual connection.

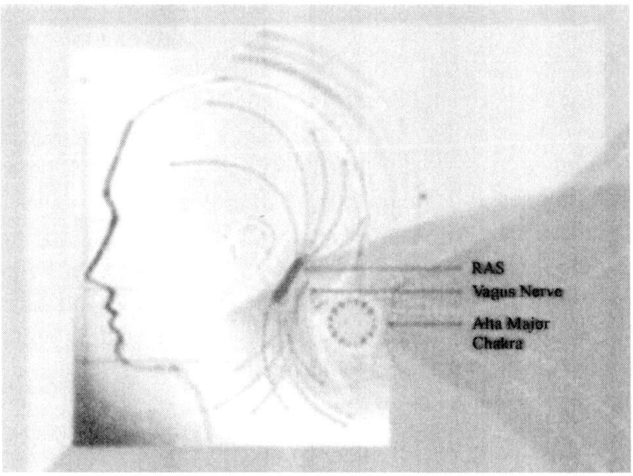

Figure 5.4: Picture displaying RAS, Vagus nerve and Alta Major Chakra

The brain is mainly composed of three segments, the cerebrum, cerebellum and the medulla oblongata. The cerebellum and medulla are the reptilian (hind) brain. Some neuroscientists postulate that they are the seat of the unconscious brain. Basically the function of the cerebellum (which aligns with the Alta major centre) is like the breaker-box (MCB box) in a house. When you build a house, all the electrical circuits connect to a breaker-box. This connection allows the electrical energy currents to flow throughout the house. If the house is not grounded, there is a strong potential for a short-circuiting to occur. This metaphor relates to the physical body's brain and nervous system. Physiologists, especially neurophysiologists, refer to these parts of the body as electrical in nature. If there is too much electrical current, as in someone who is hyperactive or hyper-stimulated/aroused, it could short-circuit the nervous system. In a similar manner, if there is reduced energy flow through the nervous system, it may result in a state of hypoactivity. "Short-circuiting" in the brain and nervous system is usually obvious, such as in cases where lesions or scars are blocking signal transmission, but even simple stress responses throughout the day can upset the body's ability to effectively communicate with itself.

To sum up, the relationship of the RAS-Vagus Nerve-Alta Major Chakra Axis is about communication with the Divine and with the self. The RAS is a communication energy centre for physical consciousness, and the vagus nerve with its nearby outcropping, is a messenger of psychological and physiological information. The Alta Major Chakra completes a life-force triad, thereby allowing a bridge to be created with the Spirit Consciousness. Each of these systems is part of an energetic feedback loop, from individual consciousness to Supreme Consciousness and back.

Following picture of the Swami Ramakrishna Paramahamsa (with aura at its back) depicts the developed Alta major chakra at the back of the head:

Figure 5.5: Aura at the back of the head of Swami Ramakrishna Paramahamsa (Guru of Swami Vivekananda) reflects the developed Alta Major Chakra

Chapter - 6

Thalamus and the Third Eye

6.1 Introduction and Illustration of Pineal, Pituitary and Thalamus

In several faiths and religions the pineal gland is linked with the 'Third Eye' – the mystical, or inner, *psychic vision*, which is believed to be man's "doorway" towards enlightenment and the "glory of god". For many mystics, the pineal is said to be associated with the sixth chakra vortex – the brow chakra or *Ajna Chakra*.

Some will say that the 'third eye' is the pituitary gland, and others will say that the 'third eye' is both the pineal gland and the pituitary gland. Many of us still believe that the so-called "third eye" doesn't really exist.

What possible reason could the ancient builders and priests of the various cultures of the globe have for including the design of the pineal, the pituitary and the thalamus within their structures? And why was the pineal, the pituitary and thalamus part of the Caduceus and snake symbolism? The answer is that **all three** (pineal, pituitary and thalamus) – as noted in the Triad and/or Holy Trinity and also personified in the god of wisdom Thoth-Hermes the "Thrice Greatest" – **were associated with the 'Third Eye' – not just the pineal.**

In the following picture, the pea-sized, pituitary and pineal glands are located within the third ventricle at the centre of the brain. The carotid and thyroid glands, the thalamus and *bindu* (dot) centre are also indicated in this picture.

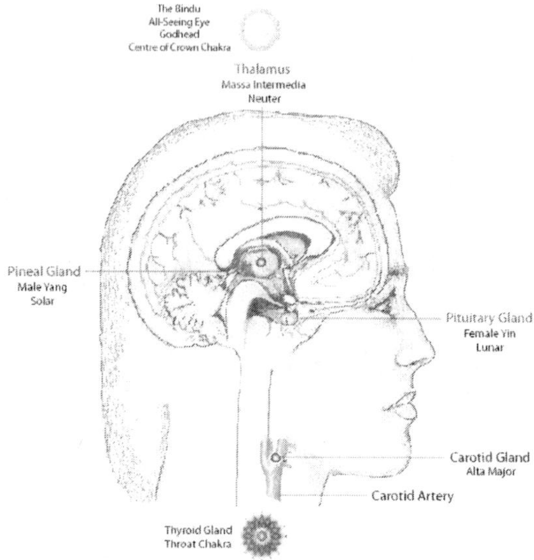

Figure 6.1: The Carotid, Pineal, and Pituitary Gland Centres in the Neck and Brain

The thalamus is the 'seed-stone' (philosopher's stone and the "cosmic egg". T*he Thalamus is the centre of consciousness and is the source of hypnagogic phenomena.*

6.2 Pituitary Gland

We have already described, in details, about the Pineal Gland in this book. We shall now describe briefly about the Pituitary Gland in this section.

The Pituitary has been called the 'Master Gland,' this is because it coordinates all the other glands, controls growth and is essential to the life and 'well-being' of the individual. It is said that removal of the pituitary from the brain will cause death in three days. Like the pineal gland associated with the day/night cycles, the pituitary gland is also dual in nature and this duality is also expressed in its physical composition. It has two lobes, each of which performs a different function. These are known as the anterior and posterior lobes. It is illustrated in the following picture:

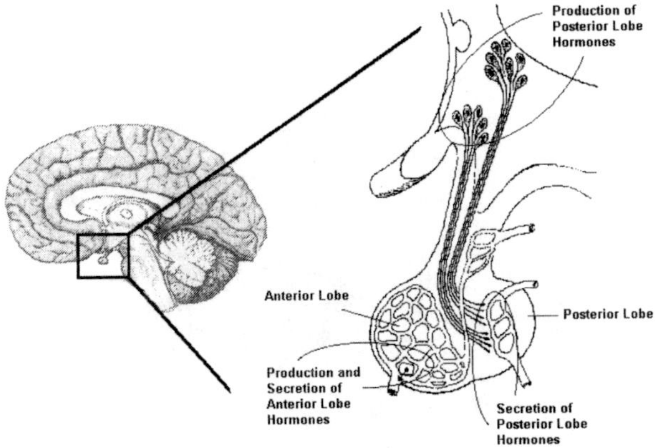

Figure 6.2: Illustration of the two Lobes of Pituitary Gland

The pituitary gland has a glowing 'phosphorescent' appearance, which is similar to the effervescent light of the 'full moon' and that it has been known that the Egyptians knew this because they called the pituitary the "Star Chamber of Isis" as the goddess Isis was associated with the moon – but there really isn't any evidence of this that Egyptologists are aware of. According to ancient esoteric tradition, the pituitary gland represents the feminine principle and the pineal the masculine. However, like the brain of both male and female individuals, the two hemispheres express the opposite traits associated with the 'logical-reasoning' male principle (left-brain) and 'emotional-intuitive female principle (right-brain.) Various esoteric traditions maintain that the predominantly, feminine-related pituitary gland, reflects this same duality. The frontal or 'anterior lobe' is associated with the reasoning and intellectual mind of the male and the 'posterior lobe' is associated with the emotional, imaginative female nature. This comes from the ancient belief that there is a connection between emotional and mental deficiency and a lack of development in the pituitary gland – and surprisingly, many endocrinologists and psychologists have expressed the same view.

6.3 The Carotid Gland (Alta Major Chakra)

Let us take a close look the Carotid Gland (Alta Major Chakra) in the neck.

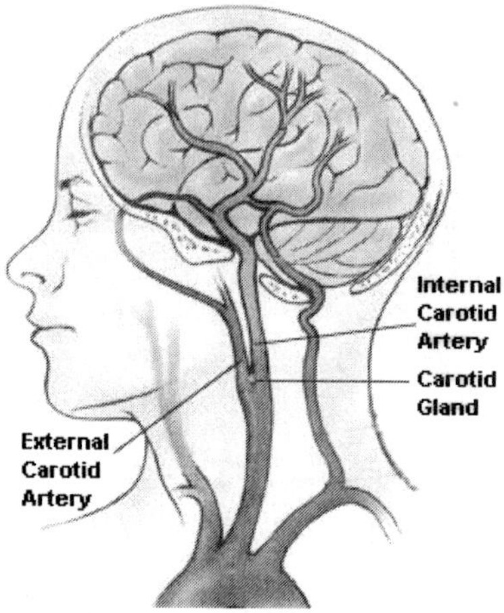

Figure 6.3: Location of Carotid Gland (Alta Major Chakra) in the Neck

In the esoteric traditions the carotid gland is known as the '***Alta major***' however, the carotid gland is hardly ever mentioned in "new-age" literature, so why would this gland be important? Importance of Alta Major Chakra has been described earlier in this book. A control over one's breathing is necessary for yoga and meditation and the carotid gland is associated with the respiratory system – i.e., breathing, and maintains homeostatic control over the levels of oxygen and carbon dioxide in the blood. The duality inherent in the cycles of opposites is again evident here in the inhalation of oxygen and the exhalation of carbon dioxide – which this gland controls.

So we are collectively concerned with the following three glands:

(i) **Pineal Gland:** The day/night cycles are also controlled with this gland and related to the waking/sleeping cycle.

(ii) **Pituitary and Hypothalamus Gland:** It regulates the body temperature – keeping a homeostatic balance between the extremes of hot and cold. These also regulate the growth of the individual.

(iii) **Carotid Gland:** The inhalation/exhalation, breathing cycles and levels of oxygen (in-breath) and carbon dioxide (out-breath) in the blood.

6.4 The Thalamus

The walnut-sized thalamus is at the centre of the brain, located on top of the brain stem or the limbic system known as the Reptilian Brain. The 'serpent's head' is a reference to the Reptilian Brain – the part of the brain which is said to be stimulated during psychic activity.

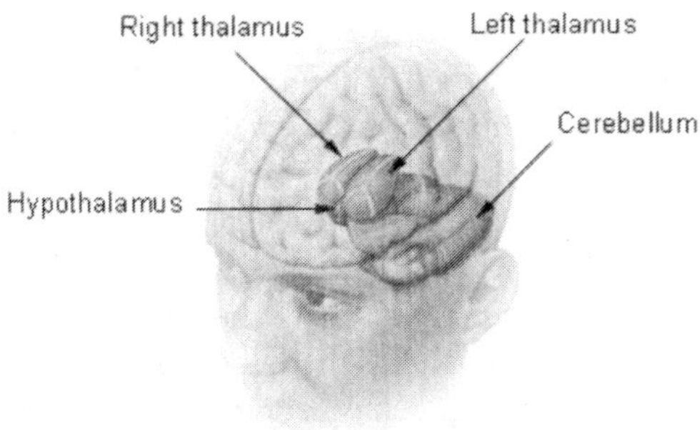

Figure 6.4: Thalamus, showing Left and Right Lobes; Also Hypothalamus, Cerebellum

The thalamus has two lobes known as the 'thalamic bodies,' which look like a smaller version of the two hemispheres of the brain known as the cerebrum. Interestingly, the name 'cerebrum' is a composite of Ceres, meaning 'cross' and RU – CerebRUm – again associated with the ancient Egyptian life symbol – the Ankh. The two lobes of the thalamus are connected together by a tubular bundle of nerve fibres at their centre, called the massa intermedia or the interthalamic adhesion.

The two halves of the thalamus are prominent bulb-shaped masses, about 5.7 cm in length, located obliquely (about 30°) and symmetrically on each side of the third ventricle. Both parts of this structure of the brain in the human are each about the size and shape of a walnut. These are about three centimetres in length, at the widest part 2.5 centimetres across and about 2 centimetres in height (the nut relative to an unshelled nut with the nut-shell join in the horizontal plane.

The thalamus is believed to process sensory information as well as relay it—each of the primary sensory relay areas receives strong "back projections" from the cerebral cortex. The thalamus also plays an important role in regulating states of sleep and wakefulness. Thalamic nuclei have strong reciprocal connections with the cerebral cortex, forming circuits that are believed to be involved with consciousness. The thalamus plays a major role in regulating arousal, the level of awareness, and activity.

Around the massa intermedia, the two thalamic bodies are separated by the 'third ventricle;' one of the few spaces in the brain which is filled with cerebral spinal fluid. The thalamic cells demonstrate high proliferative activity, frequently fusing via the massa intermedia, which is a non-neuronal structure. In other words, and in esoteric thought based on correspondences with the sexual, procreative process, the egg (thalamus) is continually being "seeded" or "fertilised" – suggesting re-creation. The term 're-creation' here means 'repeating patterns' – i.e., re-patterning. The thalamus is the major sensory and motor relay nucleus in the brain; it is our "central control box" and is our interface with the reality around us. In other words, it acts like the hub of the whole wheel. When one part of the neocortex – one "spoke" of the "wheel" – communicates with another; it does so via the thalamus – being the centre of the whole sphere. If there were anything in the physical body that would represent the centre of consciousness itself, it would be the thalamus at the centre of the brain.

To esoteric initiates the thalamus, known as the Optic Thalamus was regarded as the real 'third e ye'. Esotericist, Alice Bailey, tells us that Francis Bacon, a Rosicrucian, regarded the soul to be at the centre of the brain, and again, this could only be the thalamus.

6.5 Thalamus as the 'Third Eye'?

After examining the ancient symbols, it becomes apparent that it was believed by the ancients that we create our reality in the same way by selecting information internally from the source and projecting it, and during this same fusion-node-point in the cyclical process. So, if all the information we are picking up from the world around us is integrated within the thalamus – which selects only that information with which we are familiar and where this information is then being regulated and relayed to the rest of the brain – then we can see that during the rare 'enlightenment experience' – when one experiences all the information of the universe at once, or so it seems – the 'gateway' of the thalamus has opened up totally – or that all our energies are focused at this point in the brain. Therefore it is logical to say that this 'conscious fusion experience' takes place in the thalamus right at the centre of the brain. This fusion is also associated with the activation of the 'third eye'.

Here is the superimposition of the two realms belonging to the left and right hemispheres, that is, the conscious-self (being the energy-information which we interact with everyday) and the subconscious-self, (energy-information we usually block out) and all within the thalamus at the centre of the brain.

Going back to the Hindu symbolism: During trance and all related experiences associated with the opening of the so-called 'third eye,' the ancient Hindu texts tell us, that the heads of the two serpents (the positive and negative 'nerve channels') strike the pineal and pituitary glands. As said, the male-related pingala strikes the male-related pineal gland, and the female-related ida strikes the female-related pituitary gland. The two come together in the sushumna – the central nerve channel, which aligns with the brain stem (the Reptilian Brain) and this activates the thalamus ("the cosmic egg" in the brain) opening it up wide to absorb more information and energy. The metaphorical descriptions of these processes as known by the ancients. The sushumna, which represents this fusion, is said to emerge from the centre of the forehead like the Uraeus of the Egyptian Pharaohs – symbolising the **'third eye'** and the 'second sight' associated with the hypnagogic trance state. Symbolically, through the Uraeus serpent on the forehead, one is able to "see into the other worlds."

According to the book titled "The Symbols of Wodhanaz", Wodhanaz (Odin) turning himself into a serpent, and charming the female guardian, is an allegory for the enlightenment experience. The three vats are related to the three power centres in the brain – two of which are 'secreting' glands – the chemical secretions represented by the mead. The drops of mead then turning into mushrooms – also associated with the word 'thalamus' – reveals that these psychoactive substances were used to activate the **'third eye'** associated with these two glands as well as the thalamus.

Finally, let us take an example from Hinduism, which is depicted in the following picture:

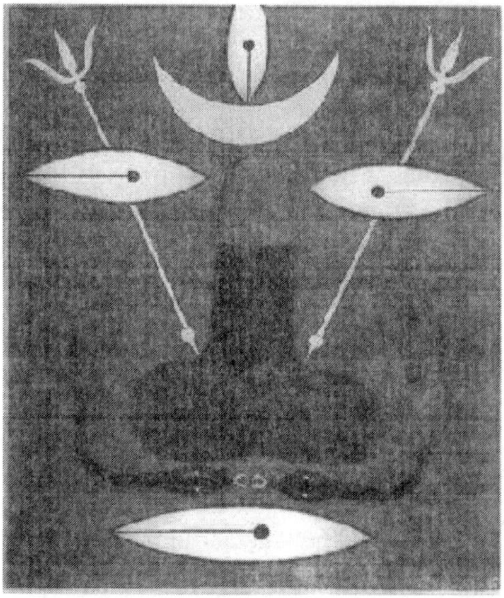

Figure 6.5: Hindu illustration encompassing many of the 'third level themes associated with the enlightenment experience

As we can see the Ru "gateway" – being the female vagina – is featured as the two eyes, the mouth and also the centre of the brain – the Hindu '**third eye**'. Further evidence that the Ru "gateway" is the vagina of the "world mother" and that it is represented by the thalamus at the centre of the brain, is the Shiva Lingam, (phallus or penis, doubling as the nose) which is depicted to be penetrating the thalamus and continually "seeding" it – but here activating it.

Between the thalamus and the penis is the 'bowl' – also shaped like the moon – representing the female ovum or egg, which is brought by the Phoenix to be put on the phallic pillar of Atum-Ra. Here the Hindu version of Atum-Ra would be Brahma or Shiva.

Chapter - 7

Third Eye In Hinduism (Lord Shiva)

7.1 Glory of Third Eye of Lord Shiva in Ancient Scripture

The following Mantra (known as: "Maha Mrityunjaya Matra"), mentioned in the Rig Veda (Mandala VII, Hymn 59), also describes the three-eyed "Lord Shiva":

ॐ त्रयम्बकं यजामहे सुगन्धिं पुष्टिवर्धनम्।
उर्वारुकमिव बन्धनान् मृत्योर्मुक्षिय मामृतात्।।

Om trayambakam yajamahe sugandhim pushtivardhanam;
Urvarukamiv bandhanan mrityormukshiya mamratat.

Meaning: I worship the three-eyed One (that is, Lord Shiva); Who is fragrant and Who nourishes all beings. May I be liberated from the bondage of mortality (death), similar to a ripe cucumber leaving effortlessly from its Creeper (a plant with long, flexible and thin stem that grows, typically along the ground or up a building, by slowly spreading out). May I never be separated from the immortality.

This third eye is the faculty of intuition and insight (insight; inner vision; subtle perception) which allows us to realise Shiva (our Essential Nature). Besides our two fleshy eyes, each of us has a third eye which lies dormant unless it is awakened by the practices of Yoga or any other transformative system. When it awakens we can live in the world of mundane affairs (with the two fleshy eyes) whilst remaining in contact with the Roots of our Being (with the third eye).

Further on Triyambakam (as mentioned in Puranas):

त्रयम्बकं यजामहे च त्रैलोक्यपितरं प्रभुम्।
त्रिमण्डलस्य पितरं त्रिगुणस्य महेश्वरम्।।

Trayambakam yajamahe cha trailokyapitaram prabhum.
Trimandalasya pitaram trigunasya maheshwaram.
– (Shiva Purana Rudra Samhita chapter 38)

Meaning: We worship lord Shiva having three eyes, who is the Lord of three worlds and the master of three gunas.

Further, in Linga Purana, it is mentioned that:

त्रयाणामपि लोकानां गुणानामपि यः प्रभुः।
वेदानामपि देवानां ब्रह्मक्षत्रविशामपि।
अकारोकारमकाराणां मात्राणामपि वाचक।।
तथा सोमस्य सूर्यस्य वह्नेरग्नित्रयस्य च।
अंबा उमा महादेवो ह्यंबकस्तु त्रियंबक।।
– (Linga Purana II.54)

Trayanaamapi lokaanaam gunaamapi yah prahuh.
Vedanamapi devanaam brahmakshatravishaamapi.
Akaarokaaramkaaraanaam maatraanaamapi vaachaka.
Tatha somasya surasya vahneragnitryasya cha.
Amba uma mahadevo hyambakastu triyambakam.
– (Linga Purana II.54)

Meaning: The word 'Tryambaka' has been defined as the one, who happens to be the Lord of the three worlds, three gunas, three Vedas, three gods, three castes— He is revealed by the three syllables 'a', 'u', 'm'. He is the lord of three fires, Viz. : the sun, the moon and the fire. He represents Amba, Uma and Mahadeva. Thus, the lord of all the sets of three is known as Tryambaka.

According to Maha Mrityunjaya Stotram:

त्र्यक्षं चतुर्भुजं शांतं जटामुकुटधारणम्।
नमामि शिरसा देवं किं नो मृत्युः करिष्यति।।
– (महामृत्युंजय स्तोत्रम्, 7)

Traiksham chathurbhujam santham jata makuta dharanam,
Namami sirasa devam, kim no mrutyu karishyathi.
– (Maha Mrityunjaya Stotram, 7)

Meaning: What can death do to the one, Who salutes with his head that god, Who has three eyes, Who has four hands, Who is peaceful, And who wears matted hair and a crown.

Sage Kashyapa prays to Bhagawan Rudra calling him Tryambaka and Pushtidam in Harivamsa Parva which is an appendix to Mahabharata as follows. Pushtidam (Health giver) is a synonym of Pushtivardhanam (health increaser). Therefore clearly this mantra cited below is a derived from Maha-Mrityunjaya Mantra alone:

त्र्यम्बकं पुष्टिदं विब्रुवाणं धर्मं विप्राणां वरदं यज्वुनां च।
वराद् वरं रणजेतारमीशं देवं देवानां शरणं यामि रुद्रम्।।
– हरिवंश पुराण विष्णु पर्व अध्याय 72 श्लोक 45

Tryambakam Pushtidam vo bruvanam |
Dharmam vipranam varadam yajvanam cha |
varadvaram ranajetaramisham |
Devam devanam sharanam yami rudram ||
– (Harivamsa Parva 2:72:45)

Meaning: I seek refuge in Lord Rudra (Mahadeva) who has three eyes, who flourishes all, who advises brahmins and wise men on dharma, who provides the wishes of the masters of the sacrifice, who is the best of the best, the lord who is the winner of battles, who is the lord of gods.

Shiva Panchakshra Stotram (शिवपञ्चाक्षरस्तोत्रं) says:

नागेंद्रहाराय त्रिलोचनाय भस्मांग रागाय महेश्वराय।
नित्याय शुद्धाय दिगंबराय तस्मै न काराय नमः शिवायः।।

Nagendraharaya trilochanaya bhasmanga ragaya maheshraya.
Nityaya shuddhaya digambaraya tasmai na karaya namah shivayah.

Meaning: Salutations to the ashes-clad, three-eyed Lord, embodied as the first letter Na, who is pure, nude and eternal and whose garland is the lord of serpents.

सर्वमङ्गलमाङ्गल्ये शिवे सर्वार्थसाधिके।
शरण्ये त्र्यम्बके गौरि नारायणि नमोऽस्तु ते।।

Sarvamanggala maanggalye shive sarvaartha saadhike |
Sharannye tryambake Gauri Naaraayanni namostu te ||

Meaning: (Salutations to You O Narayani) Who is the auspiciousness in all the auspicious, auspiciousness Herself, complete with all the auspicious attributes, and Who fulfils all the objectives of the devotees, Who is the giver of refuge, with three eyes and a shining face; Salutations to You O Narayani.

According to Ardhanari Nateshvara Stotram (अर्धनारी नटेश्वर स्तोत्रम):

विशालनीलोत्पललोचनायै विकासिपङ्केरुहलोचनाय।
समेक्षणायै विषमेक्षणाय नमः शिवायै च नमः शिवाय।।4।।

Vishalanilotpalalochanayai vikasipankeruhalochanaya.
Samekshanayai vishamekshanaya namah shivayai cha namah shivaya. (4)

Meaning: To Her with eyes as broad as the petals of the blue lotus (Nilotpala), to Him with eyes as broad as the petals of the fully blossomed lotus, to Her with an even number of eyes (two), to Him with an odd number of eyes (three), to Gauri and Lord Siva may our prostrations be.

Bhagavan Sri Krishna gifts the third-eye-vision to his dear devotee, disciple Arjuna, amidst the waging war-field of Kurukshetra during the Bhagavad Gita.

He says –

न तु मां शक्यसे द्रष्टुमनेनैव स्वचक्षुषा।
दिव्यं ददामि ते चक्षुः पश्य मे योगमैश्वरम् ।।11–8।।

na tu maam shakyase drashtum anenaiva swachakshushaa
divyam dadaami te chakshuh pashya me yogamaishwaram.
– Srimad Bhagawad Gita, 11-8

Meaning: Oh Arjuna, with your own eyes you cannot see Me. Let me give you the Divine Eyes, without which you will not be able to see the inconceivable mystic power, My sovereign Yoga power." And Lord Krishnan opened His third-eye, through which Arjuna had the rarest spiritual, cosmic experience.

Through this verse, The Lord says that Arjuna cannot see Him in the Cosmic Form with his own fleshy eyes and hence gives him the divine eye (Divya Chakshu), called the 'third eye'. Human eyes can see only the outward forms, the inner soul is perceived by the eye of the Spirit, the third eye.

There is a type of knowledge that we can acquire by our own efforts, knowledge based on the perceptions by the senses and intellectual activity. Another kind of knowledge is possible when we are under the influence of grace, a direct knowledge of spiritual realities. The god-vision is a gift of God. All these indicate the unity of the cosmic manifold in the Divine nature. The vision is not a mental construction but the disclosure of a truth from beyond the finite mind. It is the vision of the third eye.

7.2 Some Instances when Lord Shiva Opened His 'Third Eye'

Figure 7.1: Lord Shiva and His Third Eye

Lord Shiva rarely opens His third eye until it is mandatory because, the immense power from Shiva's third eye could destroy everything. Shiva opens His third eye only when He has to destroy evil.

Following are instances when Shiva opened his third eye are:

(i) To destroy Kama (lust): One day Shiva was in deep meditation, and to provoke Lust feelings in Shiva, Lord Kama hits Shiva with Kaamastra. Shiva with anger opens His third eye and destroys Kama into a pile of ash.

(ii) To destroy Lord Indra's arrogance: One day, Lord Indra gets a thought that he is far superior and powerful than Shiva. Indra goes to Kailash to meet Shiva and fight with Him.Shiva disguises himself as a Gana and stops Lord Indra at the gate of Kailash, after knowing that Indra has come to prove to the world about his supremacy over Shiva. Indra fumes at the Gana, after the Gana challenges Indra to first fight with him, before approaching Shiva. The Gana pushes Indra hard and he falls down on the ground, and Indra realizes that Gana is none other Shiva himself. As no one has the power to defeat Indra and throw him onto the ground, with a mere push. Indra falls on the Gana's feet and asks for his mercy. Then Shiva comes into his original form, but because of the attitude of Indra, Shiva in order to destroy Indra's arrogance opens his third eye. But after seeing Indra at his feet, Shiva cools down, since His third eye is already opened, the energy from his third eye gets transmitted into the ocean. And from that energy, Jalandhar is born.

(iii) For Lighting up the world: When Parvati closed His Eyes and darkness descended upon the Universe: There is one more story of Shiva opening his third eye. It is believed that one day Parvati closed Shiva's eyes and the universe went dark. Shiva had to open his third eye to provide light and energy to the world. Heat from His third caused Parvati's hand to perspire and a drop fell on the ground from her hand, which transformed into a child. It was a boy and they named him Andhaka. He was adopted by a Shiva devotee Asura. Andhaka was blessed with a boon – death would only come to him when he desired for a women he shouldn't. Once he came across Parvati, and completely smitten by her beauty, he chased her and got killed by Shiva. This episode represents the dark side of desires. When people forget to differentiate between good and bad, their world needs to be jolted apart.

(iv) Shiva accepted Nandi as His vehicle: Surabhi, the mother of all cows started giving birth to a lot of cows, and the cows started flooding mountain Kailash with their milk. Furious at this, Lord Shiva used his third eye and destroyed many of them. To calm down Lord Shiva, other gods sought to offer Nandi the magnificent bull to Lord Shiva, which He accepted as His vehicle.

(v) Significance of Varanasi as a Pilgrimage: There is an interesting story about the third eye of Lord Shiva, Lord Brahma and the importance of the sacred place Varanasi. The story goes like this: Shiva and Parvati once went to visit Brahma. Brahma began to chant hymns in Shiva's praise with all of his five mouths. One of the mouths however made mistakes in the pronunciation of the hymns. This angered Shiva and He severed the offending head of Brahma with a gaze of His third eye. But this effectively amounted to the killing of a Brahmana and therefore Shiva committed a crime. As a consequence, the severed head got stuck to Shiva's back and it would not come off, no matter wherever Siva went. But when Shiva arrived in Varanasi, the head fell off his back. Shiva realized that Varanasi was a special place and he resolved that he would always be present there. This is the reason for some people to think that Varanasi, the spiritual capital of the world, is the home of Lord Shiva. Varanasi is the DNA of Vedic tradition where death itself is liberation. 'Vara-nasi' means: Third-Eye – the space between your nose and eyebrows. Varanasi is also called the great funeral pyre, and in the mystic geography of India Varanasi is the blazing third eye of Shiva. In Varanasi, Ganga's holy city, the Ganges River is a place of meditation. The river reflects the archetypes to the visionaries' third eyes. Because the Ganges is shallow, it remains a place for reflection. Once you have visited Varanasi, it will always be with you.

(vi) To destroy the Arrogance and Falsehood of Lord Brahma: Following story is taken from 'Shiva Purana':

"Once while travelling, Lord Brahma reached the abode of Lord Vishnu. He saw lord Vishnu resting on Shesh-Nag and being attended by Garuda and other attendants. When Brahmaji saw that Vishnu did not get up to receive him, he became very angry. Very soon, Verbal dual erupted between them. It became so severe that a battle was fought between them, which continued for a very long time. All the deities arrived from the heaven to watch the battle. They became very worried when they saw no sign of battle coming to an end. They decided to go to lord Shiva, to seek his help. "Though Lord Shiva knew everything, but still feigning ignorance, he asked about the well beings of the world. The deities told him about the battle, being fought between Brahmaji and Vishnuji." "Lord Shiva then sent his one hundred Ganas to pacify both of them. Lord Shiva also went there accompanied by Parvati, boarded on a chariot.

When Lord Shiva reached there, he saw that Brahmaji and Vishnuji were about to use their deadly weapons- Maheshwar and Pashupati respectively. Fearing the destruction, which these deadly weapons might have caused, Lord Shiva manifested himself in the form of 'Analstamba' (pillar of fire) between them. Brahmaji and Vishnuji had already released their weapons. Both the weapons fell into that pillar of fire and got destroyed. "Brahmaji and Vishnuji were very surprised to see the pillar of fire, which was so enormous in size that it reached the sky and penetrated through the earth. Vishnuji transformed himself into a boar and went to the 'Patal' (below the earth) to find the base of that 'Pillar of fire'. But he was unsuccessful in his attempt and came back. Similarly Brahmaji transformed himself into a swan and flew up in the sky to find its limit. While going through the aerial route he met a withered 'Ketaki' flowers, which had still some freshness and fragrance left in it."

"Lord Shiva smiled at the futile attempts of Shri Brahmaji and Vishnuji. As a result of his smile the Ketaki flower fell down from the branch. Ketaki flower told Brahmaji that he had been present there since the beginning of the creation, but was unable to know about the origin of that 'Pillar of fine'. The flower also advised Brahmaji against making any effort in that direction, as it would be of no use." "Brahmaji then sought the help of Ketaki flower to give a false witness before lord Vishnu, that he (Brahmaji) had been successful in seeing the limit of that pillar of fire. Ketaki flower agreed. Both of them went to Vishnuji and Brahmaji told him that he had seen the limit of that Pillar of fire. Ketaki flower gave a witness. Vishnuji accepted the superiority of Brahmaji."

"Lord Shiva became very angry with Brahmaji. He proceeded to punish Brahmaji for his falsehood. Lord Vishnu requested Lord Shiva to spare the life of Brahmaji. Lord Shiva became pleased with Vishnuji and accorded him the same status as that of his own." "After according same status to Vishnuji as that of his own, Lord Shiva opened his third eye. from it manifested 'Bhairav'. He ordered Bhairav to kill Brahmaji. Bhairav severed the fifth head of Lord Brahma with his sword. Brahmaji became very terrified. He was trembling in fear. Lord Vishnu felt pity on his condition and requested Lord Shiva to forgive him. Lord Shiva then stopped Bhairav, but told Brahma. "You spoke untruth with a desire to become worshippable. It is my curse that, you will not be worshipped by anybody. You will posses only four heads." Brahmaji begged his forgiveness. Lord Shiva feeling pity on Brahmaji gave him a boon of being the presiding deity of all the yagya. Similarly the Ketaki flower also prohibited from being used during worship. But when Ketaki flower tendered his apology Shiva gave blessing that it would be fortunate to be offered to Lord Vishnu during the worship.

Lord Vishnu and Brahma made salutations to lord Shiva and offered him a seat. They then worshipped him. This was the first time, Brahma and Vishnu had worshipped Lord Shiva. Shiva was very pleased. Shivaratri has been continued to be celebrated since that day. This particular day is considered to be the most auspicious day for the worship of Lord Shiva. A devotee who fasts on Shivaratri remaining only on fruits, attain virtues equivalent to the worship done for the whole year.

Lord Shiva has himself told the deities that he had manifested in the form of 'Pillar of Fire' in the month of Agahan and during the constellation of Ardra. He also said- "One who has my darshan on this day (Shivratri) or worships me in my form of linga is dearer to me than Kartikeya. The place where, I manifested in the form of Pillar of fire, will become famous as Lingasthan. Because of its resemblance with the 'Mountain of Fire', it will also be known Arunachal." Later on Shiva brought back to life all the people who had died in the battle, fought between Brahmaji and Vishnuji.

Chapter - 8

Third Eye in Kashmir Shaivism

8.1 Introducing Kashmir Shaivsim

Kashmir Shaivism is a theistic philosophy that identifies Lord Shiva as the Absolute, Infinite, and pure Consciousness lying beyond the reach of speech, mind, and intellect. The development of Kashmir Shaivic philosophy can be traced back to Aagamas, which were written from 3rd century BC to 3rd - 4th century AD. Malinivijayattara is the most important Aagama of this period. Dating from around 850-900 CE, the Shiva Sutras and Spandakārikā were the first attempt from the Śākta Śaiva domain to present a non-dualistic metaphysics and gnostic soteriology in opposition to the dualistic exegesis of the Shaiva Siddhanta. The Shiva Sutras appeared to Vasugupta in a dream, according to tradition. The Spandakārikā was either composed by Vasugupta or his student Bhatta Kallata. Vasugupta who lived in Kashmir during the end of the 8th century AD wrote Shiv Sutra and it was his disciple Bhatta Kalatta (mid 9th century AD) who wrote Spanda Karika. Somananda wrote Shiv drishti in late 9th century AD.

Kashmir Shaivism is a group of non-dualist tantric Shaiva traditions from Kashmir that originated after 850 CE. It superseded Shaiva Siddhanta, a dualistic tradition which scholars consider normative tantric Shaivism. The Shiva Sutras and Spandakārikā were the first attempt from the Śākta Śaiva domain to present a non-dualistic metaphysics and gnostic soteriology in opposition to the dualistic exegesis of the Shaiva Siddhanta. The Tantrāloka, Mālinīślokavārttika, and Tantrasāra of the Kashmirian Abhinavagupta (975–1025 CE) are formally an exegesis on the Mālinīvijayottara Tantra, although they also drew heavily on the Kali-based Karma tradition of the Kulamārga.

While there may have been yogis and practitioners quietly following the teachings, there were no major writers or publications after perhaps the 14th century. In the 20th century Swami Lakshaman Joo, himself a Kashmiri Brahmin, helped revive both the scholarly and yogic streams of Kashmir Shaivism. He inspired a generation of scholars who made Kashmir Shaivism a legitimate field of inquiry within the academy.

While he himself not belonging to the direct lineage of Kashmir Shaivism, Muktananda felt a great affinity for the teachings which were validated by his own direct experience.

Figure 8.1: Swami Muktananda:
A Great Exponent of Kashmir Shaivism

The Vijnana Bhairava Tantra, a chapter from the Rudrayamala Tantra, was introduced to the West by Paul Reps, a student of Lakshaman Joo. Reps brought the text to wider attention by including an English translation in his popular book Zen Flesh.

While most other paths observe offering incense and external objects to the deity, this path takes on to offering breaths. The individual controls his heart and pulse by reducing it significantly. The final stage is renouncing consumption of food and water. As a result, he/she connects the state of the supreme in the form of Shiva which results in purification of the body and generation of ojas.

Tantric scholar-practitioner Christopher Wallis outlines the philosophical view of non-dual Shaiva Tantra thus:

All that exists, throughout all time and beyond, is one infinite divine Consciousness, free and blissful, which projects within the field of its awareness a vast multiplicity of apparently differentiated subjects and objects: each object an actualization of a timeless potentiality inherent in the Light of Consciousness, and each subject the same plus a contracted locus of self-awareness. This creation, a divine play, is the result of the natural impulse within Consciousness to express the totality of its self-knowledge in action, an impulse arising from love. The non-dual or monistic philosophy of Kashmir Shaivism is called Pratyabhijna. Ksemaraja, the student of Abhinavagupta, extended this philosophy to a broad range of tantric Saiva texts.

Kashmir Shaivism and Advaita Vedanta are both non-dual philosophies that give primacy to Universal Consciousness (Chit or Brahman). In Kashmir Shaivism, all things are a manifestation of this Consciousness, but the phenomenal world (Śakti) is real, existing and having its being in Consciousness (Chit).

8.2 Third Eye as mentioned in Vijnana Bhairava Tantra (विज्ञानभैरव तन्त्रम)

Vijnana Bhairava is a short manual about the Self and the means to acquire direct knowledge of the Self and ultimately reach Self-realization. Thus it is a manual of meditative practices. It is a central text of Kashmir Shaivism. It is an ancient tantric text of unknown origin and date, but it is older than the first millennia A.D. "Vijnana Bhairava "is composed of the words" "Vijnana" and "bhairava". Vijñāna means knowledge. Bhairava, in Hindu mythology, is one of many manifestations of Shiva. However, in Kashmir Shaivism Shiva/Bhairava means the Absolute, the Self. This book is said to be spoken by Bhairava in reply to Devi's questions. Devi lists a number of questions concerning the highest reality based on the contents of now lost books (tantras). These are regarding the nature of the highest reality and how to reach it.

Some of the verses in Vijnana Bhairava Tantra, related to the location of the third eye or Ajna chakra given here below.

तयापूर्याशु मूर्धान्तं भङ्क्त्वा भ्रूक्षेपसेतुना।
निर्विकल्पं मनः कृत्वा सर्वोर्ध्वे सर्वगोद्गमः।।31।।

Tayapuryashu murdhantam bhangtva bhrukshepasetuna.
Niravikalpam manah kritva sarvodhrave sarvagodgamah. (31)

Meaning: Then, having filled the tip of moordha (forehead) and crossed the bridge between the eyebrows, the mind rises above all dichotomizing thought patterns and omnipresence (prevails).

With verse 31 of Vijnana Bhairva, an additional focal point is introduced: the "third eye" region in the forehead. This focus deep behind a point between the eyebrows onto the "eye of light" grows into feeling and perceiving a brightening of energy and light from the third eye focal point, which then expands upward in feeling and awareness into the crown and beyond.

In verse 36, it mentions about the third eye:

कररुद्धदृगस्त्रेण भ्रूभेदाद् द्वाररोधनात्।
दृष्टे बिन्दौ क्रमाल् लीने तन्मध्ये परमा स्थितिः ।। 36।।

Kararuddhadrigastrena bhrubhedad dwararodhanat.
Drishte bindau kramal leene tanmadye parama sthitih. (36)

Meaning: By using the hands (as tools) to block the entrances in all directions, the eyebrow centre is pierced and bindu (or light) is seen. Being gradually absorbed within that, the supreme state is realized.

'Bindu' literally means a dot, but it is used as a synonym for the source point or origin of all manifestation. Some translate 'bindu' with light and it is likely that bindu here means seeing a dot of light in the third eye. Some maintain bindu as a centre located at the back of the scull. The technique of blocking the openings of the head with the hands is known as "shanmukhi mudra". Take a deep breath, close the ears with the thumbs, the eyes with the index fingers, the nose with the middle fingers and the mouth with the ring fingers and the little fingers, in order realize the supreme light.

Further, in verse 37, this book mentions:

धामान्तःक्षोभसम्भूतसूक्ष्माग्नितिलकाकृतिम् ।
बिन्दुं शिखान्ते हृदये लयान्ते ध्यायतो लयः ।। 37 ।।

Dhamantah kshobhasabhutasukshmagnitilakakritim.
Bindum shikhante hridaye layante dhyayato layah. (37)

Meaning: Whenever one meditates upon the subtle lire, in the form of a tilak (like the mark on the forehead), or on the bindu at the end of the shikha, a condition of agitation and shaking is produced, followed by absorption and dissolution in the cave of the heart.

"The lock of hair" could refer to the lock of hair brahmins leave at the back of the head (shikha, in Hindi), and some people do speak of a centre located there which they calls bindu. It is translated "ākritim bindum" as "similar to a small dot", and the previous word "tilaka" locates it to between the eyebrows. It refers to the crown of the head. This verse is also sometimes translated that one should meditate on the "cave of the heart". But heart is here a metaphor for pure Being, as it most commonly is. Since the verse states that one should meditate on the heart after one has transcended meditation on the contraction produced by agitation, it makes most sense to understand heart to mean utter freedom from contraction, which means the Self.

The bindu refers to the source, to the primal borderline to pure Being. This is also what Bindu technically refers to, despite that it literally means "dot" or "drop". In the aftermath of agitation one may merge into pure Being by meditating on the sense of contraction which the agitation has left as an imprint on consciousness. In the midst of agitation one should focus on the third eye. One can then look at the contraction inherent in agitation from a witness stance, disengaged. Then one should recognize the contraction as Shakti, as the bliss of the Self in an agitated and contracted state. Then one should move from the contraction to the heart, which means to move from contraction and limitation to freedom and the Self. The contraction will then dissolve. Any agitation will do: physical or emotional, though emotional agitation is typical.

In verse 76, Vijnana Bhairava mentions:

तेजसा सूर्यदीपादेर् आकाशे शबलीकृते ।
दृष्टिर् निवेश्या तत्रैव स्वात्मरूपम् प्रकाशते ।। 76 ।।

Tejasasuryadeepader aakashe shabalikrite.
Drishtir niveshya tatraiva svatmarupam prakashate. (76)

Meaning: By gazing on the space that appears variegated by the rays of the sun or an oil lamp, there the nature of one's essential Self is illumined.

This practice is not what is known as tratak, in which one fixes the gaze at a steady flame for a prolonged period. In tratak one stares at the flame for a while until the image of the flame is imprinted on the mind. Then one closes the eyes and visualizes the flame in the third eye. This verse, however, speaks of "variegated" ("shabaleekrite") space or light, not the steady light used in tratak. On should gaze into the room (for example) with the sense that the light illuminating from the various things in it, is the light of the Self.

In verse 85, Vijnana Bhairava mentions:

लीनं मूर्ध्नि वियत् सर्वम् भैरवत्वेन भावयेत् ।
तत् सर्वम् भैरवाकारतेजस्तत्त्वं समाविशेत् ।। 85 ।।

Leenam muridhna viyat sarvam bhairavatvena bhavayet.
Tat sarvam bhairavakaratejastattvam samavishet. (85)

Meaning: One should contemplate on the sky as the form of bhairava (until it is) all absorbed in the forehead (at the location of the third eye). Then all that (space) will be entered by the essence of light in the state of bhairava.

8.3 Third Eye in Netra Tantra

The Netra Tantra is one of the authoritative scriptures of non-dualist Kashmir Shaivism (dated not later than 700 AD) with important sections on Yoga. It is attributed to the school of Kashmir Shaivism and is usually printed with a commentary by Kshemaraja. It is the only Tantra on the Third Eye of Shiva, and it is also called Mrityujit or Mrityunjaya, "The Overcomer of Death", relating to the form of Shiva revealed in it and to his mantra. The commentary by Kṣemarāja (early 11th century) is an important help in understanding this profound text and its practice.

Mentioned in 'Netra Tantra' 19.3-6, the term 'chhaya-chhidra' is introduced, which is the sole comprehensive treatment of the 'evil eye' (another phase of the 'third eye') In Her formulation of a question to Shiva concerning the evil eye (literally,

the 'casting of the gaze': drishti-pata), the Goddess States:

"Now, those innumerable "goddesses" are indeed possessed of immeasurable powers. The Yoginis who are more powerful, oppress by means of the 'chhaya-chhidra'. They are exceptionally filthy, violent, merciless, fearless, [and] mighty. They are injurious to all creatures, and especially to children. Their number is not found. Tell me the strategy against them. The trick they always play, which takes the form of the chhaya, is likewise the trick [they play in] the casting of the gaze. This chhaya: how manifold is it declared [to be]? What is there to fear from the casting of the gaze, and how does one avert it?

In the case of powerful beings such as gods, demons, and human yogis, such rays of perception can actually penetrate the surface of their objects, and enter into them: this is possession (avesha) or, as described in 'Netra Tantra', 20.23-27, 'subtle yoga' (sukshma yoga).

Chapter - 9

Five Eyes in Buddhism

Buddhism classifies the eye into five categories; namely, the (i) Physical eye, (ii) Heavenly eye, (iii) Wisdom eye, (iv) Dharma eye, and the (v) Buddha eye. It should be pointed out first that the term 'eye' used here does not refer to the ordinary human eye. The human eye is but first kind of eye that is the physical eye. As a matter of fact, the human eye is not the best example of this category. An eagle has eyes which can see much farther than can those of a human. An owl has eyes which are much more sensitive to light than our eyes, and can see things in the darkness that we cannot see.

9.1 Physical Eye

With the help of the physical eye, we can see only within the visible part of the electromagnetic spectrum (popularly called as VIBGYOR). We cannot see infrared wavelengths and beyond, nor ultraviolet wavelengths and beyond. This means that before man invented the instruments to assist his naked eye in detecting the universe beyond the visible band, the world that he saw and considered complete, true, and real was actually incomplete and a very small portion of the whole universe. It is really amazing to realize that more than 2,500 years ago Buddha drew this same conclusion without the assistance of any of the instruments we now have.

The following example may illustrate more clearly the inferiority of our human (physical) eye, and how it compares with the heavenly eye:

Imagine that there is a totally enclosed dark house in the middle of a big city, with one very small window from which one can see only crowded tall buildings, a little blue sky above, and a few limited human activities. Suppose a child is born and grows up in this house. What would be his impressions of his world? They would no doubt be based on what he sees through the small opening. No matter how eloquently one might describe to him the beauty of the vastness of a seascape and the wonder of a view at sunrise and sunset he could hardly understand and appreciate them.

This is precisely how our human eye limits us. We are actually in a dark house, viewing the universe through a very small opening which is our physical eye. Yet we insist that what we see is the complete, real, and true world.

Now imagine that there is another house on top of a mountain. The house has a large picture window from which one can see the unlimited sky and infinite horizon. Maybe we can make it even more romantic by saying that numerous flower gardens and dancing girls surround the place. Again, a child is born and grows up in this house. Is it not conceivable that the world he envisions is much greater and more beautiful than the one seen through the small window facing a crowded city? According to this analogy, the second child possesses the heavenly eye whereas the first one has only the physical eye.

9.2 Heavenly Eye (Divine Eye)

Usually it is said that the heavenly eye is possessed by gods or goddesses in heaven. According to Buddhism, however, this statement is not entirely correct because we human beings can also obtain the heavenly eye. There are two ways to achieve it. One way is through 'dhyana,' a Sanskrit word which is commonly (but incompletely) translated as 'meditation.' The other way is to add an instrument to the naked eye (which is also a kind of instrument that can itself be transplanted). Although the first way, meditation, is a much superior method, the second way is probably easier for modern man to understand. Modern man is able to see into remote space by employing a powerful telescope. Modern man can watch the activities of bacteria by using a microscope. Today, one can observe events happening millions of kilometres away by means of space vehicles and television, and can see many other wonders which in the Buddha's time were exclusive to the heavenly eye. In those days, dhyana was the only means of enabling a human being to transcend the boundary set forth by the physical eye. It is clear that Buddha realized that although man's ability to see is infinite, that ability is actually limited by the physical eye. However, through years of meditation, Buddha discovered that the barrier of the physical eye can be broken and that the original ability of man to see can be fully developed. When that occurs, there will be no difficulty in extending one's vision as far as the realm perceived by the heavenly eye.

In Buddha's time, it was much more difficult for man to understand the heavenly eye; today, practically speaking, everyone possesses the heavenly eye to some degree. It is, therefore, comprehensible to us. Heavenly eye perceives things in the darkness, at a distance, or beyond the physical limits of obstruction.

9.3 Wisdom Eye

To describe the wisdom eye we need to introduce a very important and fundamental concept in Buddhism, which in Sanskrit is called 'shunyata' and may be translated as 'emptiness.' This is a unique teaching that cannot be found in any other religion. Voluminous scriptures in Buddhism are devoted to the study of emptiness. What can be described in this chapter is really a drop of water from a vast ocean.

There are three analytical modes of thinking, described by Buddha, which lead to the understanding of emptiness:

(i) Analytical method of disintegration

Let us take a radio as an example. Imagine that you have a radio here. If you take out the loud-speaker, can you call the loud-speaker the radio? The answer is no. You call it the loud-speaker. Now take out the transistor. Do you call the transistor the radio? Again no; it is the transistor. How about the condenser, the resister, the plastic case, the wire, etc.? None of these parts are called the radio. Now note carefully. When all the parts are separate, can you tell me where the radio is? There is no radio. Therefore, 'radio' is simply a name given to a group of parts put together temporarily. When one dismantles it, the radio loses its existence. A radio is not a permanent entity. The true nature of the radio is emptiness.

Not only is the radio emptiness; the loud-speaker is too. If you take the magnet out of the loud-speaker, do you call it a loud-speaker? No, you call it a magnet. If I remove the frame, do you call it a loud-speaker? Again no, you call it a frame. When all the parts are taken apart where is the loud-speaker? So, if we dismantle the loud-speaker, it loses its existence. A loud-speaker is not a permanent entity. In reality, a loud-speaker is emptiness.

Now, this analytical method of disintegration can be applied to everything in the world, and will lead to the same conclusion: Everything can disintegrate; therefore, nothing is a permanent entity. So, no matter what name we call a thing, it is, in reality, emptiness.

Buddha applies the method of disintegration to himself. In his imagination he removes his head from his body and asks if the head would be called the human body or self. The answer is no. It is a head. He takes his arm off his body. Would this be called the human body or self? The answer is again no. It is an arm. He takes the heart out and asks whether this is the human body or self. The answer is again no, which we understand now even more precisely since a heart can be removed from one body and transplanted into another without changing one person into another person. Buddha takes every piece of his body apart and finds that none of the parts can be called the human body or self. Finally, after every part is removed, where is the self? Buddha therefore concludes that not only is the physical body emptiness, but the very concept of self is emptiness.

(ii) Analytical method of integration

Although we see hundreds of thousands of different things in the world, man is able to integrate them into a few basic elements. For example, based upon chemical characteristics man has classified gold as a basic element. We are able to name thousands of golden articles ranging from a complicated golden statue to a simple gold bar, but all of these articles could be melted and remolded into other forms. They are changeable and impermanent. The things which remain unchanged are the common chemical characteristics, due to which we call all of these articles 'gold.' In other words, all of these articles are integrated under the category of the element which we call 'gold'.

In Buddha's time, Indian philosophers integrated everything into four basic elements, namely, solids, liquids, gas, and heat (agni). Buddha went further and declared that the four elements could be integrated into emptiness. Continuing with our example of gold, Buddha's statement means that we can also question the existence of gold as a permanent entity, even though we have recognized it as a common characteristic of the various golden articles. Whatever we can show is but a specific form of gold, such as a gold bar which is basically changeable and impermanent. Therefore, gold is simply a name given to certain characteristics. Gold itself is emptiness.

By the same reasoning, Buddha concluded that all solids are emptiness. Not only are solids emptiness, but liquids are too, since the characteristics of fluidity are formless, ungraspable, and empty of independent existence. Thus, 2,500 years ago, Buddha concluded that everything in the universe can be integrated into emptiness.

It is certainly interesting to note that the western scientists have reached a similar conclusion. Before Albert Einstein discovered the theory of relativity, scientists integrated everything in the universe into two basic elements, namely, matter and energy. Einstein unified these two elements and proved mathematically that matter is a form of energy. By doing so, he concluded that everything in the universe is simply a different form of energy.

But what is the original nature of energy? Although it would not be ventured to assert that energy is the same as emptiness, we would at least like to say that energy is also formless, ungraspable, and analogous to emptiness.

(iii) Analytical method of penetration

Buddha performed this method by means of meditation. Meditation may be difficult for most of us, but fortunately today's scientific technology furnishes us with certain analogies which can give us some comprehension of this method. Let us refer back to the electromagnetic spectrum. We know that our naked eye can see only the small portion of the universe which is visible to us, but with the aid of certain instruments, such as an infrared device, x-ray, microscope, etc., modern man is able to see other realms of the universe. So we see an ordinary man as he would be detected by different instruments at different wavelengths.

Now just imagine that your eyes are able to detect infrared. What you see standing in front of you is a red, yellow, and green coloured image. Now shift back to the instrument you use daily; my external form is perceived by your naked eyes. Next imagine that your eyes can see with an x-ray. My skin, flesh, and blood disappear and what you see now is the bone structure of my body. Changing to another instrument, the microscopic eye, the man standing in front of you is a complicated chain structure of molecules. Now penetrate a bit further. Modern science teaches us that molecules consist of atoms, and atoms consist of particles, and ultimately all mass can be converted into energy, the original nature of which is something that we cannot see or hold. Let us call it formless form, which is represented by the empty space.

Your attention is invited to the fact that I am the same man in the ordinary sense, but that I can appear to you in different forms: colourful image, fleshly body, and structure of bones, assembly of molecules, many other forms, corresponding to different realms or instruments, and finally the formless form.

This third method, the analytical method of penetration, again leads to the same conclusion that everything in the universe can be penetrated to its foundation, called energy by scientists, and emptiness by Buddha.

However, emptiness is a state of direct experience. It is said that when one reaches that state, there is an experience of tremendous bliss which is hundreds of times stronger than any kind of bliss ever experienced by ordinary man. Furthermore, emptiness is a state in which one transcends the sense of change and impermanence.

Now let us go a step further. As you may know, the realization of human suffering was the direct cause which led the Buddha-to-be, Prince Siddhartha, to renounce his palace and to become an ascetic in search of the way leading to the emancipation of mankind. Buddha listed eight kinds of human suffering, called 'dukha' in Sanskrit, which has a somewhat more extensive meaning than the word 'suffering.' The eight sufferings are (i) birth, (ii) old age, (iii) sickness, (iv) death, (v) loss of loved ones and pleasant conditions, (vi) association with unpleasant persons and conditions, (vii) failure to obtain what one wants, and (viii) impermanence. If you carefully analyze them you can conclude that all the eight sufferings are related to, or have originated from, the physical body and consciousness that we call self. The physical body and consciousness of the self are the foundations upon which all human sufferings are built.

Now, if the physical body and the consciousness of self are no longer in existence when the state of emptiness is achieved, how can suffering still exist? When one reaches that stage, everything in the universe, including oneself, is seen as emptiness. All human sufferings disappear, and one is said to possess the wisdom eye.

It is like sudden relief from a deadly heavy burden. It is like the unexpected reunion of a mother with her son who had disappeared for years. It is like the discovery of land on the horizon while one is sailing desperately on a stormy sea. These are a few of the descriptions of the great delights that are experienced when the wisdom eye is gained.

Many disciples of Buddha reached this stage. Such people were called arhats. Although they were saints, Buddha issued a stern warning to them: "Don't stop at the wisdom eye." Buddha explained that with the physical or heavenly eye we see the incomplete, changeable, and unreal world as complete, permanent, and real. Thus we become attached to the world, which is why we suffer. This is one extreme. With the wisdom eye we see everything in the universe as impermanent, unreal, and empty, and like to remain in that state of emptiness. This becomes an attachment to emptiness, and is the opposite extreme. Once there is attachment, whether to a substance or to emptiness, the consciousness of self, which is the root of all ignorance and suffering, cannot be completely eliminated. To obtain the Dharma eye is, therefore, the ultimate teaching of Buddha.

A Note about Arhat

Arhat is a Sanskrit word that means "worthy," "venerable" and "deserving." In Theravada Buddhism, an arhat is defined as one who has reached a state of nirvana through extreme self-discipline and abstention from worldly pleasure. Depending on the school of Buddhism and the evolution of the term over the centuries, arhats may be considered as similar to buddhas or enlightened ones. Some traditions, like Mahayana Buddhism, consider arhats imperfect when compared to buddhas. In contrast, the Pali Tipitaka text describes arhat as the goal of the Buddha's path to liberation. Some early scriptures refer to the historical Buddha, or Siddhartha Gautama, as an arhat. Theravada Buddhists believe that all enlightened beings are arhats, but that just one in each eon is a Buddha — distinguished by his learning and ability to teach others. In Mahayana Buddhism, arhat may describe an enlightened being or a Buddhist who is spiritually advanced, but has not reached buddhahood. In Tibetan and Chinese Buddhism, arhats are revered like saints. They are believed to have been chosen from the Buddha's disciples to remain in the world and protect the dharma.

9.4 Dharma Eye (or Dhamma Eye)

What is Dharma eye (Dhamma in 'Pali' and Dharma in Sanskrit)? A man is said to have Dharma eye when he does not stay in emptiness after gaining the wisdom eye. Instead, he recognizes that although whatever he sees in different realms is only a manifestation, it is nevertheless real with respect to its realm.

One who has only the physical eye will insist that only the physical body is real, since he lacks the knowledge of all other realms. One who possesses the wisdom eye sees that these forms are phantoms which are impermanent, insubstantial, and unreal, and that emptiness is the only state which is real and permanent. Thus one becomes attached to emptiness.

Now, one who possesses the Dharma eye will say that although it is true that all such forms are manifestations, they are not entities separate from emptiness, and they are real with respect to the realm they are in. This realization automatically generates an unconditional, nondiscriminative universal love and compassion. Such a person is said to possess the Dharma eye; in Buddhism that person is called a ***bodhisattva***.

Once one overcomes the attachment to emptiness, the unconditional, nondiscriminating love and compassion arising spontaneously from a direct experience of emptiness is truly a wonder of mankind. This teaching makes Buddhism a most unique and profound practical religion.

Let us take the help of a story to illustrate the difference between an arhat who has achieved the wisdom eye and a bodhisattva who possesses the Dharma eye:

A huge mansion is on fire. There is only one door which leads to safety. Many men, women, and children are playing in the mansion but only a few of them are aware of the danger of fire. Those few who are aware of the danger try desperately to find a way out. The way is long and tricky. They finally get out of the mansion through the heavy smoke. Breathing in the fresh open air again, they are so delighted that they just lie on the ground and do not want to do anything more. One of them, however, thinks differently. He remembers that many people are still inside and are not aware of the danger of the fire. He knows that even if they are aware, they do not know the way that leads to safety. So, without considering his own fatigue and risk he goes back into the mansion again and again to lead the other people out of that dangerous place.

This person is a bodhisattva

There is another famous Buddhist story which has been introduced to the readers by Professor Huston Smith in his distinguished book, 'The Religions of Man'. It goes as follows: Many people are travelling across a desert in search of a treasure at a remote location. They have walked a long distance under the hot sun, and are tired, thirsty, and desperately in need of a shaded place to rest and some water or fruit to quench their burning thirst. Suddenly three of them reach a compound surrounded by walls. One of them climbs to the top of the wall, cries out joyfully, and jumps into the compound. The second traveller follows and also jumps inside. Then the third traveller climbs to the top of the wall where he sees a beautiful garden, shaded by palm trees, with a large pond of spring water. What a temptation! However, while preparing to jump into the compound, he remembers that many other travellers are still wandering in the horrible desert without knowledge of this oasis. He refuses the temptation to jump into the compound, climbs down from the wall, and goes back into the immense, burning desert to lead the other travellers to this resting place.

I believe that everyone here will have no difficulty in understanding that the third person is a bodhisattva.

It should be pointed out here that such compassion is not superficial but is deep and fathomless. It has no pre-requisite such as "because I like you" or "because you obey me." It is nondiscriminating and unconditional. Such compassion and love arises spontaneously from the direct experience of emptiness, the state of perfect harmony, equality, and lack of attachment of any sort.

By this point I hope that you have some understanding of the four kinds of eyes. Here is a story about two famous verses in Zen Buddhism:

The Fifth Patriarch in the Tang Dynasty of China once asked his disciples to write a verse to present their understanding of Buddhism. The head monk Shen Hsiu presented one as follows:

The body is a wisdom tree,
The mind a standing mirror bright.
At all times diligently wipe it,
and let no dust alight.

The Fifth Patriarch commented that Shen Hsiu had only arrived at the gate and had not entered the hall.

A layman called Hui Neng was also in the monastery. Although he had not yet received instruction from the Fifth Patriarch, he was nevertheless a highly gifted person. When Hui Neng heard the verse, he disagreed with Shen Hsiu and said, "I have one also." He submitted this verse:

Wisdom is no tree,
Nor a standing mirror bright.
Since all is empty,
Where comes the dust to alight?

Later, Hui Neng became the Fifth Patriarch's disciple and achieved enlightenment. He became the famous Sixth Patriarch of Zen Buddhism. He gave different teachings to persons of different capacities.

9.5 Buddha Eye

So far we have discussed about the four kinds of eyes, but there is something beyond this: the Buddha eye.

You will notice that in our discussions about the first four kinds of eyes, there was always a subject and an object. For example, with the physical eye we have a human being as subject and worldly phenomena as object. With the heavenly eye we have divine beings as subject and the vast realms of space as object. With the wisdom eye we have arhat as subject and emptiness as object. Bodhisattva is the subject and the various realms of the universe are the objects when we refer to the Dharma eye. When we talk about the Buddha eye, however, it would be quite incorrect to say that Buddha is the subject and the universe is the object, because the distinction no longer exists between Buddha and the universe. Buddha is universe and universe is Buddha. It would be equally wrong to say that Buddha possesses the Buddha eye because there is again no distinction between the Buddha eye and Buddha. Buddha eye is Buddha and Buddha is Buddha eye. In short, any duality you can construct is not relevant to the Buddha eye.

The second point about the Buddha eye concerns the nature of infinite infinity. What is meant by infinite infinity? Although we say that the human concept of the cosmos is infinity, such a concept is just like a bubble in the vast sea when compared with Buddha's experience of the cosmos. Is it incredible? Yes, it is incredible. But let us think of what we have in mathematics. You know that the first degree of power is a line. The second degree of power is a plane. The third degree of power represents a three-dimensional space. All of these shapes could already be infinite in size. Now how about the fourth degree of power, the fifth degree of power, up to the nth degree of power? If you are able to explain what the nth degree of power represents, you might have some understanding of Buddha's cosmology: the infinite infinity.

Thirdly, let us something about the nature of instantaneity and spontaneity. This is again a concept that is very difficult for human beings to understand. To us, the duration of time is a solid fact. Moving through this time factor, man grows up from an infant, to a youth, to maturity, to old age, etc. It is beyond our comprehension to say that time does not exist for the Buddha eye, but that is what the Buddha eye entails. Billions of years are no different from one second. A world which is measured as billions of light years away from the earth according to our cosmology can be reached in just one instant. What a wonder this is!

The final point we discuss about the Buddha eye is its nature of totality and all-inclusiveness. Some of you might have seen a movie called "Yellow Submarine." A monster which is like a vacuum machine sucks in everything it encounters. After it has sucked in everything in the universe, it begins to suck in the earth on which it stands. The vacuum machine is so powerful that it sucks the whole earth into itself and finally it sucks itself in. This image illustrates the all-inclusiveness of the Buddha eye.

Now, let us summarize what we have mentioned four points about the Buddha eye:

1. no subject and no object; that is, no duality
2. infinite infinity; that is, no space
3. instantaneity and spontaneity; that is no time
4. all-inclusiveness and totality; that is, no nothingness.

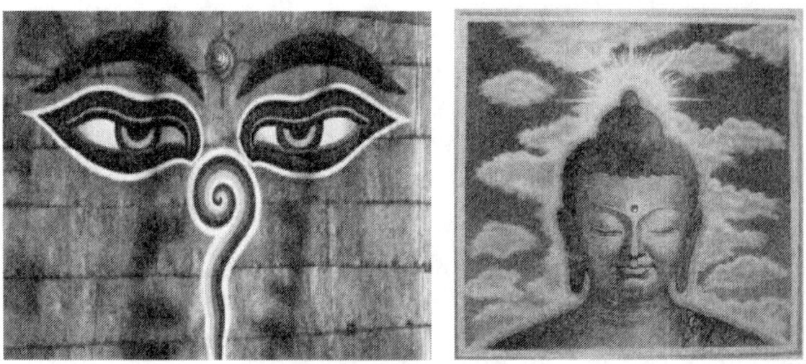

Figure 9.1: The Buddha Eye

The Buddha eye includes all the other four eyes, or perceptive faculties. In other words, Buddhas possess all five types of vision.

On virtually every Buddha statues, Buddha heads and Buddha stupa (Buddhist shrines) from countries like India, Nepal, Thailand, Burma, China and others, there are pairs of eyes casting down as if in a meditation state, and enriched with a spiritual aura. This style has been a model for various generations of artists while depicting them in various Buddha heads and Buddha images. Between the two outer eyes of Wisdom, a curly symbol is depicted symbolizing the nose which looks like question mark. These curly symbol symbolizes the unity of all things existed in the world as well as the only path to enlightenment though the teachings of Lord Buddha. These depictions can mostly be found in the Buddha stupa such as Swayambhunath Stupa, Boudhanath Stupa. Every Buddhist Stupa and monasteries all over world have various important features and eyes of Buddha are believed to one of the important features of Buddha stupa and are quite important in Buddhist tradition. In most of stupa, these eyes are depicted in all four directions to show all seeing omnipotent ability of Lord Buddha. These eyes are the representation of Lord Buddha's omnipotent powers of seeing all that can be in the past, present as well as in futures. Eyes of Buddha also symbolize important part of Enlightenment. After attaining Nirvana in Bodh Gaya, Lord Buddha sees all the sentient beings in all realms i.e. human realm, god realm, hell realm, etc.

In Buddhism, the protuberance depicted at the top of the head of the Buddha known as "ushnisha" is interpreted as a symbol of the spiritual power of the Buddha's enlightenment. Some say it is a protuberance or the skull or the flesh, while others say it is just a knot of hair. Some also interpret it as the opening of the Sahasrara chakra (the crown chakra) during the Buddha's enlightenment experience. In South-East Asia the protuberance is replaced by either a flame or a lotus flower. According to Madam Blavatsky, the ushnisha represents the third eye.

Ushnisha is explained as "a protuberance on Buddha's cranium, forming a hair-tuft". This curious description is given by the Orientalists, which states that Ushnisha was "originally a conical or flame-shaped hair tuft on the crown of a Buddha, in later ages represented as a fleshy excrescence on the skull itself". This ought to read quite the reverse; for esoteric philosophy would say: Originally an orb with the third eye in it, which degenerated later in the human race into a fleshy protuberance, to disappear gradually, leaving in its place but an occasional flame-coloured aura, perceived only through clairvoyance, and when the exuberance of spiritual energy causes the (now concealed) "third eye to radiate its superfluous magnetic power.

Chapter - 10

Third Eye in Daoist or Taoist Practice

What is the difference between Taoism and Daoism?

Taoism is a great philosophical and religious tradition that originated in China; it is sometimes also referred to as Daoism. In Chinese, the word 'Tao' means 'the way', the force that flows through all life in the universe. It is considered to be the driving force behind everything that exists. The objective of Taoism is for a person to align harmoniously with the 'Tao' i.e. to achieve immortality by taking the right path in life.

Taoism is based on the writings of a mythical figure named Laozi who lived some 2,500 years ago. It calls for an adherence to "the way", which practitioners have long interpreted as a return to the natural world. The core of the basic belief and doctrine of Taoism is that "Tao" is the origin and law of all things in the universe. Taoists believe that people can become deities or live forever through practicing certain rituals and austerities.

In linguistics, the term 'Taoism' and 'Daoism' are different English phonetic adaptations of that word. The term 'Tao' is from a Romanization created by the early European traders to help them understand the Chinese language. Phonetically, it is close but not always identical to the word in their sound. In 1958, the Chinese government adopted pinyin, a Romanization that is more consistent with the phonetic sounds in the, government accepted, Mandarin dialect. In pinyin, the character is spelled and pronounced as 'Dao'.

In English, the difference between the terms 'Taoism' and 'Daoism' is based on their sinology, phonemes, loanwords, and pronunciation. The root meaning of the terms, 'the way', is Romanized as 'Tao' in the older Wade–Giles system, while the term 'Dao' is used in the modern Pinyin system.

Even though the oldest system for transcribing Chinese into the Roman alphabet is the Wade-Giles, and the term 'Taoism' is more familiar and older than 'Daoism', the modern Pinyin system is fast gaining grounds in the international standards. It is the official system of Romanization used by the governments of the People's Republic of China, Singapore and Taiwan. Though, many sinologists increasingly prefer the term Daoism, traditionalists continue using the well-known Taoism.

In Taoism and many traditional Chinese religious sects such as Chan (called Zen in Japanese), "third eye training" involves focusing attention on the point between the eyebrows with the eyes closed, and while the body is in various qigong postures. The goal of this training is to allow students to tune into the correct "vibration" of the universe and gain a solid foundation on which to reach more advanced meditation levels. Taoism teaches that the third eye, also called the mind's eye, is situated between the two physical eyes, and expands up to the middle of the forehead when opened. Taoism claims that the third eye is one of the main energy centres of the body located at the sixth Chakra, forming a part of the main meridian, the line separating left and right hemispheres of the body. In Taoist alchemical traditions, the third eye is the frontal part of the "Upper Dan Tien" (upper cinnabar field) and is given the evocative name "muddy pellet".

10.1 Pineal Gland Activation in Cranio-sacral Work and Daoist Practice

In both Cranio-sacral work and Daoist practice, the endocrine system is a critical gateway joining physical function with spiritual experience. The endocrine system includes the following glands: the pituitary, pineal, hypothalamus, thyroid, parathyroid, adrenals, pancreas, and ovaries/testes.

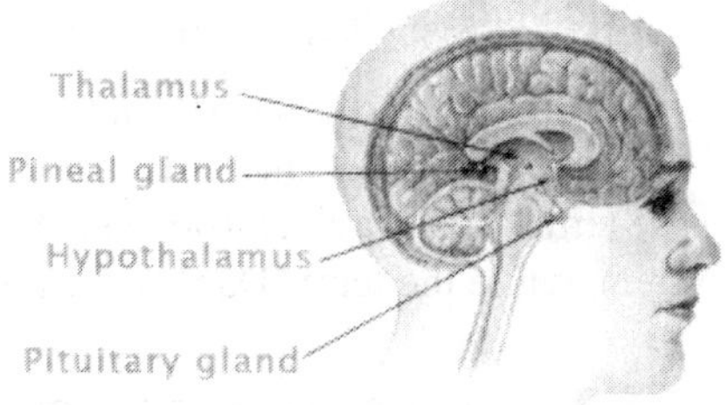

Figure 10.1: Display of pituitary, pineal, hypothalamus

These glands use hormones (rather than the electrical impulses used by the nervous system) to effect changes in our body, emotions, cognition, and energy. Hormones are chemical messengers that circulate through the body via the bloodstream and coordinate critical body functions. They increase or reduce nerve impulses and can also act as neurotransmitters. The hypothalamus, pituitary, and pineal glands play particularly important roles in spiritual experience and will be explored in greater detail in the following.

10.1.1 The Hypothalamus / Pituitary Relationship

With access to both the nervous and endocrine systems, the hypothalamus plays a central role in linking the two and in activating the pineal gland. It is also connected with the limbic system, a centre for our feelings and emotions. When entrained with the pituitary gland, the hypothalamus has the ability to affect most of the major systems and organ functions in the body as well as our emotions. Together, the hypothalamus and pituitary regulate all of our basic survival processes including body temperature, hunger, thirst, fatigue, growth, sleep, weight, sexual function, pain relief, blood pressure, circadian rhythms, and stress responses such as fight or flight.

The hypothalamus is about the size of an almond and is located just behind the optic chiasm. It secretes neuro-hormones that communicate with the pituitary gland, signalling the release or inhibition of key pituitary hormones, which in turn harmonize and activate pineal gland function. The pituitary gland has two major lobes, which are distinctly different embryologically, anatomically, and functionally. Altogether, the pituitary is about the size of a pea; it sits below the hypothalamus, cradled in the sella turcica of the sphenoid bone. Because the pituitary is enclosed by the sphenoid, it is highly sensitive to misalignments or restrictions in the movement of that bone. If you press your tongue to the roof of your mouth at the soft palate, you are pressing on the underside of the pituitary.

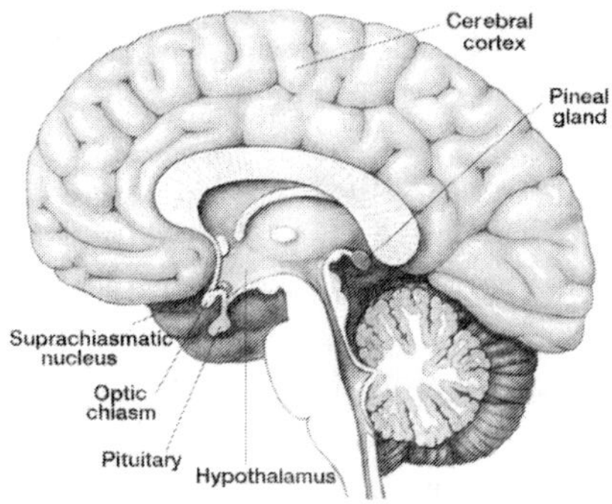

Figure 10.2: Display of Optic Chiasm, hypothalamus and Pineal Gland

The hypothalamus communicates with the anterior lobe of the pituitary via blood vessels, and connects directly with the posterior lobe through the pituitary stalk or infundibulum. Although the pituitary gland has often been referred to as the master gland because it appears to control the endocrine system, the hypothalamus plays a more crucial role in this system than previously thought. The hypothalamus receives and integrates information from the rest of the body and then secretes the neuro-hormones that release or inhibit key pituitary hormones. By signalling and directing the pituitary, the hypothalamus plays a critical part in the endocrine system and is important in a larger sense for pineal gland activation.

10.1.2 Functions of the Pituitary in Physical Health and Spiritual Awakening

The anterior lobe of the pituitary secretes seven key hormones that are related to lactation, the release of testosterone, and the production of sex, thyroid, and human growth hormones. The posterior lobe does not produce hormones, but stores and releases two important ones, which are made in the brain: oxytocin and vasopressin. Oxytocin fosters maternal instincts, bonding between mates, trust, and sexual pleasure. Vasopressin influences circadian rhythms, the reabsorption of water into the bloodstream, and also stimulates paternal protective and caring instincts. The pituitary relates to our growth and its health is also important for pineal gland activation. When it begins to vibrate in synchrony with the pineal gland, we are inspired to grow and renew ourselves both physically and spiritually.

10.2 The Pineal Gland

The pineal gland is located in the centre of the brain, behind and above the pituitary gland. Because the pineal is bathed in highly charged cerebrospinal fluid (CSF) and has more blood flow per cubic volume than any other organ, it may well be the gland with the highest concentration of energy in the body. In addition to its high concentrations of CSF and blood, the pineal gland is also the dominant source of the body's melatonin.

10.2.1 Melatonin and the Pineal Gland

Melatonin is significant for its effects on our mood, immune function, circadian rhythms, and the quality and quantity of our sleep. Melatonin is known as an anti-aging and anti-stress agent because it both suppresses cortisol and is a powerful antioxidant. The production of melatonin by the pineal gland is activated by darkness and inhibited by light. Once released, melatonin circulates through the brain via the CSF and enters nearby blood vessels for distribution to the rest of the body. When melatonin levels are disrupted, people can experience mood swings, depression, and seasonal disorders.

10.2.2 Serotonin and other Consciousness Enhancing Neuro-chemicals secreted by the Pineal Gland

In addition to producing melatonin, a healthy, activated pineal gland also metabolizes other neurochemicals that coordinate physical and emotional processes on a cellular level. These neurochemicals, including pinoline and Dimethyltryptamine (DMT), are said to connect the mind and body. The pineal plays a key role in the production of these neurochemicals because it has one of the highest concentrations of serotonin in the body, and serotonin is a critical precursor to them.

10.3 Spiritual Aspects of the Pineal Gland

Given its important role, it is not surprising that a healthy, activated pineal gland has been connected with spirituality for millennia. Its pinecone shape is found in art and artefacts of many ancient traditions, where it is associated with enlightenment and immortality. Ancient Egyptians revered this tiny gland and even preserved it separately during the process of mummification. With its spines and spirals, the pinecone illustrates a perfect Fibonacci sequence—symbolizing growth and the unifying force that underlies creation, all embodied in an activated pineal gland.

10.3.1 The Pineal Gland: Key to Opening the Third Eye

Spiritual traditions associate and activate pineal gland with the opening of the third eye of inner vision, insight, and wisdom. Scientific research is beginning to validate the relationship between the pineal gland and vision: comparative research into the anatomy, physiology, and biochemistry of the pineal gland and the retina across a wide range of animal species suggests that the two organs share evolutionary and developmental paths. Modern living fossils such as the tuatara have a photosensitive pineal eye with a rudimentary lens, cornea, and retina. Other species such as frogs and lampreys also have pineal eyes. In humans, pineal cells resemble retinal cells in composition and in the presence of proteins not found elsewhere in the body. Pineal light sensitivity is common across diverse species and in humans is connected with the opening of the third eye.

10.4 Melatonin and the Spirit Molecules

In terms of spiritual experience, melatonin quiets the body and mind, allowing access to higher consciousness. Both pinoline and DMT, secreted by a healthy, activated pineal gland, are psychoactive, causing changes in perception, mood, consciousness, cognition, and behaviour. Pinoline enables visions and dream states in the conscious mind and has been used by ancient Egyptians and Zoroastrians in their rituals. It assists in DNA replication and is said to resonate with the pulse of life at ~8 cycles per second.

DMT is produced in the pineal gland during deep meditation and extraordinary conditions of birth, sexual ecstasy, extreme physical stress, and near-death experiences. It also alters our dream consciousness when it is released into the bloodstream during the Rapid Eye Movement phase of sleep. DMT links the body and spirit because of its relationship to visionary experiences and nonordinary states of transcendent consciousness. Dr. Rick Strassman calls DMT the Spirit Molecule.

10.5 The Pineal Gland and Vibration

The activated pineal gland can also influence our experience through vibration. With the heart, rhythmic vibrations can have a powerful effect on our cognition, emotions, and physical state. We know this intuitively, and we experience it directly when we sense the effects that music has our mood, memory, and physiology. In the early 1980s, the French musician Fabien Maman researched the effect of sound vibrations on cells; he found that sounds can destroy cancer cells and invigorate healthy ones. Today, it is common for parents to play classical music to stimulate brain development in their children before and after birth. Rhythm entrainment, also called resonance, happens when two wave forms begin to oscillate together at exactly the same rate. When the hypothalamus and pituitary entrain with the pulsing vibration of the pineal gland, our whole system can shift toward harmony.

Daoists believe that the North Star is the source of the original pulse. Vibrations from this star were crucial in the evolution of the first forms of life on Earth. It is said that Earth's ability to support life is related to the planet's tilt toward the North Star (rather than being oriented directly toward the sun). This orientation maximizes the habitable surface and optimizes the environment for plant and animal life. Because of the North Star's strong power and influence, many Qi Gong exercises intentionally connect with the North Star. According to Daoists, the North Star emits pulsing vibrations which affect and activate the pineal gland. When the pineal gland pulses in synchrony with the North Star, it receives cosmic information and relays it to the hypothalamus and pituitary through resonance. In turn, they send messages to the heart which communicates with the rest of the body through its own electromagnetic pulsing.

10.6 Magnetic Fields and the Pineal Gland

Besides being sensitive to light and vibration, the pineal gland activates in part due to exposure to magnetic fields. Studies with birds and other animals conclude that the pineal gland monitors magnetic fields and assists the body in orienting in space, by acting as a navigational centre. This magneto receptive capacity also explains why geomagnetic storms and environmental stress can affect the pineal gland, leading to problems with circadian rhythms and melatonin secretion.

As we discussed earlier, the heart generates a strong electromagnetic field that permeates the whole body. When the heart is activated with the high frequencies of love and compassion, its electromagnetic field is amplified and expanded. The pineal gland's sensitivity to electromagnetic energy causes it to begin vibrating and activating in concert with the heart. As these two organs entrain together, their high vibration opens the third eye to greater inspiration, intuition, and inner vision. Because of the pineal gland's connection with spatial orientation and circadian rhythms, our perception of space and time often shifts when the pineal is in a highly aroused state. Such experiences have been mentioned by meditators and Chi Kung practitioners for millennia, and research is now providing explanations for these phenomena.

10.7 Hypothalamus, Pituitary, and Pineal Gland

In Daoist practices, the region of the brain bounded by the pineal, the pituitary, and hypothalamus glands is called the Crystal Palace. The Crystal Palace sits between the left and right hemispheres of the brain and between the forebrain of reason and the hind brain of instinct. Many meditation practices mention the Crystal Palace, but some people have difficulty sensing it because these structures are inside the skull and cannot be touched directly.

However, with a little practice, it is simple to connect with and activate these spiritual glands through our awareness and intention. The location of the pineal gland is often described as the centre of the head—it is at the level of the eyebrows, above and behind the pituitary and hypothalamus. Behind the eyes, the optic nerves cross at the optic chiasm. Below the optic chiasm is the pituitary gland, which sits in the sella turcica of the sphenoid. Above and behind the optic chiasm is the hypothalamus.

10.8 Crystal Palace, The Pineal Gland and Its Relationship with Light

All three glands of the Crystal Palace are extremely sensitive and responsive to light. Prior to 2002, science was aware of two forms of light receptors in the eye: cones (for colour vision) and rods (for low light vision). In 2002, however, scientists discovered a third photoreceptor: cells in the retina that contain a light-sensitive pigment called melanopsin. These cells send messages to the suprachiasmatic nucleus (SCN) of the hypothalamus. The SCN is responsible for controlling circadian rhythms, which influence our sleep, alertness, hormones, temperature, and digestive functions.

When the hypothalamus receives information about the presence or absence of light, it signals the pineal gland to activate and to start or inhibit cortisol and melatonin production. Variation in melatonin levels causes a cascade of changes in the SCN, pituitary, and retina. The pituitary also responds to light through its release of vasopressin, which influences the SCN to adjust our circadian clock.

In addition to the light detected by our eyes, studies now show that the whole body acts as a light receptor. Light shining on any part of the body can be detected, signalling the SCN and pineal gland to shut down melatonin production. Because there is so much ambient light these days, our systems rarely receive the deep relaxation that occurs in total darkness. Many people find that removing light sources from the bedroom can be helpful in optimizing sleep cycles, improving general health and powerfully stimulating pineal gland activation and rebalancing.

10.9 Qi Gong Practices for Activating the Pineal Gland and Harmonizing the Crystal Palace

Many Chi Kung (also known as Qi Gong) practices contain simple elements like breathing or tapping that can be used to activate the bones and glands of the Crystal Palace.

(i) Breathing

Various breath practices move the pumps, activating the pineal and pituitary glands as well as stimulating the flow of cerebrospinal fluid. Breathing is said to ionize the CSF and therefore increase its potency.

(ii) Tapping

Gently tapping your forehead in between your eyebrows activates the pineal gland and all three structures of the Crystal Palace. The vibration sends a wave directly back to the pineal gland, activating it in the process. The same vibration also moves through the bones to the sphenoid, which in turn stimulates the pituitary gland that rests in the sella turcica. The vibration of the pituitary awakens the hypothalamus through the pituitary stalk.

(iii) Toning

Toning or chanting sends vibrations into the Crystal Palace, activating the pineal and other glands and energizing the CSF. Chanting the eight forces of the pakua to draw in elemental energies is an exceptionally powerful exercise for activating the Crystal Palace. See Cosmic Fusion (Destiny Books, 2007) for complete instructions on chanting the eight forces.

(iv) Pressing

Pressing your tongue to the roof of your mouth activates the pituitary gland and, through its physical and chemical connections, activated the pineal gland and hypothalamus as well.

(v) Squeezing

When we squeeze our eyes, the muscular connection with the sphenoid activates the pituitary. Sucking in our cheeks moves the jaw, which stimulates the neck and cranial pumps. Contracting the anal sphincter and perineum sends vibrations to the muscles that envelop the anus and form the pelvic floor. From the pelvis, the vibration then travels up the spine and dural tube to the occiput. The intracranial membrane system transfers the vibration to the centre of the head, activating the pineal and pituitary glands.

(vi) Spiralling

Spiralling movements such as spinning the pakua, the Tai Chi symbol, or our Dantians creates an electromagnetic field that energizes the CSF and enhances the power of the heart field, thereby activating the pineal gland and other glands of the Crystal Palace.

(vii) Being in Darkness

Darkness triggers increased production and release of melatonin, and eventually of pinoline and DMT as a result of its effect of activating the pineal gland and helping to stimulate function of and open the third eye.

(viii) Laughing and Smiling

Smiling opens both the heart and the crown, allowing more light to penetrate while also increasing the vibration of the organs. Laughing and smiling reduce stress and relax the body, which increases the flow of chi. Laughter also triggers the release of endorphins, promoting feelings of well-being. Relaxation increases blood flow, which amplifies the effects of the hormones released in the Crystal Palace and has an effect of pineal gland activation.

(ix) Focusing

Since energy flows where our attention goes, bringing our attention to the structures of the Crystal Palace will activate them.

Note: The Tao also emphasizes the importance of good diet and hydration. We are 70–80 percent water, and water is highly conductive. To increase the activation of the pineal gland and the Crystal Palace, sufficient hydration is critical. Additionally, a good, balanced diet high in tryptophan is helpful in providing the building blocks for these important biochemicals. Tryptophan is plentiful in many foods including chocolate, seaweed, almonds, bananas, dried dates, sesame seeds, chickpeas, and peanuts.

As we practice Spinal Cord Breathing, the rhythmic pulsing of the spinal cord creates an electromagnetic field that charges the cerebrospinal fluid and enhances the circulation of this important fluid throughout the body, resulting in pineal gland activation. Increased flow shifts the electrolyte balance, the means by which the CSF regulates the body's ability to conduct electricity. The greater the conductivity, the more energy can flow through the nervous system, charging the cells and priming them for activation. Any psychoactive substances (such as DMT) that are released by the activated pineal gland also enter into the CSF, charging it even further.

10.10 Spinal Cord Breathing

In Spinal Cord Breathing, the movement of the sacrum transfers vibration up the spine and to the occiput through the dural tube. Connected with the occiput at the sphenobasilar joint (SBJ), the sphenoid also begins to vibrate, stimulating the pituitary. At the same time, the rocking wavelike movement of the pituitary stalk activates the hypothalamus and milks the pituitary gland, which as we know is connected to the health and activation of the pineal gland. The milking of the pituitary releases more oxytocin and vasopressin, which heighten feelings of trust, relaxation, peace, and empathy while reducing fear, anxiety, and aggression.

The pituitary gland is located above the sphenoid sinus, which drains almost directly down the throat. During high levels of excitement, CSF may be excreted into the sphenoid sinus. Here, vasopressin and oxytocin mix with the already highly charged CSF and drip down into the throat, giving us the nectar (frequently referred to as Soma) that is often described in spiritual experiences. Both vasopressin and oxytocin are critical hormones during the birth process; their presence in the nectar may contribute to birth-like experiences. The effects of these hormones on bonding may also explain the feeling of deep connection and unconditional love that is part of many enlightenment experiences.

This potent brew travels down the back of the throat and into the stomach, where it is absorbed directly through the mucous membranes. Some of this fluid also enters the bloodstream later in the digestive process. In this way, the nectar is brought to the lower Dantian for integration into the physical body, uniting heaven and earth.

During spiritual experiences, the activated pineal gland affects the rest of the brain through its influence on CSF, which completely immerses both the brain and the spinal cord. After bathing the brain, approximately half of the CSF gets reabsorbed into the bloodstream in the head. The other half leaves the head through lymphatic drainage. From the lymph, the supercharged CSF enters the body's bloodstream and is carried to the heart. Blood flows through the heart and vessels in a spiral motion, boosting the CSF's electromagnetic charge. These neural, biochemical, and electromagnetic connections between the brain and heart may lead to ecstatic heart-mind expanding sensations.

The heart field is the strongest electromagnetic field of the body: when consciousness moves from the head to the heart, the field becomes stronger and more organized. When the head resonates with the heart's vibration, neurons in the brain fire differently, reducing mind chatter, increasing the communication between mind and body and inducing further pineal gland activation. Thus, during spiritual experiences, the liquid-light ambrosia of the CSF is active in all three Dantians, enhancing their powers. Because the pineal gland is itself bathed in CSF, there can be a self-amplifying positive feedback loop that creates peak experiences. Moreover, since the heart field extends and can be felt at least ten feet from the body, our experiences also have the potential for a ripple effect to our communities.

10.11 Lights and Music

Research by neurosurgeon Wilder Penfield reported in 1958 that stimulation of the right temporal lobe of the brain led to patients reporting spiritual experiences such as seeing God, leaving their bodies, hearing music, and seeing the dead. Since then, studies by Peter Fenwick and Vernon Neppe also show connections between mystical experiences and the temporal lobes. Although the exact mechanism by which the temporals are stimulated is not yet known, it may be that the CSF present in the interpeduncular cistern situated between the temporal lobes may be involved.

A structure called the colliculus helps to orient the head to what is seen or heard. It receives visual and auditory stimuli and has sensorimotor connections to assist with orienting movement. It surrounds the pineal gland and is activated by its secretions. As the pineal awakens, releasing biochemicals such as serotonin, tryptamine, pinoline, melatonin, or Dimethyltryptamine (DMT), it affects the colliculus, which can explain some of the lights, visions, and celestial music that people report when the third eye is open and the Crystal Palace is active.

10.12 Awakening the Core Link between the Cranium and Sacrum

Earlier we mentioned the soft tissue dura mater connection between the cranium and the sacrum—the Core Link. For good flow in the physical body, there must be good connection and communication between heaven (the cranium) and earth (the sacrum). Spinal Cord Breathing is one of the best ways to awaken this connection and keep it healthy and also has the added effect of inducing pineal gland activation.

Spinal Cord Breathing enlivens the spine, promotes good range of motion and flexibility, activates the cranial and sacral pumps, and enhances the flow of cerebral spinal fluid, which in turn stimulates pineal gland activation. It also helps to relax the back muscles so meditation is comfortable, and increases the flow of chi through the spine.

In modern life, many people work at a desk and sit for many hours a day. Additionally, many people also sit watching television or playing on the internet once they are home. So much sitting hinders the motion of the sacrum and reduces Flow. Spinal Cord Breathing is a great way to counteract the ill effects of prolonged sitting.

10.13 U Spinal Cord Breathing

1. Stand with your feet shoulder-width apart and your knees slightly bent.
2. Relax, and begin to notice how you feel.
3. Begin natural breathing.
4. On your next inhalation, keeping your elbows bent and your fingers toward the sky, bring your arms level with your shoulders and pulled slightly back. Gently tilt your sacrum backward, arching your spine. Open your chest and allow the rib cage to expand, activating the thymus and adrenal glands. Allow your head to drop backward and allow your jaw to soften.

5. As you exhale, tilt your sacrum forward, tucking your tailbone and rounding your spine as if curling into a ball. Bring your elbows together in front of your chest, and let your chin drop toward your chest as you lightly clench your teeth.
6. Repeat 9 or 18 times, then return your head and spine to neutral and rest.

10.14 Taoist Technique for opening the Third Eye

The focus of Taoism is the individual in nature rather than the individual in society. It holds that the goal of life for each individual is to find one's own personal adjustment to the rhythm of the natural (and supernatural) world and to follow the Way (dao) of the universe. In many ways the opposite of rigid Confucian moralism, Taoism served many of its adherents as a complement to their ordered daily lives. A scholar on duty as an official would usually follow Confucian teachings but at leisure or in retirement might seek harmony with nature as a Taoist recluse.

Taoists stress the importance of harmonizing with nature by balancing yin and yang, and developing chi through meditation and disengagement. The human body is regarded as a source of chi-derived energy, which some people have the power to concentrate and congeal into an essence. Chi (also spelled ch'i or qi) is variously known as the "breath of heaven," "mystical breath," the "breath of nature" and the "quality of spirit"

One way to think of the 'third eye' is as a 'meta' organ that consists of our mind and all of our senses working together as a larger, more powerful sensory organ that the pineal gland then acts as a focal point to create a vision. Seers use their third eye to understand hidden connections and answer questions. Energy workers 'feel' the energies around them and to then consciously manipulate that energy. And every time you have empathy, you are using your third eye to touch and feel the emotions of others.

The two primary guidelines in Taoist meditation are jing ('quiet, stillness, calm') and ding ('concentration, focus'). The purpose of stillness, both mental and physical, is to turn attention inwards and cut off external sensory input, thereby muzzling the "Five Thieves". Within that silent stillness, one concentrates the mind and focuses attention, usually on the breath, in order to develop what is called 'one-pointed awareness', a totally undistracted, undisturbed, undifferentiated state of mind which permits intuitive insights to arise spontaneously.

The primary hallmark of Taoist meditation is the generation, transformation, and circulation of internal energy. Once the meditator has 'achieved energy' (deh-chee), or opened his 'third eye', it can be applied to promoting health and longevity, nurturing the 'spiritual embryo' of immortality, martial arts, healing, painting and poetry, sensual self-indulgence, or whatever else the adept wishes to do with it.

To understand how the third eye works, let's look at how it is possible to use the Third Eye to sense and visually interpret energy around us. It's possible to see Motion (for example a car moving), Activity (you driving the car) and Exchange of Energy (burning the gas). Add in our capacity of sensing & projecting potential (being able to predict where the car goes based on the roads and knowing the driver), in other words seeing where energy, motion, and activities will flow to over time. Add all this together into an internal visual map, and you have just expanded how you see Energy playing out (the results of using the car/gasoline/intention to drive you up the hill). By seeing energy as a mental overlay rather than just an abstract concept, it becomes a tangible property of life that we can learn how to sense and interact within a deeper manner.

Consider a person who sees auras or light. Auras are in fact such an information overlay. Your brain has the ability to process visual information, but the image it creates for you is not limited to what comes from your eyes. Consider what you see on this page as you read it. You aren't seeing black lines. You are seeing words and then concepts and ideas overlaid on top of them. Now envision yourself looking at another person. You don't just see what he or she is wearing. Your whole neural network, mind and sense organs form a larger more sensitive antenna that picks up on energy and patterns before you. There are so many clues in front of you that tell you about the person's emotional state, well-being, level of distraction, and so many other factors. Your third eye has a lot to share with you and so it puts this information into what you see by adding an aura. In reality what you are seeing is slightly different over what is happening: but your mind is always altering your experience to give you extra information to work with. If you look at the scientific research you will discover the mind is constantly editing our perception. So the third eye uses this natural mental capacity to alter our perception to add in extra data more than we realize.

The third eye is a sense. It returns information on what might be and also energetic states. With it you can sense another person's emotions: that's empathy. The third eye you can let you feel how a person is doing. It can show you how a person's life story is flowing. With the third eye, you can get inklings of what might be ahead, behind or out of sight.

Different cultures use many varied techniques to develop this skill. Taoists, for example, are very patient, taking decades to define and refine this ability to help them become a Sage / Seer with the extra information they can see. The nature of the interpretive aspects of this ability means experience helps improve its capabilities and accuracy. As a consequence, it is a slow process to master.

Lesson One: Pause. That's right the first step to learning how to use the third eye is simply to pause. You cannot listen to your heart if you cannot pause. The third eye requires cantering and patience. Without pause, you will not truly connect to any deeper third eye experience. Yes, you may have visions or have intuitive hints, but you will miss most of the full experience without pausing into your heart.

Lesson Two: Don't make a vision bigger than life. All too many people blow out of proportion a vision they experience. Be Calm!

Lesson Three: Practice just watching life flow around you. The third eye reveals patterns of the world unfolding around you. As a result, the more you understand the patterns of nature, the easier it is to understand what a vision can represent.

Lesson Four: Back to Pause. You pause when receiving an intuition. The third eye isn't using the logical thinking part of the mind. As a result, if you begin to think the moment you get a vision it disrupts the third eye process. So you pause to stop the rest of your mind from ruining the third eye moment.

Lesson Five: The third eye is a beautiful sense; it expands how a person connects to the world, adds another dimension to how we connect to everything. But it's only one of many senses. People tend to focus a bit too much only on one sense, and that limits a person quite a bit then. So you have to be patient and learn to use all of the senses together, or you are missing the larger world.

After you get a vision with the third eye you check all your other senses, even use your logic, you poke about and add in other pieces of information to create an even more complete picture if possible.

When your other senses return contradictory information, then you slow down. Remember to allow your intuition to tell you when to slow down to pause and look again at everything around you. If other information extends and validates what you sense, then you move ahead with a bit more surety.

The third eye is a natural sense we all possess. The third eye is a sense to detect "what might be" or our sense of potential. To open the third eye means to further develop that sense to the point of being aware and conscious of the sense. Once the third eye is opened, it doesn't come with an eyelid that we can just shut. It's more· like our ear, always on. The problem is this: some people get overwhelmed by their senses.

Chapter - 11

Third Eye in Jainism

11.1 Jyoti Kendra as 'Third Eye'

According to Jainism, in the front part of the head, in the sliding line of Jnan Kendra, the Centre of Knowledge, there is located a special psychic centre, which has been identified as the Centre of Tranquillity, Peace. This centre accounts for man's strong emotions. It regulates human passions and body-temperature. With the purification of the Centre of Tranquillity, all passions and strong emotions are extinguished of themselves. This centre is therefore also called the Centre of Passions and Their Extinction. As long as it remains unrefined, it is known as the Centre of Passions. But on being purified, it becomes the Centre of Tranquillity.

Man's consciousness, his dispositions, habits and illusory actions have all their respective centres for manifestation present in the body. However, it has not yet been discovered as to where precisely a particular centre for the manifestation of a particular disposition is located. The physiologists and the psychologists did some research on this subject and found out the centre which regulates passions. The ancient masters of spiritual too, had undertaken research on this topic but their discoveries were forgotten during the middle ages. Through a comparative study of the conclusions arrived at by the modern and ancient researchers it has been located. To some extent this effort has been successful and people have been able to, identify them.

This discovery has increased the utility of meditation on the psychic centres.

According to the psychologists, emotion is man's fundamental disposition. There are two kinds of emotion---internal (urge or impulse) and external. The control of external emotion is not good from health point of view. But if the urges and impulses are not controlled, the situation becomes positively harmful. Those who have meditated long on the Centre of Tranquillity, have been found to succeed in controlling their urges.

Just below the Centre of Tranquillity is another important centre called Jyoti Kendra, the Centre of Enlightenment. Here is located the pineal gland. The physiologists have not been able to gather much information about it. Recently, some discoveries have been made about it on the basis of which its importance is being assessed. As a matter of fact this Jyoti Kendra, the Centre of Enlightenment, is called the third eye.

The location of Darshan Kendra (The Centre of Intuition) is the pituitary gland. It is positioned between the two eyebrows. Concentration on this centre turns preksha into inner preksha, and it turns wisdom into intuition. At this stage, a man's personality becomes wholly introversive. With the evolution of introversion, outside factors cease to be obstructions. From the point of view of sadhana, this point on the forehead, may be said to be a great boon. If we make use of it with full consciousness, concentration and will-power, it can transform our lives beyond imagination.

Some people recognise, Darshan-Kendra (The Centre of Intuition) or Ajna-Chakra (The Centre of Command) to be the third eye. From another point of view, Darshan Kendra (The Centre of Intuition) and Jyoti Kendra (The Centre of Enlightenment), may both be called the third eye, but the latter, because of its usefulness has a greater importance. Jyoti Kendra (The Centre of Enlightenment) is the centre which annihilates anger. By meditating on this centre, wrath dissolves very soon. From the point of view of brahmcharya, too, this centre has great utility. It has been recognized as the controlling or master-gland. It controls the secretions of all the lower glands. The purification of these centres resolves many of our physical and psychological problems.

These centres have been named on the basis of their functions and the results achieved through them. In the ancient texts are to be found names of the body-chakras. In the Tantra-Shastra and Hatha-Yoga, for example are mentioned certain names. But our finding is that there are not only six or seven chakras in the body; rather there are to be found there hundreds of centres of power and consciousness. Out of these some important centres were selected and experiments of meditation performed on them. The experience thereof naturally formed the basis of the present nomenclature. No texts were consulted, nor any deliberations held for finding suitable names for the psychic centres. In the very process of their exposition, certain names happened to suggest themselves and these appeared to be appropriate. What results does meditation on a particular centre produce in the body, in the mind and in life? With such a basis formulation, the objective of making the names of the psychic centres was significant and intelligible.

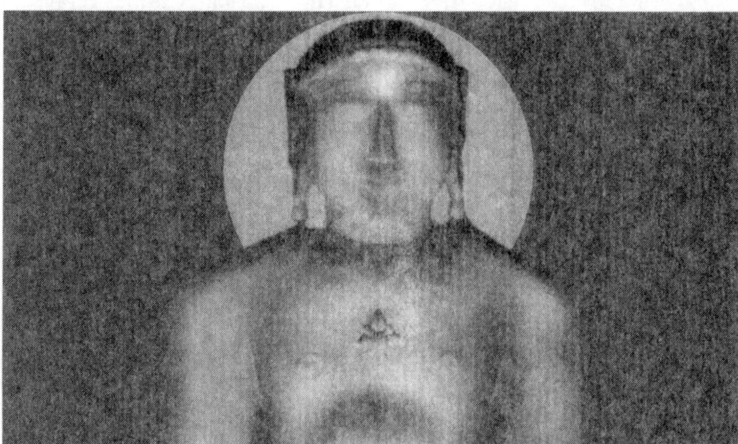

Figure 11.1: Third Eye of Lord Mahavira

11.2 Leshyas

In Jainism, there is a great deal of importance given to Leshya. Leshya refers to the state of Mind. Our activities reflect our state of mind. The following illustration shows how our activities vary with the state of our mind.

Two Stories for illustration of Leshyas:

First Story: Once there were six friends who were going on a trip, but along the way got lost in a forest. Soon they became hungry and thirsty. They searched for food for some time and finally found a fruit tree. As they ran to the tree, the first man said, "Let us cut the tree down and get the fruits." The second one said, "Don't cut the whole tree down, cut off a big branch instead." The third friend said, "Why do we need a big branch? A small branch has enough fruit." The fourth one said, "We do not need to cut any branches, just climb up and take the bunches of fruit." The fifth man said, "Why pick that many fruits and waste them, instead just pick the fruits that you want to eat." The sixth friend said quietly, "There are plenty of good fruits on the ground, so let us just eat them first."

You can see that the states of minds of these six friends cause a range of thoughts which begin with the destruction of a tree and end with picking up what is on the ground. The six friends' minds represent six types of leshyas.

The first friend's state of mind represents Krishna (black) leshya. The second friend's state of mind represents neel (blue) leshya. The third friend's state of mind represents kapot (brown) leshya. The fourth friend's state of mind represents tejo (red) leshya. The fifth friend's state of mind represents padma (yellow) leshya. The sixth friend's state of mind represents shukla (white) leshya.

The first leshya is the worst and the sixth leshya is the best. The first three leshyas lead the soul to ruin and the last three lead the soul to spiritual prosperity. Therefore, people should strive for the white leshya and not the red leshya. It is not so that a person's state of mind remains the same at all times and therefore, it can be changed for the better or for the worst.

Second Story: The popular story of King Prasanraj, who lived during Lord Mahavira's time, illustrates the effects of leshays:

One day King Shrenik was on his way to pay homage to Lord Mahavira and on the way he saw a sage who was meditating and illuminating very brightly. He bowed down to the sage and continued on his way to pay homage to Lord Mahavira. After reaching Lord Mahavira, King Shrenik asked the Lord, "Oh Lord, I saw a very illuminated sage who was engaged in meditation on the way here.

Supposing he died at that moment, what state would he have acquired?" The Lord replied, "He would have been hurled down to the seventh hell-region." The king was much astonished to hear this reply from the Lord. He thought, "Why would such a sage go to hell? Perhaps the Lord might have misunderstood me." He asked the Lord again, "Oh Lord, if the sage leaves this body just now, then what state will he attain?" The Lord replied, "He will be an angel in Sarvarthasidha, a heavenly region." The king was much surprised at this reply, too. He thought, "The Lord first said he would attain the seventh hell and now he says that the sage would be an angel." The king was perplexed.

At that very moment drums began sounding in the sky and voices of `victory' were proclaimed. The king asked the Lord, "What is the cause of these sounds?" The Lord said, "Oh king, the sage about whom you were inquiring has acquired omniscience and so the angels are beating the drums and proclaiming `Victory'." The king was extremely surprised by these answers and therefore, he requested the Lord to explain them. Thereupon the Lord said, "Oh king, right before you approached the sage, two soldiers leading your procession diverted the mind of the sage by their conversation. His mind began thinking about his kingdom where his ministers turned out to be untrustworthy and would eventually kill his son. He was inflamed with rage and he lost his mental equanimity. Therefore, he started mentally fighting against his ministers. He violently discharged his weapons one after the other against his ministers. Soon his weapons were exhausted and his foes were not destroyed. So he thought of throwing his steel helmet against them in order to destroy them. You bowed down to him at that time when he was reflecting on such thoughts. I, therefore, replied that he would attain the seventh hell.

Thereafter, when the sage placed his hand on his head for the steel helmet, he realized that he was not King Prasanraj but that he was a sage. His anger calmed down immediately. He remembered that he has been initiated into the vow of equanimity and of non-violence to any living being mentally, verbally, and physically. He deeply regretted and repented for the breach of his vow and indulgence in acute anger. He further thought that he ought to have maintained love for all creatures of the world, ought to have no malice for the ministers, and no attachment for his son. He severely condemned his mental act. He despised it and withdrew himself from such a feat of anger and malice.

Oh king, when he thought this way, you asked me the next question and I replied that he would be born in the Savartha Siddha (heaven) as an angel. Even thereafter, he continued the purification of his mental reflections and gradually he reached the stage of `Kshapaka', where he annihilated all of his ghati karmas, and attained omniscience."

King Shrenik's doubts were resolved and he learned how mental reflections can fluctuate. He also learned that not only can physical acts or verbal abuses have such devastating effects, but so can mental acts.

Let us understand the characteristic of personalities and the outcomes resulting different leshyas.

11.2.1 Krishna (Black) Leshya:

People in this state of mind do not show any compassion or mercy. Everyone is afraid of them as their anger turns into violence. They always burn with jealousy and have ill-will for everyone. They are filled with animosity and malice and do not believe in religion. This state of mind is the worst and most dangerous. If anyone dies in this state of mind, they will go to hell.

11.2.2 Neel (Blue) Leshya:

People in this state of mind are proud, haughty, and lazy. They are unreliable and other people avoid their company. They are cheaters, cowards, and hypocrites. Such people also avoid the religious lectures. If anyone dies in this state of mind, they will be reborn as a plant.

11.2.3 Kapot (Brown) Leshya:

People in this state of mind always remain sad and gloomy. They find faults in others and are vindictive. They boast about themselves, become excited over small matters, and lack mental balance. If anyone dies in this state of mind, they will be reborn as a bird or an animal.

11.2.4 Tejo (Red) Leshya:

People in this state of mind are very careful about their actions and discriminate between good and evil. They know the difference between what is right and what is wrong. They are kind, benevolent, and religious and lead a harmonious life. If anyone dies in this state of mind, they will be reborn as a human being.

11.2.5 Padma (Yellow) Leshya:

People in this state of mind are kind and benevolent and forgive everyone, even their enemies. They observe some austerities and are vigilant in keeping their vows till their last breath. They remain unaffected by joys and sorrows. If anyone dies in this leshya, they will be reborn in heaven as a celestial being.

11.2.6 Shukla (White) Leshya:

People in this state of mind strictly observe the principles of non-violence, truth, non-stealing, celibacy, and non-attachment. They are trustworthy, treat every soul as if it was their own soul, and do not have ill feelings even for their enemies. They remain calm even if someone abuses them. People who perfect this state of mind have no attachment or hatred and treat everyone alike. They do not become happy or sad. Their state of mind is the purest. If anyone dies in this perfected state of mind, they will be liberated from the cycle of birth and death.

Figure 11.2: Leshya Dhyana (Coloured Meditation)

11.3 Correlation of Leshyas in Jainism with Chakras in Hinduism

Vedic Chakras of Hindu tradition and Leshyas of Jainism are the similar concepts in Indian Religious traditions. In Hinduism these Leshyas are known as Chakras. The Chakras in human bodies are located at several places starting from muladhara to ajna (third eye), that is forehead and above the head. There was originally a concept of Sadchakra (six chakras) in Indian spiritual tradition but generally seven chakras are described. The Sahasrar chakra is beyond the corporeal body the Indian Seers thought of Sadchakras. The number six is very much important in Hindu religious traditions. There are Sad-darshanas, six systems of philosophy, Sad Chakras (six wheels of energy rooted in the human body), sadrasas (six tastes of balanced food) and Sadgunas (six attributes). Seen in this way we can come across the same concepts in Jainism, that is, Sad Leshyas (Six states of mind).

If we look into the scriptures of Jainism such as Bhagwati Sutra, Uttaradhyayan Sutra, Tatvarth Sutra, and Aagam literature we find many such similar concepts that stand in line to Chakras. The six Leshyas or rather mental tendencies as described in Jainism can well be equated with Chakras. There are six Leshyas as there are six chakras.

11.4 Shukla Dhyana and Third Eye Opening

Jain sages have described various forms of meditation, but have mostly elaborated on the shukla dhyana, the meditation of light. In the Vedic literature this is known as the Yoga of light, and as meditation on the third eye. According to Shukla Dhyana, the soul in the mundane form is known as sentient soul and when this soul attains substances, space, time and inner feelings inwardly and outwardly, then it attains right faith, right knowledge and right conduct. From its assistance, there is gradual decrease in the worldly attachments which produces Shukla Dhyan. Consequently the bad karmas are quashed away from the soul and there is development of four infinites, namely infinite faith, infinite knowledge, infinite pleasure and infinite strength and hence the soul gets the name GOD- Siddha.

11.5 Preksha Dhyana and Activation of Third Eye

Besides this, Preksha Dhyana (Schwas Presksha) can also activate the third eye. According to this, when the breath is inhaled and exhaled, the vibrations are generated throughout the body which stimulate inner body organs, knowledge-centres, consciousness-centres and internal power-centres. When all these centres are visualized with fullest concentration, it is known as Preksha-dhyan or Schwas preksha (breath meditation), which could lead to the opening of the 'third eye'.

CHAPTER - 12

Third Eye as the Single Eye in Christianity

12.1 Single Eye of Jesus Christ

According to the Christian teaching of Father Richard Rohr, the concept of the third eye is a metaphor for non-dualistic thinking; the way the mystics see. In Rohr's concept, mystics employ the first eye (sensory input such as sight) and the second eye (the eye of reason, meditation, and reflection), "but they know not to confuse knowledge with depth, or mere correct information with the transformation of consciousness itself. The mystical gaze builds upon the first two eyes—and yet goes further." Rohr refers to this level of awareness as "having the mind of Christ".

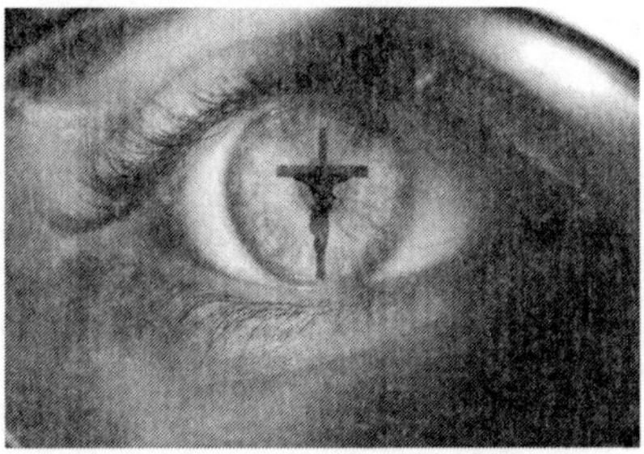

Figure 12.1: Symbolic Display of the Single Eye of Jesus Christ

Jesus said, "The light of the body is the eye: if therefore thine eye be single, thy whole body shall be full of light." (Matthew 6:

22). When Jesus said this, he was not speaking of our physical eyes. He was speaking of the spiritual, third eye. The original Greek word for "single" is "haplous". It is an adjective that means "good" and "sound".

This statement is mirrored in Luke 11:33-36:

"No man, when he hath lighted a candle, putteth it in a secret place, neither under a bushel, but on a candlestick, that they which come in may see the light. The light of the body is the eye: therefore when thine eye is single, thy whole body also is full of light; but when thine eye is evil, thy body also is full of darkness. Take heed therefore that the light which is in thee be not darkness. If thy whole body therefore be full of light, having no part dark, the whole shall be full of light, as when the bright shining of a candle doth give thee light."

John 1:5. "This then is the message which we have heard of him, and declare unto you, that God is light, and in him is no darkness at all."

Here the Bible clearly identifies God as a light being: a photon. The Bible connects God with the light. The Pineal Gland is the light receptor of the Body. Some people believe that the single eye Jesus is referring to is the 'pineal gland' of the brain to be activated during meditation. How?

Jacob of the Old Testament has an experience with God and what does he call the place where this experience occurs?

Genesis 32:30. "And Jacob called the name of the place Peniel: for I have seen God face to face, and my life is preserved."

Jacob sees God face to face and calls the place Peniel. Jesus says if your eye be single your body will fill with light. Therefore the single eye is the Pineal Gland of the brain. So, according to the Bible itself, Jesus was talking about the Pineal Gland of the brain and meditation through activating that Pineal. The ancient ancestors clearly had a healthy awareness of our pineal gland and the mysticism surrounding its purpose and connection to a higher level of consciousness. Its pine cone shape adds to the mysterious symbolism seen across various cultures. It comes as no surprise that the pine cone also forms in a sacred geometric pattern from Fibonacci golden ratio.

The pineal gland is a small (8 mm in human) reddish-gray body located above the superior colliculus and behind and beneath the stria medullaris, between the laterally positioned thalamic bodies. It is responsible for the production of melatonin, which has a role in regulating the circadian rhythm. Melatonin is a derivative of the amino acid tryptophan. The production of melatonin by the pineal gland is stimulated by darkness and inhibited by light.

Two things of interest here. (i) Pineal gland is responsible for the production of melatonin. Melatonin is a skin lightener in amphibians. That would give a little credence to the statement that if your eye be single your body will fill with light. (ii) More important than that is the fact that melatonin is actually the light carrier of the body. The other point as you can see is that the pineal gland flow of melatonin is stimulated by darkness and inhibited or closed down by light. So it is in darkness when the melatonin flows from the pineal. Considering that, let us look at another scripture. Another statement by Jesus:

Matthew 4:16. "The people whom sat in darkness saw great light; and to them which sat in the region and shadow of death light is sprung up."

Also, let's take a look at what Jesus says here:

John 3:19-21:

"And this is the condemnation, that light is come into the world, and men loved darkness rather than light, because their deeds were evil. For every one that doeth evil hateth the light, neither cometh to the light, lest his deeds should be reproved. But he that doeth truth cometh to the light that his deeds may be made manifest, that they are wrought in God."

Consider that: Jesus says if your eye be single your body will fill with light. The single eye is the Pineal Gland which only activates in darkness. The same Jesus says the people who sat in darkness saw great light. Is it not obvious what is being said? That means the single eye referred by Jesus is nothing the 'Pineal gland' producing melatonin in the darkness.

The third eye, or pineal gland, is activated by light. Just as our eyes on our face turn light into information so we may see what's around us and the colours of the objects, light that passes through our eyes on our face also goes to the pineal gland. The light the pineal gland receives allows the pineal gland to heal itself, to activate, and to function. When our "eye is single", we are allowing the proper rays from the sun to pass through the eyes on our face to the third eye, the pineal gland. In doing this, along with holding faith, a spiritual belief, the third eye opens. Our eye, therefore, is single.

The following verse is interesting. It describes the moving of the energy as it reaches the pineal gland:

Matthew 3:16:

"And Jesus, when he was baptized, went up straightway out of the water: and, lo, the heavens were opened unto him, and he saw the Spirit of God descending like a dove, and lighting upon him."

When the third eye is opened, as stated above, it is said you may see a flash of a bright white light. Some say it is more like an orb that appears far off at first, appearing to get closer as it increases in size. This very well may be what Paul experienced when he was knocked off his horse before Jesus met him in the road. He may have, in actuality, experienced the activation and opening of the pineal gland, which allowed him to realize the Christ within.

The pine cone is a standard reference to the pineal gland which is shaped as a pine cone. Many cultures have used a pine cone as a representation of a spiritual link to God. The Freemasons also use the pine cone in a lot of their symbolic references. Freemasonry can also explain the meaning of the rod to represent the spinal column which has 33 vertebrae. The masons have 33 steps leading to enlightenment. In this case enlightenment is represented by a pine cone which in turn represents the pineal gland situated at the head of the spinal column.

Following picture is that of the Pigna sculpture. It is the largest pine cone statue in the world. The bronze sculpture is three stories tall. Legend has it that the sculpture originally stood on top of the Pantheon. It was then brought to Rome where it was a water fountain next to the Temple of Isis. Now it sits in front of the Vatican in a courtyard called the Court of the Pine Cone.

Figure 12.2: Court of the Pine Cone in the Vatican City

Following figure shows the Pope carrying a staff, with a crucified Jesus arising out of a pine cone, a symbol of the third eye.

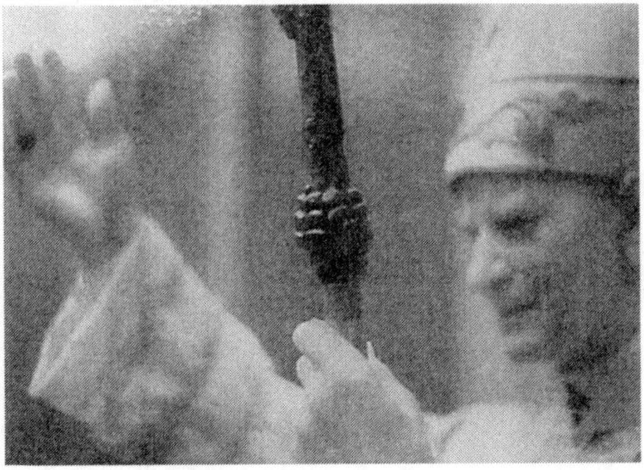

Figure 12.3: Pope carrying a staff

Following is another image of the Pope's staff. Also notice the pine cones on his chest plate and that the shape of his 'crown' resembles a pine cone as well. The pine cones on his chest are pointed forward, the way the pineal sits in the brain.

Figure 12.4: Pope's staff, the pine cones on his chest plate and on crown

Further indication of how we correlate Jesus Christ follows here. Jesus Christ was nailed to the cross on the hill of Golgotha which in Hebrew means "the place of the skull." In Latin we find the word Calvary, which also means skull. The name of the place in ancient Greek texts is Kranion from which we derive the modern word, cranium. So we have the connection to the head in which you find the brain. The pineal gland is in the centre of the brain.

The cross, another symbol rich in meaning, is a derivation of the Egyptian Ankh (eye), which incidentally better explains its relationship to the third eye chakra. Bear in mind here how much symbolism Christianity has borrowed from ancient Egypt and earlier cultures.

If you position the arms of the Ankh across your eyebrows, the rounded head will rest on your brow, where the third eye chakra is. Furthermore, Matthew 27:38 tells us that when Jesus was killed, "two robbers were crucified with Him, one on the right and one on the left."

The depiction of three crosses on Calvary represents the third eye and two physical eyes

The "two robbers" this passage speaks of are the optical eyes we view the world through, the same eyes which give us a false perception of reality that is created for us by the governors of society.

Only by opening the "all-seeing, all-knowing" eye do we understand the truth about ourselves. This is the true inner wisdom that Jesus explains throughout his teachings.

And have you ever noticed how three crosses are often grouped together? Whilst travelling through South America one encounters numerous places called Los Tres Cruces – the three crosses. And the middle cross is always positioned slightly higher than the "one on the right, and one on the left." Further, a thread of number three symbolism runs through the story of the crucifixion. The number three of course is central to third eye symbolism for obvious reasons.

12.2 The Staff of Dionysus

Dionysus, the Greek god and son of Zeus and Persephone, was the god of wine, and the god of epiphany and mysticism. He had a cult which followed him that sought to reach altered states of perception through intoxicants. The Romans named him Bacchus. Dionysus always carried a staff or rod with a spiral vine coiled around it, which was capped with a pine cone. The staff is depicted in the following picture.

Figure 12.5: The Staff of Dionysus

12.3 The Eye of Providence

The Eye of Providence (or the all-seeing eye of God) is a symbol, having its origin in Christian iconography, showing an eye often surrounded by rays of light or a glory and usually enclosed by a triangle. It represents the eye of God watching over humanity (the concept of divine providence).

Figure 12.6: Symbol of the 'Eye of Providence'

In 1782, the Eye of Providence was adopted as part of the symbolism on the reverse side of the Great Seal of the United States. It was first suggested as an element of the Great Seal by the first of three design committees in 1776 and is thought to be the suggestion of the artistic consultant.

The third eye is symbolized by the "Eye of Providence" in apyramid's capstone on the U.S. one-dollar bill.

Figure 12.7: US One-dollar bill depicting the 'Eye of Providence'

Today the Eye of Providence is sometimes associated with Freemasonry, although it is a Christian symbol. Following picture depicts the single eye in the Masonic Temple, Newfoundland and Labrador.

Figure 12.8: Masonic Temple, Newfoundland and Labrador. Note the 'Single Eye' inside the middle triangle on the top of the middle building.

Chapter - 13

Third Eye in Theosophy

13.1 Introduction to Theosophy

Theosophy is the body of truths which forms the basis of all religions, and which cannot be claimed as the exclusive possession of any. It offers a philosophy which renders life intelligible, and which demonstrates the justice and the love which guide its evolution. It puts death in its rightful place, as a recurring incident in an endless life, opening the gateway to a fuller and more radiant existence. It restores to the world the Science of the Spirit, teaching man to know the Spirit as himself and the mind and body as his servants. It illuminates the scriptures and doctrines of religions by unveiling their hidden meanings, and thus justifying them at the bar of intelligence, as they are ever justified in the eyes of intuition.

We may see evidence of the inroad being made by the principles and doctrines of the esoteric philosophy into the human consciousness in 'The Secret Doctrine' books by Madam H. P. Blavatsky. Although the concept of 'Theosophy' was known for the last six hundred years or so, it was Ms Helena Blavatsky who revived it in 1879. In a newsletter (published in 1879) she wrote that: "according to lexicographers, the term theosophia is composed of two Greek words—theos ("god") and sophos ("wise"). She then writes that Noah Webster defines it as "a supposed intercourse with God and superior spirits, and consequent attainment of superhuman knowledge. In her opinion, Robert Vaughan proposed "a far better, more philosophical" definition: "A Theosophist is one who gives you a theory of God or the works of God, which does have not revelation, but an inspiration of its own for its basis."

Lemuria is the name of a hypothetical "lost land" variously located in the Indian and Pacific Oceans. Lemuria was the huge Pacific continent and Atlantis the huge Atlantic continent. The great watery masses of the Pacific and Atlantic Oceans are where these continents once located . It is said in Tamil legend to have been civilized for over 20,000 years, with its population speaking Tamil. "Lemuria" entered the lexicon of the occult through the works of Helena Blavatsky, who claimed that the Mahatmas had shown her an ancient, pre-Atlantean Book of Dzyan.

Lemurians – who are said to have possessed a "Third Eye" in the back of their heads, which in modern man has been degenerated into and represented by the pineal gland. These Lemurians never even developed any form of speech or verbal communication beyond a basic monosyllabic grunt and imitations of the shrieks and cries of the animals around them. The majority of their communications were through psychic means of clairvoyance and perceiving the thoughts of those around them. It was with the Atlanteans that proper language and proper speech were finally developed. So, those who we call "Lemurians" did not call themselves Lemurians and those who we call "Atlanteans" did not call themselves Atlanteans. These are just convenient terms of reference. In this vast Lemurian Epoch, many important and interesting things must have happened but there are three in particular which we should pay attention to. And it was over the course of this Root Race that human bodies went from being asexual or having no gender at all to being dual- or double-sexed, androgynous, and then underwent the separation of the sexes, resulting in single individual genders of male and female as we have it today. But while the Lemurians were still androgynous, some of the Lords of Wisdom – or high divine beings – chose to incarnate in some of the androgynous Lemurians and after doing so they utilized the power of Kriyashakti – the divine energy of creative thought, will and imagination – to create higher and more developed physical forms as vehicles for the incarnation of still higher beings, referred to as the "Sons of Ad," "Sons of the Fire Mist," and "Sons of Will and Yoga."

According to Madam Blavatsky, "Dogmatic religions are the antithesis of objectivity and dull thinking that does not correspond to the theosophical principles. And she says that the main task of the Theosophical movement has always been a struggle with such beliefs.

13.2 'Third Eye' in Theosophy

The term the 'third eye' in Theosophy was first used by Madam Blavatsky in 1884 when she wrote "their spiritual vision became dim; and co-ordinately the third eye commenced to lose its power". Her use of the term is specifically derived from its use in Hindu mythology as Shiva's frontal eye, the eye of higher perception as described in the Mahabharata. For the artists associated with the Theosophical Society the third eye was a practical reality. Its enhanced operation was the subject of daily meditation and anxious speculation. The reality of a world invisible to the physical /scientific eye was routine. This altered visionary experience was played out in the work of the artists associated with the Theosophical Society in ways that were occasionally stylistically consistent with European modernism but were often not recuperable within this framework.

The Pituitary Body is the organ per se of the psychic plane. Pure psychic vision is caused by the molecular motion of this body, which is directly connected with the optic nerve, and thus affects the sight, and gives rise to hallucinations. Its motion may readily cause flashes of light, seen within the head, similar to those that may be obtained on pressing the eyeballs, and so causing molecular motion in the optic nerve. When molecular action is set up in the Pituitary Body these flashes are seen, and further action gives psychic vision, as similar motion in the Pineal Gland gives Spiritual Clairvoyance. Drunkenness and fever cause disorderly motion in the Pituitary Body, and so produce illusions of sight, visions, and hallucinations. This body is sometimes so affected by drunkenness that it is paralyzed. (CW XII:698). Blavatsky further states that the pituitary corresponds to the Manas-Antahkarna, while the pineal is the Manas itself.

The third eye is the inner spiritual eye of the seer, and the faculty which manifests through it is not clairvoyance as ordinarily understood, that is, the power of seeing at a distance, but rather the faculty of spiritual intuition, through which direct and higher knowledge is obtainable.

As artists and Theosophists they came to valorise the experience of the 'third eye' above the 'normal' eye. They drew on a particular interpretation of Indian art; not as a primitivist vocabulary to be plundered for stylistic purposes, but as indicating the way forward to a more accurate depiction of reality. The practice of visualisation was manifested through a variety of stylistic vocabularies.

The ancient shamanistic tradition in Hebrew culture was established as the Merkabah Tradition representing an intellectual sophistication to a more primitive-seeming Magic. Its core element was to "see in the spirit vision" as is the root method of all ancient shamanism. These visions were called "apocalypses" from which prophecy was gleaned as medicine was practiced.

The 'third eye', in Hindu esotericism it is called the 'Eye of Shiva', while in the esoteric Buddhism of Tibet and the Trans-Himalayan regions it is referred to as the 'Eye of Dangma'. Dangma means a purified soul, one who has become a Jivanmukta (free from life and death cycle), the highest adept, or rather a Mahatma so-called. His "opened eye" is the inner spiritual eye of the seer, and the faculty which manifests through it is not clairvoyance as ordinarily understood, that is, the power of seeing at a distance, but rather the faculty of spiritual intuition, through which direct and certain knowledge is obtainable. This faculty is intimately connected with the third eye, which mythological tradition ascribes to certain races of men.

The Theosophical view does not connect the third eye with the "brow chakra". It states that this was a real eye in early Root-Races, which in the course of evolution retreated into the skull and became the pineal gland, while the Ajna chakra was never a real eye. In regards to its position, Madam Blavatsky affirmed that it was at the back of the head, its depiction on the forehead being an exoteric license. Thus, Theosophy does not connect the powers of the third eye with those of the brow chakra, but rather with the faculty of spiritual intuition. This is explained by Madam Blavatsky when commenting on "the 'Opened Eye' of the Dangma", mentioned in the Shloka I.8 of Cosmogenesis:

His "opened eye" is the inner spiritual eye of the seer, and the faculty which manifests through it is not clairvoyance as ordinarily understood, that is, the power of seeing at a distance, but rather the faculty of spiritual intuition, through which direct and certain knowledge is obtainable. This faculty is intimately connected with the "third eye," which mythological tradition ascribes to certain races of men.

A short note on 'Clairvoyance':

Clairvoyance is the ability to use your 'third eye' to tune into subtle energy levels of physical reality, as well as the astral dimension. It is also the power to receive visions of the past, present, and future, inside the Mind's Eye. It is about accessing visual information that reveals emotional and mental facts about a person's character and history. For example, If you know what a person is thinking, feeling, or doing at any time, then you can assume that your third is awakened. This is 'clairvoyance'. But if you don't open your Third Eye and see through your Mind's Eye, then you won't ever get to use all of your natural powers of perception.

A short note on 'Aura':

When a clairvoyant psychic uses the word "Aura", he is actually talking about a tangible energy field surrounding the physical body. He is talking about perceiving the colours, shapes, textures, and symbols that appear around the human body when it is viewed or sensed energetically. For a clairvoyant, Auras are a veritable window into the soul. Not only does the human energy field and Aura exist, but visual clairvoyants can 'see' this aura, and the emotions of the person being viewed, no matter what their beliefs are.

According to 'The Secret Doctrine' by Madam Blavatsky, The Third Eye was situated in the back of the head, not the front.

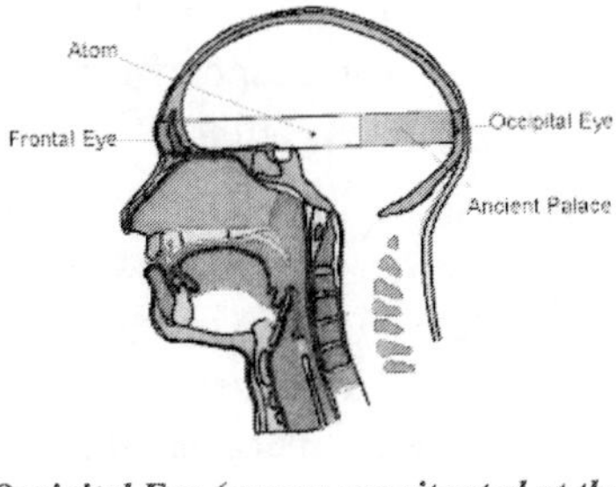

Figure 13.1: Occipital Eye (means eye situated at the back of head)

It is only for illustrative purposes, and often out of ignorance, that it has been portrayed as being between the two physical eyes or in the forehead. The Third Eye deteriorated, withdrew inside the head, and ceased to function, during the Atlantean Root Race, which is known as the Fourth Root Race. When the Fourth (Race) arrived at its middle age, the inner vision had to be awakened, and acquired by artificial stimuli, the process of which was known to the old sages.... The third eye, likewise, getting gradually petrified, soon disappeared. The double-faced became the one-faced, and the eye was drawn deep into the head and is now buried under the hair.

Then, "the third eye acted no longer," says the Stanza, because man had sunk too deep into the mire of matter. A few more occult teachings were then to be given with reference to this point as well as some others. "The third eye retreated inwards when its course was run." [Secret Doctrine, 2:295]

"The possession of a physical third eye, we are told, was enjoyed by the men of the Third Root-Race down to nearly the middle period of Third sub-race of the Fourth Root-Race, when the consolidation and perfection of the human frame made it disappear from the outward anatomy of man. Psychically and spiritually, however, its mental and visual perceptions lasted till nearly the end of the Fourth Race, when its functions, owing to the materiality and depraved condition of mankind, died out altogether before the submersion of the bulk of the Atlantean continent."

The third eye remains latent and dormant within all human beings today, as the Pineal Gland. The "deva-eye" does not exist anymore for the majority of mankind. The third eye is dead, and acts no longer; but it has left behind a witness to its existence. This witness is now the 'Pineal Gland'. During the activity of the inner man (during trances and spiritual visions) the eye swells and expands. The Arhat sees and feels it, and regulates his action accordingly.

The third eye was an active organ at that stage of evolution when the spiritual element in man reigned supreme over the hardly nascent intellectual and psychic elements. And, as the cycle ran down toward that point when the physiological senses were developed, the growth and consolidation of the physical man, the interminable and complex vicissitudes and tribulations of zoological development, that median "eye" ended by atrophying along with the early spiritual and purely psychic characteristics in man.

And there was a day when all that which in our modern times is regarded as phenomena, so puzzling to the physiologists now compelled to believe in them – such as thought transference, clairvoyance, clairaudience, etc.; in short, all that which is called now "wonderful and abnormal" – all that and much more belonged to the senses and faculties common to all humanity. We are, however, cycling back and cycling forward; i.e., having lost in spirituality that which we acquired in physical development until almost the end of the Fourth Race, we (mankind) are as gradually and imperceptibly losing now in the physical all that we regain once more in the spiritual re-evolution. This process must go on until the period which will bring the Sixth Root-Race on a parallel line with the spirituality of the Second, long extinct mankind." [Secret Doctrine 1:536-537]

This throws also a light on the mystery – incomprehensible to some – of the connection between abnormal, or Spiritual Seer ship, and the physiological purity of the Seer. The question is often asked, "Why should celibacy and chastity be a sine qua non rule and condition of regular chelaship, or the development of psychic and occult powers? The answer is contained in the Commentary. When we learn that the "third eye" was once a physiological organ, and that later on, owing to the gradual disappearance of spirituality and increase of materiality (Spiritual nature being extinguished by the physical), it became an atrophied organ, as little understood now by physiologists as the spleen is. During human life the greatest impediment in the way of spiritual development, and especially to the acquirement of Yoga powers, is the activity of our physiological senses. Sexual action being closely connected, by interaction, with the spinal cord and the grey matter of the brain, it is useless to give any longer explanation. Of course, the normal and abnormal state of the brain, and the degree of active work in the medulla oblongata, reacts powerfully on the pineal gland, for, owing to the number of "centres" in that region, which controls by far the greater majority of the physiological actions of the animal economy, and also owing to the close and intimate neighbourhood of the two, there must be exerted a very powerful "inductive" action by the medulla on the pineal gland. All this is quite plain to the Occultist, but is very vague in the sight of the general reader.

This is what Theosophy teaches and when we stop to think about the fact that it was the increasing materiality and sensuality of human beings that resulted in the obscuration and deterioration of the Third Eye and its faculties in the first place, it becomes plainly obvious that its reawakening or "re-opening" is dependent on the decrease of that materiality and sensuality on the part of the spiritual aspirant.

In Christianity, the seven neshamot (subtleties) within us which correspond to the first seven "Let there be" instances of Genesis. They can be briefly stated as under:

(1) Neshamah-behemot: The subtlety of our physical body.
(2) Neshamah-nepheshi: The subtlety of our self, our soul.
(3) Neshamah-lev: The subtlety of our heart.
(4) Neshamah-sod halev: The subtlety of our secret heart.
(5) Neshamah-ruach: The subtlety of our spirit man.
(6) Neshamah-chayim: The subtlety of our spiritual life.
(7) Neshamah-yachidah: The subtlety of our oneness with the One.

The Chakras of Hindu spirituality and Leshyas of Jainism represent the same thing in one way or the other. All have colour systems of their own. Different Leshyas are represented by different colours. The colour has a specific importance and function in religious traditions. Why did God opt to create the universe and what is the Will of God, which He intends to accomplish? Reflection of all these things is found in the Great Soul. One side of Great Soul is the Obscure Subtlety (akhfa). Great Soul is the storehouse of eleven thousand beatific visions of God. The person who attains communion with these two subtleties can observe these visions. These subtleties of akhfa are found in every human being irrespective of who he is, what he is, or whatever his station in life is. "Great Soul", "Human Soul", and "Animal Soul" are really levels of functioning of the same soul and are not different souls. These three components are like three rings of light infused in one another and are collectively called the soul, the inseparable entity, the Lord's decree, or simply the man. Man gets acquainted with them one by one by purification from negative thoughts patterns such as fear, depression, negative emotions such as hate, contempt, anger, lust and negative practices such as hurting others psychologically or physically. Loving God and loving every human being irrespective of his race, religion, or nationality, and without consideration for any possible reward.

Chapter - 14

The Eye of Horus

The Eye of Horus is an ancient Egyptian symbol of protection, royal power and good health. The eye is personified in the goddess Wadjet. The Eye of Horus is similar to the Eye of Ra, which belongs to a different god, Ra, but represents many of the same concepts. The Eye of Horus Activation (EOH) is a gateway that connects us to the fifth dimensional energy of light and higher frequencies.

A long time ago, the god Osiris came to Egypt to rule as king. He brought the Egyptian people new laws and taught them how to farm well and live peacefully in their villages. Osiris was a very wise and powerful king, and was loved and respected by the Egyptian people. Unfortunately, his brother Seth, was very jealous of his brother's power in Egypt, and began to form a plan to kill Osiris and take over his throne. Late one night, Seth tiptoed into Osiris's bedroom. Careful to not wake up Osiris, or his queen, the goddess, Isis, Seth measured Osiris's body from top to bottom and from side to side. The next morning, Seth took the measurements to a carpenter who made a beautiful wooden chest decorated with bright paint and sheets of gold. That night, Seth threw a huge party, and invited Osiris as the guest of honour. The night was spent feasting, singing, dancing, and playing games. For the final game, Seth brought out the huge wooden chest. He announced that the first person to fit perfectly into the chest would be allowed to keep it. One by one, each of Seth's friends climbed into the chest. Unsurprisingly, no one was able to fit into the chest, which was made perfectly for Osiris. Finally, Seth and his friends convinced Osiris to try his luck with the chest. Osiris stepped into the chest and lay down. The chest fit him perfectly, just as Seth had planned. Just as Osiris lay down, Seth slammed the lid and sealed it shut. Seth and his friends took the chest down to the Nile River and dumped it in, knowing that Osiris would never be able to survive. When Isis heard the news of her husband's death she was extremely upset. She rushed to the riverbank, and after several days of searching, found the wooden chest. Isis opened it and removed the dead body of her beloved Osiris. Crying, Isis hid Osiris' body in the river grass. She didn't want Seth to find Osiris's corpse before she could perform the proper rituals that would allow him to pass into the Afterlife. Late that night, Seth returned to the Nile, to make sure Osiris's body had washed away. The chest was nowhere to be found, but after searching the riverbank grass, he found the body of his late brother. Furious, Seth cut Osiris's body into fourteen pieces. To make sure that the body was never found again, he hurled the pieces all over Egypt. The next morning, Isis returned to the river with her sister, Nepthys and her friends, to perform the necessary rituals, only to find Osiris's body gone! Isis transformed into a huge bird and flew high over Egypt. Using her sharp vision, she was able to find all the pieces of the body to put Osiris back together. With the help of Nepthys, Thoth, and Anubis, Isis performed a great act of magic. Very carefully, they began to sew Osiris's body back together. They worked together night after night. When the body was whole once again, they wrapped it head to toe in strips of linen, creating a mummy. On the night of the full moon, Isis used powerful magic to bring her husband back to life. Osiris embraced Isis, and thanked her sister and her friends. He told them he would not be able to stay in the world of the living. He explained that having died; he needed to travel to the world of the dead, where he would become the King of the Afterlife. Before he left, Osiris told Isis not to worry. He told her that she would soon give birth to a son, Horus, who would defeat Seth and become a great protector of the Egyptian people. By taking back the throne from Seth, Horus would restore order and peace to the Universe. When Horus was born, he was hidden away and kept safe from his evil uncle Seth. When he became of age, Horus finally confronted Seth, and they violently fought. During the fight Horus' left eye was poked out, but magically came to life. Later on, the Wadjet, or eye of Horus became a powerful symbol to promote healing. Although Horus emerged victorious, there was still a large question of who legally had power to the throne. Seth believed that as Osiris' brother, he was the rightful ruler, but Horus argued that he should be proclaimed king, since he was Osiris' legitimate heir. Ultimately, it was decided that Horus would rule on earth as King. Seth was banished forever.

Horus was the ancient Egyptian sky god who was usually depicted as a falcon, most likely a lanner or peregrine falcon. His right eye was associated with the sun god, Ra. The eye symbol represents the marking around the eye of the falcon, including the "teardrop" marking sometimes found below the eye. The mirror image, or left eye, sometimes represented the moon and the god Djehuti (Thoth). It was believed by the Greeks and Romans that an evil heart could get to the eye. The thought to be powerful effects of eyes and optics created the myth that the energy-producing power of eye had the ability to cast evil spells with just a glance. Because the ancients believed the evil eye could be counteracted with a 'good eye', myths about Horus arose.

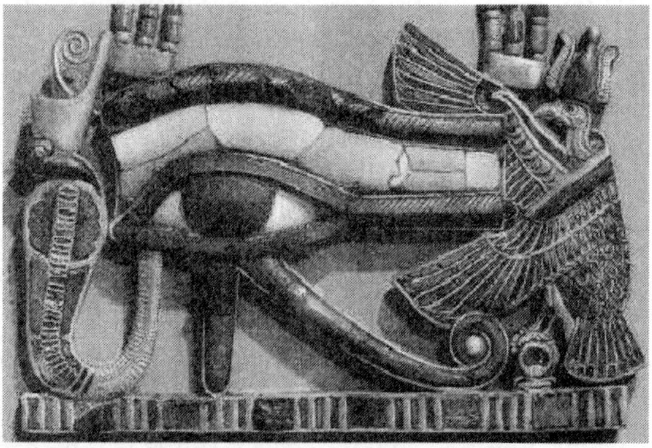

Figure 14.1: The Eye of Horus (EOH)

The EOH Activation provides the opening that creates a reservoir of celestial energy within our own energy field. This reservoir of celestial energy then anchors and infuses our energy field then continuing the journey by going out to the universe and returning to us on a constant basis renewing itself within us. Our connection with our Sacred Mother Earth is also strengthened and aligned and we are nurtured by our divine earth mother.

14.1 More on the Eye of Horus

The Eye of Horus refers to the ancient Mystery School Teachings of Creational Geometry encoded by Isis and Osiris and left behind with their priests in Egypt. These are the same souls who are the priests in Atlantis and other programs. They carry this genetically encoded information in their DNA. There is additional information kept hidden in the ancient mystery school teachings since the beginning of this reality/program. All hidden information will come forward at this time, as the Hall of Records - Golden Capstone was activated on December 12 - 12:12 at 12:12 am and pm in the Kings Chamber of the Great Pyramid and brings our healing, enlightenment and ascension. The calibration for the time clock of our reality was reset and consciousness shifted.

The ancient Egyptians believed that the pharaoh was a living god, a personification of the forces of heaven meant to be their ruler because divine blood ran through his veins. Sometimes, the pharaoh was even referred to as the 'Living Horus'. It was said that with each pharaoh's passing, the spirit of Horus passed from the deceased to his successor. This explains why the Eye of Horus was so often, and so prominently, displayed in royal courts and costumes. Even the funeral ceremonies of the pharaohs gave pride of place to the Eye of Horus. Some of the most precious and intricate funerary amulets recovered from pyramids and sarcophagi were of the Eye of Horus. The symbol was meant to be a guiding eye as the pharaoh made his journey from the land of the living to the land of the dead.

The eye is a recurring theme in ancient symbology. The five senses with which we perceive all of existence around us held great wonder for people long ago, and the sense of sight was perhaps the one most highly regarded of them all. For that reason, we often see the eye depicted in symbols whose origins lie far back in mankind's shared history. Many of us recognize the all-seeing eye (Eye of Providence) that is today most readily associated with the Illumination.

There are theories that the Egyptian Eye also played a part in mathematics. Ancient Egyptian priests excelled in mathematics, something that is fairly obvious from the fantastic monuments that they have left behind.

Their mathematical system used to depict all fractions as unit fractions (one divided by a whole number). For example, ¾ would not be simply that; it would be written as '½ + ¼'.

Some scholars believe that the individual elements of the Egyptian Eye are representations of the unit fractions ½, ¼, 1/8, 1/16, 1/32 and 1/64 (which are 1 divided by the first six powers of 2). It also ties in to the inherent structure of the 'Golden Ratio' which we see materialized in nature so often. They attributed that remaining, indecipherable and unknowable portion to magic. Although we cannot know for certain, it is possible that the Egyptian Eye was the precursor to depictions of the eye that have appeared in cultures across the world.

Shiva, one of the gods of the Hindu trinity, is always depicted with a third eye on his forehead, aligned with the crown chakra. In Buddhism, the Buddha himself is referred to as the 'Eye of the World' or the 'Eye of Truth'. It may actually astonish you to recognize that the 'Rx' symbol we so often find on pharmaceutical products is actually constructed around the Egyptian Eye of Horus.

As an amulet the Eye of Horus has three versions: a left eye, a right eye, and two eyes. The eye is constructed in fractional parts, with 1/64 missing, a piece that Thoth added with magic. The Eye of Horus is depicted as a human eye embellished with a typical Egyptian cosmetic extension and subtended by the markings of a falcon's cheek. When worn as jewellery fashioned of gold, silver, lapis, wood, porcelain, or carnelian the eye served to ensure safety, protect health, and provide the wearer with wisdom and prosperity; it was called the "all-seeing Eye." We can find eye of Horus jewellery as a pendant, necklace and as a ring, both silver and gold versions. Silver and Gold Ring with regeneration and health protection properties. Silver and gold pendant, provide protection and health regeneration properties.

14.2 The Eye of Horus (Originally the Eye of Ra)

The Eye of Horus is shown as an ancient Egyptian Hieroglyphic Symbol and the story about Osiris and Isis and the birth of Horus their son, is known. That the story was a parable meant to keep alive the energies until humanity was ready. The Eye is the Eternal Eye through which a template of vibratory patterns is used by the Masters and Lords of Light to generate physical creation. The Father's Eye of divine creation coordinates the minds of the Elohim so that the divine image can be passed on to all generations of creations. The Eternal Eye allows the Father's Living Light to make visible His garment so that it can form the Light substances.

Light is transmitted through the Eye of Horus to the human being to transform him into a Light Being. This is known as a remembrance as far back as Lemuria and is a very ancient system that had been used on the Earth Plane but forgotten until now. When it is said that through the Eye of Horus we are transformed into a Light Being, it does not mean that this is the only method. It is believed that everyone is receiving the accelerated energies that are present on the Earth now. The people who are drawn to activate through the Eye of Horus energies receive the showers. The Eye of Horus refers to the ancient Mystery School Teachings of Creational Geometry encoded by Isis and Osiris and left behind with their priests in Egypt. These are the same souls who are the priests in Atlantis and other programs. They carry this genetically encoded information in their DNA. There is additional information kept hidden in the ancient mystery school teachings since the beginning of this reality/program.

The Eye of Horus (originally, The Eye of Ra) is an ancient Egyptian symbol of protection and power, from the deity Horus or Ra. The Eye was a symbol that signified royal power, yet on the numeration side denoted a decimal system where round off was set to the first 6-terms. The ancients believed this symbol of indestructibility would assist in rebirth, due to their beliefs about the soul. The more recent tradition of freemasonry adopted the symbol in the form of the Eye of Providence and as such it has survived to this day. The Eye of Horus (flanked by Nekhbet and Wadjet) was found under the 12th layer of bandages on Tutankhamun's mummy. The ancient Egyptian word wedjet signifies blue, and the same word is used for the human eye. Horus was an ancient god in Egyptian mythology who dramatically evolved over the whole of Egyptian history. Early on, he became identified as a sky god, where one of his eyes was the sun, and the other the moon. His weaker eye later became less important in his mythology, and he became more strongly aligned with the sun, particularly when the cult of Thoth, a moon god, arose. As the sun, or rather, with his eye as the sun, his eye had a special meaning, and became a symbol of power when combined with the hieratic aspects of the subject. Originally,

Ra held this position, but as Horus gradually became more important, he transformed into a sun god, so Horus became thought of as Ra, or rather Ra-Herakhty ("Ra, who is Horus of the two horizons").

Later Horus-Eye numeration decreased in importance in Egyptian life, with hieratic, demotic and later improvements in Egyptian arithmetic solving the oldest Horus-Eye problem. The oldest Horus-Eye problem was to write any number, like one (1), exactly, without throwing away any piece of the number. It represents a peregrine falcon's eye and the markings round it, including the "teardrop" marking sometimes found below the eye.

The Eye of Horus was intimately associated with the gods and their rule over the realm of men. Part of this rule involved protection and the Eye of Horus was an omnipresent symbol of that protection. It is said that Egyptian sailors painted the Eye of Horus on the bows of their boats before setting sail on long and perilous voyages. In this sense, the eye both guided the vessel in its journey through unfamiliar waters and served as a deterrent to malefic forces.

The other widespread use of the Eye of Horus was in funerary ceremonies. Besides being a symbol of divine protection, it was also taken to be a representation of the will of the gods over the mortal world.

14.3 Light Body

14.3.1 What is our light body?

Figure 14.2: Light Body

Our light body is an energy body that exists at a higher level, closer to our Source, than our chakras. We have seven vibrational energy body centres (chakras) and three light body centres, for a total of ten centres (chakras) that power and make up our light body. The first three centres regulate the amount of energy we take in from of our environment; they change less harmonious energies into harmonious ones, and use all the energy around us to go higher. These three centres form the power base of our light body. As we work with these centres, we may experience a stronger sense of personal power and an increased ability to stay centred and to release stuck emotional energy. The upper vibrational energy body centres create flow and harmony, and take us to the higher mental realms and other dimensions that are beyond time and space. As we work with these centres, we can add light to our thoughts and open our channel to the higher dimensions. We can experience many illumined, expanded states of awareness that can feel deeply insightful, blissful, and take us beyond thought into direct experiences of being-ness. There are three light body centres. As we awaken these centres and connect with your Source, we can increase the balance, clarity, and harmony in our life. Awakening our light body is like having a new kind of vision, where we can see, sense or feel the higher, more beautiful energies of our Universe, and make them a part of our daily life. The EOH Activation awakens our Light Body as it has been done in ancient temples long ago and is still practiced between a teacher and a student on the inner planes today. It is an initiation process and much, much more. The ancient knowledge of this EOH initiation process has been passed on to generations is and it the sacred duty of the initiated soul to conduct this initiation for each and every person who finds their calling to receive it.

14.3.2 Why Awaken Your Light Body?

Our light body is the body of light we are developing as our next evolutionary step. Awakening our light body brings higher, finer frequencies of light into our physical, emotional and mental energy bodies. With these finer frequencies of light we are building step-by-step an awareness of the higher dimensions and ourselves as we exist in them. As we awaken your light body we can experience many heightened, blissful, peaceful, loving, joyful and insightful states of consciousness. We can reach higher, expanded states, open our channel upward, and expand our consciousness to experience our Source directly. We can use these energies in many practical ways as well as to create the life we want. We feel a strong, inner desire to make significant changes in the way we experience your life. We can expand our consciousness, deepen our sense of your life's purpose and grow in our ability to connect to our Source and our own inner knowing. We learn to merge our willpower with our heart and mind for balanced, harmonious living. We learn to surf the chaos and navigate the flow of the energies that make up our Universe.

If we are on a path of accelerated self-growth along with the higher vibrations of light, we receive from initiation, by accessing and holding more 5-D light as we operate in our daily lives, with conscious intention to be a vehicle of that light for the Earth, we can help stabilize and support her increase in frequency and vibration. The upcoming earth changes that have been prophesied by many, including the Hopi, Edgar Cayce, Gordon Michael Scallion and many others, will be altered by the higher frequencies that each one of us are striving to hold for ourselves, our planet and humanity. We are the Light workers of this planet and we know that being of higher consciousness and moving towards the 5th Dimension we can in fact hold the energy. It means not only anchoring this light when our lives or environment are calm, during times of temporary disruption, upset or change. By adapting and surviving we model the true meaning of "Readiness to Evolve."

14.4 Eye Symbology

Everything is myth, math, and metaphor, laced with 'eye' symbology in the matrix of time. All things are viewed through an eye of creation - conscious creation - projected illusion in the alchemy of time. Everything sweeps forth from the 'eye' - experience consciously - then returns to the eye as the patterns of reality create and recreate in loops - think spiralling galaxies. Eyes are windows to soul experience - think virtual reality. The eye is a lens which allows us to see and become consciously aware of our experiment in third dimension.

The eye has a pupil. We are pupils/students in a university experiencing consciously through the lens of time or virtual reality. The eye is the window to the soul and all aspects of our soul experiencing in other grids. The third eye is the 6th chakra (Ajna chakra or eyebrows chakra). As it begins to activate and open - it is a common experience that one sees an eye - or eyes - looking back at them. Our perspective in dreams - of colours - our personal life and relationships - will be seen through a 'new light.' We are then moving into a higher frequency that enables us to expand our consciousness and see reality on many levels and dimensions. This can be a quantum leap in perception and can be life changing as we discard patterns that no longer work in higher frequency. Our total perception changes in this acceleration of time. The opening of the eye - is symbolic of a time of awakening - the evolution of consciousness -- the activation of our DNA.

14.5 Opening of the eye of Horus

It can be the physical eye or what is called the 'third eye' - which looks up and out - has a lens and is the pineal gland. The camera slows down the action allowing us to experience events as linear in nature - when indeed they are not. Exploring in linear time allows us to experience emotions through an electromagnetic field - duality - polarity - love vs. fear. We see balance as we awaken and remember that we are soul-sparks - the twinkling lights we see - who are in a physical form that is evolving back to its original creation - pole shifts of consciousness - earth changes as both physical and as metaphors. There is much symbology linked with the image of the 'eye' - all linking to the eye as a metaphor for the source of creation - God - Eye of God When people dream or are meditating they sometimes see an Eye that is either opened or closed. Symbolically it is the opened eye that is awakened consciousness.

14.6 The Eye of Horus with Fractions

The Eye of Horus or the udjat, is a symbol of the god Horus as both the son of Osiris and Isis and as the sun-god. Egyptian myths state that Horus lost his left eye in his war with Seth to avenge the death of his father. Seth tore the eye of Horus into pieces. The left eye, being the moon was discovered by Thoth (the god of wisdom and magic) lying in pieces, but he was able to reassemble them into the full moon. Each piece of the udjat represents a fraction of the descending geometric series 1/2, 1/4, 1/8, etc., put together they make 63/64 or approximately 1. Having been reassembled, Thoth gave the Eye to Horus. Horus, in turn, gave the eye to his murdered father Osiris, thereby bringing him back to life. The Eye of Horus was used a form of fractional notation, each of the parts of the eye representing a different fraction. The parts of the eye were divided as follows:

- ½ was represented by smell, symbolized by the right side of the eye in a form of the nose. The pyramid text says: "Behold [the fire] rises in Abydos and it comes; I cause it to come, the Eye of Horus. It is set in order upon thy brow, O Osiris Khenti-Amenti; it is set in the shrine and rises on thy brow."
- ¼ was represented by sight or the sensation of light, symbolized by the pupil. The pyramid text says: "Perfect is the Eye of Horus. I have delivered the Eye of Horus, the shining one, the ornament of the Eye of Ra, the Father of the Gods."
- 1/8 was represented by thought, symbolized by the eyebrow. The pyramid text says: "...the Eye of Horus hath made me holy...I will hide myself among you, O ye stars which are imperishable. My brow is the brow of Ra."
- 1/16 was represented by hearing, symbolized by right side of the eye in the form of an arrow pointing towards the ear. The pyramid text says: "That which has been shut fast/dead hath been opened by the command of the Eye of Horus, which hath delivered me. Established are the beauties of the forehead of Ra."
- 1/32 was represented by taste, by the sprouting of wheat or grain from the planted stalk, symbolized by a curved tail. The pyramid text says: "Come, the Eye of Horus hath delivered for me my soul, my ornaments are established on the brow of Ra. Light is on the faces of those who are in the members of Osiris."
- 1/64 was represented by touch, symbolized by a leg touching the ground. The pyramid text says: "I shall see the Gods and the Eye of Horus burning with fire before my eyes."

Figure 14.3: Eye of Horus in Fraction

Chapter - 15

Third Eye in Other Faiths and Religions

15.1 Third Eye in Sufism

If you stand in one place and whirl around, the world begins to look tired and dull, a mirage that's losing power, because it was never really there. Or so say the Sufis, who do just that as a way to break from this mortal coil. In the book Sufism and Wisdom, Molana-al-Moazum Salaheddin Ali Nader Shah Angha says, "the human quest for knowledge is only valid when the goal is to discover the reality behind the surface value of words, things, entities, etc." Staring at an ocean, imagine the waves as life's unsolved mysteries; a vast majority of believers are concerned with what the wave has left behind, but it is the Sufis who are concerned with plunging into the ebb and tracing it back to its Eternal and Infinite Source. Sufism is known as the "Way of the Heart, the Way of the Pure, the Mystical Path of Islam." It is also called the "School of Self Knowledge." Sufism is the way to remove the gravity of the lower self (which weighs down the spirit) and ascend through methods and practices to the state wherein the "Vision of God" is presented. It is the art of discovering the eternity within ourselves. The Sufi path takes the seeker to the Divine Essence, the ultimate goal being to dissolve in the Absolute Truth – God. The ways to God are as numerous as the number of breaths of mankind, and each individual has his own way. Sufism stresses the need to cut through the veils of existence while here on earth, because "Whoever is blind in this world will be blind in the next and go yet further astray."

Derived from Islamic mysticism, Sufism's biggest tool is the Quran ("The Instrument of Discernment") known as "The Uncreated Word of God." Sufis speak of "seeking to drown themselves" within its verses. They want to drink in as much as they can hold, for they realize their internal emptiness and ache to fill their Spirits rather than their Minds. Sufis continually strive to live the explicit Quran, recognizing that God is omnipresent. "We (God) are nearer to him (man) than his jugular vein." To the Sufis, God is everything that is "Majestic" and "Beautiful." By embodying these two divine qualities, Sufis live in Heaven, on earth. To them, the physical world is merely a projection of the heavenly world. Martin Lings' What is Sufism? explains, "Pleasures of the senses are shadows of the paradisal archetypes that God is seeking to convey." To the Sufi, the feeling of Wonder that comes from looking at a beautiful landscape is God. God is continually of and in us, so much within and without, that we do not recognize Him but turn around searching. "It is hidden in Its own outward manifestation wherein It doth appear as veil after veil made to cover Its glory." As we all live and breathe the same air, Mother Nature joins all of us together and screams out all the secrets between us so loud that we do not hear Her!

Sufis are Islams who have had a mystical experience. For entrance into a Sufi order or brotherhood, termed a Tar'quah, the individual must be "haunted by the thought of God" and have a "presentiment of one's higher states." The aim from the beginning is no less than sainthood; Sufis strive for Perfection. Of the Five Pillars of Islam (the Shahadah, prayer, almsgiving, fasting and pilgrimage to Mecca), Sufis only practice the First, which can be summed up as, "There is no God but God and Mohammed is His messenger." The Sufis are more concerned with the supple sincerity of devotion, as opposed to the rigid Islamic concern with ritualized prayer. Sufis are wrapped in a continual struggle of non-stop striving in their pursuit of the Full Knowledge of God. Above all, the Sufis aim is to lose their sense of self.

Individuality, the Sufis say, is the sum of everything that has ever been learned by a person. As proud as we are, Sufism begs us to deliver ourselves away from this deception. The Sufi says, "let go of yourself in order to be free." Adepts have reached Fana, the state of "self-having-passed-away," where the Sufi has completely lost his "self" and reached the spiritual station of the "tavern of ruin."

From an old fable: Byazid was in his station when someone knocked at his door. Byazid asked, "Who do you want?' The man answered that he was looking for Byazid. Byazid replied, 'h! It has been years since I have had any news of him.'" Byazid is so completely possessed of God, so full of spirituality that the physical world has become secondary and meaningless to him.

Sufism is "Heart Wakefulness." As the bodily heart receives Life from the Divinity which floods the body with Life, so too is it the focal point of concentration of all the powers of the soul in its aspiration towards the Infinite. To the Sufi, Heart is Intellect and Spirit. This is Intellect in terms of the Latin intellectus, which is, "the faculty which perceives the transcendent." What is Sufism? describes The Heart as, "the centre and summit of mankind, it is the direct faculty of spiritual (or intellectual) vision." We see fine with our eyes, it is our Heart that falls blind. The emphasis is on thinking with the Heart rather than the mind. Shaykh `Al' al Jamal said, "Relax the mind and learn to swim." The mind is a one-dimensional trap, it is only by letting go that the soul can experience intuition.

In **Sufism, the third eye is called 'Khafi'**. There is a term called ***'Lataif'*** in Sufism, which means the subtle centres or elements of creation or psycho spiritual energy centres (as chakras in Hinduism). The concept of Lataif is drawn from the Holy Quran by Sufis. All Sufis distinguish Lataif-as-Sitta-the six subtleties namely Latifat-an-Nafsi, Latifat-al-Qalbi, Latifat-as-Sirri, Latifat-ar-Ruhi, Latifat-al-Khafi, and Latifat-al-Akhfa. Out of this Latifat-al-Khafi means inexplicable, arcane or latent subtlety. It represents intuition. **Khafi is located in the middle of the forehead between the eyes or on the point of third eye.** Its colour is black or darkest blue. Some believe that it is located to the right of the chest and it is darkest green in colour. Some Sufis compare it with Kitab-e-Marqoom the divine codices. The invocation or activation of this latifa leads to the realm of unification with ultimate reality. Khafi is a 'meta' organ, which means that the khafi consists of collective and coherent functioning of all the senses and the mind for a higher consciousness.

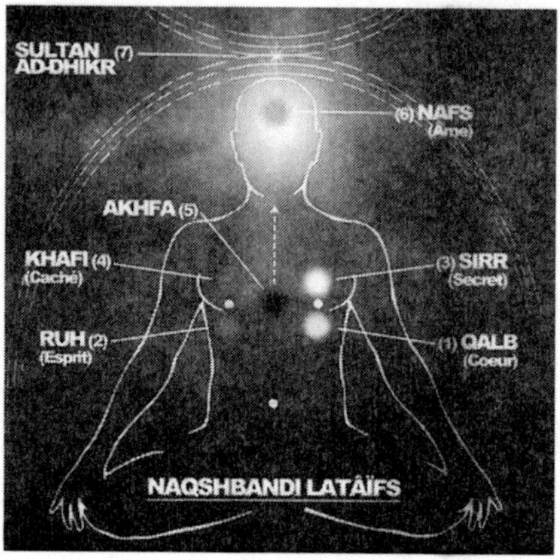

Figure 15.1: Third Eye in Sufism (Khafi)

Being similar to a pinecone in shape (thus its name), the pineal gland is constructed in a three dimensional Fibonaccian spiral (that is close to a Golden Mean spiral). This shape in sacred geometry is considered a portal system onto itself, helping a person transcend dimensions in many mystery schools. A prime example of this is the mystical group called the **Sufi**. They do a spiral dance to get close to God and the heavens. Inside the pineal gland not only do we find the manufacturing of several 'mind altering' hormones such as melatonin, serotonin and possibly the psychedelic dimethyltryptamine (DMT), we find extremely coherent water with piezoelectric crystals. This extremely coherent water, encased in a sacred geometry chamber, has deep interest to us. The piezoelectric quality of this chamber is a great candidate for an event horizon to project us into other dimensions. This could be a connection to many things including: dreams, astral projection, remote viewing, visions and even the connection to higher self, the soul/spirit worlds. Some authorities have gone as far as calling it a Star Gate.

15.2 'Third Eye' termed as 'Dasam Dwar' in Sikhism

In Gurmat (Sikhism), Dasam Dwar is the tenth door situated in the subtle body. Gurbani says that place is called Tirkuti. Tirkuti is a place where we listen, breathe, and see. The Dasam Dwaar also Dasamadvara is the Tenth Door or Gate in addition to the physical body having nine openings: two eyes, two ears, two nostrils, one mouth and the organs of procreation (sexual organ) and excretion. The third eye, according to Sikhism, is at the top of the head, the Brahmarandhra that opens upon awakening of Kundalini and we feel the cool breeze. The third eye is open in all the new-born babies with a soft spot called the anterior fontenal. Sikhs believe that there are 10 'gates' to the body; Some understand 'gates' as another word for 'chakras' or energy centres. These gates are also understood as chand-suraj (sight), pavan (air), pani (water) signifying eyes, ears/nose and mouth. The topmost energy level is the called the tenth gate or dasam dwaar where Anhad Bani: The unstruck sound current of the Shabad vibrates.

Figure 15.2: Shri Guru Nanak Dev ji, the Founder of Sikhism

According to Sikhism, the Tenth Gate can only be opened by the Guru's grace and is vital for Self-realization and enlightenment. Sikhism forbids meditation on the lower chakras, the tenth gate is the starting point for Sikhs; it is the final goal in Hinduism. The Dasam dwar appears in Guru Granth Sahib (the most sacred book in Sikhism) at many places. As an example:

Bhanai nanak bharam pat khulhei gur parsadi janiya.
Sachi liva lagi hei bhitari sataguru sio man maniya.
– (Shri Guru Granth Sahib, Mohalla: 3, p 666)

Meaning: With the Guru's grace the mask of delusion lifts and one is able to know about God; following the guru's instructions facilitates being absorbed in Him within the mind.

This verse of the third Guru refers to the phenomenon of delusions caused by temptations resulting in the human soul being separated from the Creator within the mind. The verse advises how the veil thus created can be lifted with the guru's help. This lifting of the veil or mask enables one to see within the mind by opening a hidden gate (the tenth gate).

The shabd-dhun or spiritual sound vibrates from Sach Khand, directly from Akal Purukh. This spiritual sound can be heard in meditation at the tenth gate when one reaches that high stage and at that point, the soul envisions the light of God within and tastes the nectar of the Lord--this is the beginning of brahmgyan (Supreme Knowledge).

Dasam duara aagam apara param purakh ki ghati.
Upari hatu hat pari aala aale bhitari baati.
(Beni, SGGS, p 974)

Meaning: Dasam Duar (Tenth gate) is the abode of the inaccessible, Infinite Supreme Being; in the body there is a niche where He abides.

Nau ghar thape thapanharei.
Daswein vasa alakh aparei.
(M: 1, SGGS, p 1036)

Meaning: The creator established nine gates (for the body); the unfathomable Lord resides in the tenth.

Mani tani ravi rahiya jagadisur pekhat sada hazure.
(M: 5, SGGS, p 1269).

Meaning: The Master of the universe abides in the mind and body. Thus the Dasam Duar is the gate that when opened enables vision of the Creator in the mind.

Nau dart hake yavatu rahai.
Dasvei nij vasa paye.
Uthe anahad shabad wahahi dinu rti gurmati shabad sunavaniya.
(M: 3, SGGS, p 124).

Meaning: One, who controls the nine organs, gets to enter the tenth, the abode of the Creator; there the unstruck celestial music continues day and night; it is heard through the Guru's word.

Hari jio gupha andari rahi kei vaja pawan vajaiya.
Vajaiya vaja paun nau duare paragatu kiye daswa gupatu rakhaiya.
Gurduare lai bhavni ikana daswa durau dikhaiya.
(M: 3, SGGS, p 922)

Meaning: The Creator put the soul in the body and gave it life; the body has nine manifest openings and a tenth is concealed; the tenth gate is shown to those who approach the Guru with devotion.

Ram namu rattan kothari gada eik lukani.
Satguru milei ta khojiye mili jeti jeti samani.
(M: 4, SGGS, p 1178)

Meaning: The jewel of God's Naam remains concealed in a chamber in the body- fortress; when we find a true guru we are motivated to search for it; once it is found the soul merges in Him.

Nagari eikei nau darwje yavatu baraji rahai.
Trikuti chhutei daswa daru khulhei ta manu khiva bhai.
(Kabir, SGGS, p 1123).

Meaning: The body has nine gates, they should be constrained from wandering; when one comes out of the grip of the three gunas, the tenth gate opens, one gets the Vision and the mind becomes ecstatic.

Dasami das duar basi kinei. Mani santokhu naam japi leene.
Karani suniye jasu gopal. Naini pekhat sai daeeyal.
Rasana gun gavei beant. Man mahi chitave puran bhagawany.
Gasat charan sant tahal kamaeeye. Nanak ihu sanjamu prabh kirpa paeeye.
(M: 5, SGGS, p 298-99).

Meaning: Remembering Naam gives contentment; with the ears one listens to the Creator's praises, with the eyes sees the compassionate Guru; with the tongue praises the Infinite Lord, in the mind thinks of the perfect beloved Master; serves the Guru using hands and feet. All this is possible only with Divine grace, which when received opens the tenth gate, the Dasam Duar. A closed gate needs a code or key to open it. This key is with the Guru.

Guru kunji pahu nivalu manu kotha chhati.
Nanak gur binu man ka taku na ughadei na kunji hathi.
(M: 2, SGGS, p 1237).

Meaning: The body is the cover for the chamber that contains the mind which is locked up behind worldly attachments; the Guru is the key to the lock; the door of the mind cannot be opened except by the Guru since none else has the key.

Daswei duari kunchi jab dijei.
Tau daeeyal ko darasanu kijei.

(Kabir, SGGS, p 341).

Meaning: When the key is applied to the Tenth gate, one is able to have vision of the compassionate Lord.

15.3 Third Eye Evidence in Ancient America

The Third Eye was also known to the religions of the Maya, Olmec, Aztec, Inca, pre-Inca, and other ancient American cultures. The symbolic Third Eye "forehead dot", present in Hinduism, Buddhism and Taoism is also abundant in the archaeology of ancient civilizations in America. This Third Eye symbolism evolved and flourished in present-day Mexico, Peru, Columbia, Panama and even the United States (that is, the Olmec, Toltec, Maya, Zapotec, Aztec, Inca, pre-Inca, and Mississippian cultures, among others).

There is a long history of the Third Eye in the so-called "occult tradition" or "hermetic tradition," and this tradition teaches that during a long-ago Golden Age our ancestors had a "Third Eye" in the centre of their foreheads. As humans evolved, this Third Eye atrophied, becoming the modern "pineal gland," located precisely in the geometric centre of the human brain.

Many examples don´t necessarily depict a "forehead dot," but nevertheless still express Third Eye symbolism. For example, in Peru the Inca king was often depicted in art with a semi-circular "solar" motif around his head—an illustration, perhaps, of his spiritual Third Eye awakening:

The ceremonial knives called Tumis show human beings crowned with a semi-circular "solar halo," which portrays them as being illuminated by the rising sun around their heads. The Inca king also wore a golden orb necklace across his chest, which may have symbolized his knowing or "gnosis" of the "inner sun" or "higher Self" within. Such representations may have implied that sunlight or soul-light resides inside every human being. Interestingly, the Incas understood the doctrine of duality—the ida and pingala of Kundalini Yoga—believing a totality is comprised of two opposing and contrasting forces locked in equilibrium. They associated the male /pingala "side" with the sun and the female/ida "side" with the moon. In Peru…a silver image of the moon, associated with the female sovereign, was the complement to the golden effigy of the sun, associated with the Inca [King]. Two forms of cult prevailed: the Inca lords and warriors were associated with the cult of which the emblems were golden images of the Creator and of the Sun, "the lord of the day". The silver huaca or image of the moon…was in the figure of a woman and was kept under the charge of women, the reason for this being "that the moon was a woman."

Like the ancient Hindus, the Incas understood the sun was spiritual and masculine while the moon material and feminine. It was on the basis of this male/female relationship between the sun and moon that the Incas perceived the entire universe as a duality, which they called hanan and hurin. Hanan expressed the Sun, High, Strong, Aggressive, Right, and Masculine. Hurin denoted the Moon, Low, Weak, Passive, Left, and Feminine.

More importantly, the Incas knew that it wasn't just "duality" that was important; it was the "union" of this duality, the "joining" of these hanan/hurin opposites, that enabled the magic of "balance" and "transcendence" to take place. This "joining" of "opposites" "sometimes around a central point or entity" precisely parallels the union of ida and pingala in Kundalini Yoga. This is the so-called "alchemical marriage" (to borrow an alchemical term) that stimulates the sushumna and awakens the Third Eye chakra; hence the gold Tumi in the photo above.

The indigenous Toltec people of Mexico did not make that mistake. They knew that we are double beings. They knew about the double nature of the world. That is why they call the world Omeyocan, or "the place of duality." Those ancient Toltecs were aware of our dual nature and envisioned the integration of the two sides of our being as the goal of human existence. Like the ancient Hindus, the Maya also believed that the world and everything inside it is made of duality, including our own physical bodies. Throughout Maya history the left and right sides of the human body, left/right spatial orientation, and handedness have had important cultural and symbolic meanings. For the Classic Maya, as with contemporary Maya peoples, the right hand or side of the body often signified "pure, powerful, or super-ordinate, and the left frequently symbolized "weaker, lame, or subordinate" in particular cultural contexts. The Maya too believed that to touch the alchemical gold we must understand and balance this duality; in fact, this was the fundamental "religion" of the Mayan people. This idea of "harmony of opposites" is also visible in pre-Inca art and architecture across western South America. In some cases, it was directly related to the Third Eye. In some pre-Inca cultures, like the Moche, the Third Eye was depicted as an owl´s face; this is because the owl is an ambivalent symbol, encompassing both sides of the duality and thus symbolizing a "union" or "reconciliation" of the opposites as one.

15.4 Unicorn Power of the Third Eye

Unicorn is a mythical animal typically represented as a horse four legged animal with a single straight horn projecting from its forehead. The first mention of the unicorn was in a book about India in the 4th century BC. The earliest description is from Ctesias, who in his book Indika ("On India") described them as wild asses, fleet of foot, having a horn a cubit and a half (700 mm, 28 inches) in length, and colored white, red and black.

The third eye is an enigmatic appendage having a universal mythological history. It is the horn of the unicorn, it is the middle eye of Shiva, and it is the eye of Horus of Egyptian tradition.

Awakening of the third eye is the birth right of every individual, which gives vision to those who choose to harness this birth right. While the two physical eyes see the past and the present, the third eye reveals the insight of the future with this item you can awaken the third eye.

A man, this was a real man who had a desire to try and turn horses into unicorn by trying to get them to grow horns from the skull. Unknowingly he tapped into the pineal gland and was able to make a horn grow from the horse's skull accidentally creating many real unicorns that held power. This was not a mystical thing but more scientific because of the gland being tapped into by force. Ajna chakra is the location of the third eye which is the conscience.

Figure 15.3: Unicorn with the Single Horn, representing the 'Third Eye'

The horns that grew gave power of the third eye and the legend was true for magic from a unicorn. Sightings of this elusive creature have been reported throughout history and recorded in ancient folklore, artwork, poems, and songs for centuries.

Unicorns have been revered in Chinese Mythology for thousands of years. Culturally it is depicted as a creature with the body of a deer often covered in fish-like scales or feathers, cloven hooves, and a single spiral horn protruding from the centre of the forehead. It is known as the Qilin, honored and respected for its power and wisdom. It would appear only in very special times, often in a Glade or at the time of death or birth of a great leader, and was always a sign of great fortune.

The earliest known recorded appearance of the Unicorn is found in Chinese Folklore. The Chinese sovereign known as Fu Hsi (c.2900 BC) was resting on the bank of the Yellow River one day near the end of his life. He was thinking about his mortality and trying to find a way to record his thoughts for following generations. Suddenly a Qilin rose from the waters of the river and came towards him. On its back it carried magical sigils from which Fu Hsi devised the very first written Chinese language. Over time, this "magical" script has evolved so naturally that readers of modern day Chinese are able to understand something which was written 2,000 years ago.

In the encyclopedias, the horn of the unicorn was said to have the power to render poisoned water potable and to heal sickness. In medieval and Renaissance times, the tusk of the narwhal was sometimes sold as unicorn horn. Even in the twenty-first century, the unicorn holds a place in popular culture. It is often used as a symbol of fantasy or rarity. The unicorn was depicted in ancient seals of the Indus Valley Civilization and was mentioned by the ancient Greeks in accounts of natural history by various writers, including Ctesias, Strabo, Pliny the Younger, and Aelian.

Figure 15.4: 'Unicorn Seal' during Indus Valley Civilization

The Bible also describes an animal, the re'em, which some versions translate as unicorn.

Figure 15.5: Unicorn as the National Animal of Scotland

Unicorn is best known as the symbol of Scotland. The unicorn was chosen because it was seen as a proud and haughty beast which would rather die than be captured, just as Scots would fight to remain sovereign and unconquered. Two unicorns supported the royal arms of the King of Scots, and since the 1707 union of England and Scotland, the royal arms of the United Kingdom have been supported by a unicorn along with an English lion. Two versions of the royal arms exist: that used in Scotland gives more emphasis to the Scottish elements, placing the unicorn on the left and giving it a crown, whereas the version used in England and elsewhere gives the English elements more prominence.

Golden coins known as the unicorn and half-unicorn, both with a unicorn on the obverse, were used in Scotland in the 15th and 16th century. In the same realm, carved unicorns were often used as finials on the pillars of Mercat crosses, and denoted that the settlement was a royal burgh. Certain noblemen such as the Earl of Kinnoull were given special permission to use the unicorn in their arms, as an augmentation of honour. The crest for Clan Cunningham bears a unicorn head.

15.5 Third Eye in Neo-Gnosticism

According to the neo-gnostic teachings of Samael Aun Weor, the third eye is referenced symbolically and functionally several times in the Book of Revelation 3:7-13, a work which, as a whole, he believes describes Kundalini and its progression upwards through three and a half turns and seven chakras.

Figure 15.6: Third Eye in Neo-Gnosticism

This interpretation equates the third eye with the sixth of the seven churches of Asia detailed therein, also the Church of Philadelphia.

Figure 15.7: Interior of the St. Peter and St. Paul in Philadelphia

15.5.1 Ammon's Horn as the Third Eye in Gnosticism

The Ammon is the Abraxas, and place of Sophia (wisdom); to the Gnostics, Christos (or Gnosis), and the 'Third Eye' to many people today. The Ammon's Horn is also known in science as our hippocampus located in a section of our brain in which we access the hidden supreme power to obtain gnosis, intuition, wisdom, and to

Figure 15.8: Ammon's Horn

relearn from our past lives. It is an ancient connection to a god who was known in Egypt as Ammon (Amun, Amon Ra, Amen etc.), and a place in our brain, known as the Ammon's horn, or hippocampus. Following is an image of the ancient Egyptian ram-horned Jupiter Ammon connecting to his third eye in order to obtain enlightenment which is depicted in the planetary disk that represents Jupiter.

Following is an image of an ammon's horn or hippocampus.

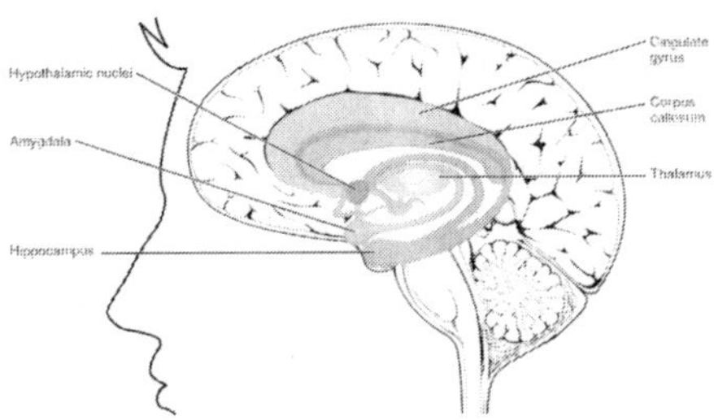

Figure 15.9: Hippocampus (Ammon's horn)

Ammon's horn is said to have represented the 'Third Eye'.

The word hippocampus is derived from the Ancient Greek ἱππόκαμπος (hippokampos), ἵππος (hippos, "horse") and κάμπος (kampos, "sea monster"). Following is the image of an actual a sea horse with its third eye.

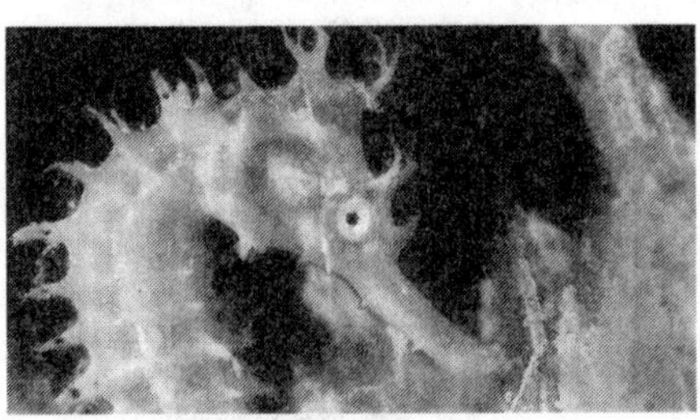

Figure 15.10: Seahorse (Third eye is also in the picture)

It is assumed by some people that in the Bible; "The word 'amen' is from Ammon, the father god of Egypt, and was an ancient Egyptian salutation to the supreme power of the universe." According to Plutarch, Ammon is the first being and all things, and Ra is the sun-god.

What many people have failed to realize in reading these descriptions, is that this first being and supreme power is actually within all of us. It is our real third eye, and it is not the pineal gland. This is why Ammon (Amen) is described by the Egyptians who were master alchemists and knew this science, as the King of Gods; Father of the Gods; Lord of the Thrones of the Two Lands; Lord of Truth whose shrine is hidden; and Amun ra, the Lord of Wisdom. Amon is "The Hidden One" of the visible and the invisible worlds, who is the "Creator God" and the mysterious soul of the universe which reveals itself in light. Amon is the light, creator, builder and grand architect of the house and temple.

This science was often depicted with Gods riding a sea-horse such as Hippius, a name of Neptune. The Hippocampus was Neptune's favourite horse. Neptune (Latin: Neptūnus) was the Roman god of water and the sea in Roman mythology and religion, a brother of Jupiter and Pluto. He is the counterpart of the Greek sea god, and one of the ancient gods of Phoenicia under the name of Poseidon. Neptune or Poseidon is often riding a hippocampus or has his chariot drawn by two of them, and his babies are called tadfoals. All humans have Ammon's horn which in the medial temporal lobe, underneath the cortical surface. It contains two main interlocking parts: Ammon's horn and the gyrus.

How does the Ammon's Horn or hippocampus act as our Third Eye or seat of our soul?

If you research the brain and the hippocampus, you will find that there are an extensive amount of studies and articles from scientists that have been completed on this subject. In almost all this information it has been concluded that this area of the brain is what we use for the ability to recall memories guide adaptive behaviour past experiences as they evolved over time. When the hippocampus is damaged, a person can't create new memories. There are several studies both government and private that verify its role in all memory and even learning. These facts along with the ancient images and gods are the reason why it is believed that it is the true third eye.

Chapter - 16

Some Shiva Temples and other 'Third Eye' Shrines in the World

A. SOME SHIVA TEMPLES IN INDIA

16.1 Maha Mrityunjaya Temple at Jageshwar Dham, Uttarakhand

Jageshwar is a Hindu pilgrimage town and one of the Dams (pilgrimage region) in the Shaivism tradition. Jageshwar Temples are a group of over 100 Hindu temples dated between 7th and 12th century near Almora, in the Himalayan Indian state of Uttarakhand. The valley has a number of temple clusters such as the Dandeshwar and Jageshwar sites. Some locations have attracted construction of new temples through the 20th-century. Together these clusters consist of over 200 structural temples built from the cut stone. Many are small, while a few are substantial. These temples predominantly illustrate North Indian Nagara style of architecture with a few exceptions that show South and Central Indian style designs. Many are dedicated to Lord Shiva, while others in the immediate vicinity are dedicated to Lord Vishnu, Shakti goddesses and Surya traditions of Hinduism.

Temple # 76, found at the Jageshwar site, also called the Mrityunjaya Mahadeva temple, is a large temple with the latina Nagara style architecture. This temple is eastern facing and the Linga is worshipped as the saviour from death. The unique linga has an ***eye*** (third eye) shaped opening. Pilgrims believe that reciting the Maha mritunjaya Mantra is a fruitful, auspicious and powerful method for self realisation, removal of evil effects, and freedom from all kinds of fears, illness and negativity.

Figure 16.1: Third-Eye Shiva Linga at Maha Mrityunjaya Temple, Jageshwari

This temple has a four-pillared entry mandapa, then the mukha-mandapa (main hall) which leads to an antarala (vestibule), then on to the square sanctum. The tower is curvilinear. Its wall is covered with frieze and niches in a format that belongs to the 850-950 CE. The temple tower is a multi-storey structure, but in the modern era is covered with a wooden canopy. Inside the canopy is the original cogged disc shaped amalaka which is then topped with hyperthral linga finial. The Maha Mrityunjaya temple follows the vastupurusha-mandala plan and elevation found in Hindu temple architecture texts. It has 16 central squares like the Mahua Hindu temple, the sanctum length equals the central offset, and the wall thickness equals the corner unit's length, proportions taught in the symmetric 16-grid plan. The temple was the first that included a pillared hall (mandapa) in front, and this hall was used for communal rituals and as shelter for pilgrims to rest in. This temple is also notable for its short inscriptions found on its mouldings, walls, pilasters and pillars.

16.2 Trimbakeshwar Shiva Temple, Nashik, Maharashtra

Figure 16.2: Trimbakeshwar Shiva Temple, Nashik, Maharashtra

Trimbakeshwar or Tryambakeshwar is an ancient Hindu temple in the town of Trimbak in the Nashik District of Maharashtra, India, 28 km from the city of Nashik. It is dedicated to the Lord Shiva and is one of the twelve Jyotirlingas. The current temple was built by Peshwa Balaji Baji Rao (Nanasaheb). The temple is located between three hills namely Brahmagiri, Nilagiri and Kalagiri. The temple has three lingams (an iconic form of Lord Shiva) representing Shiva, Vishnu and Brahma. The temple tank is called Amritavarshini. There are three other bodies of water, namely, Bilvatheertha, Viswananthirtha and Mukundathirtha.

As per the Shiv Purana, once Brahma (the Hindu God of creation) and Vishnu (the Hindu God of preservation) had an argument in terms of supremacy of creation. To test them, Shiva pierced the three worlds as a huge endless pillar of light, the jyotirlinga. Vishnu and Brahma split their ways to downwards and upwards respectively to find the end of the light in the opposite directions. Brahma lied that he found out the end, while Vishnu conceded his defeat. Shiva appeared as a second pillar of light and cursed Brahma that he would have no place in ceremonies while Vishnu would be worshipped till the end of eternity. Brahmadev worshipped God Trivikram when he came to Satya Loka (on earth) with the same holy water of the Ganges, to get the river Ganges held up by God Shankar on his head, to flow.

There was a famine lasting 24 years and people were affected by the pangs of hunger. However, Varun - the God of Rains, pleased with Sage Gautama arranged rains every day in Gautama's Ashram (dwelling place) which was in Trimbakeshwar. Gautama used to sow rice in the surrounding fields of his Ashram in the morning, reap the crop in the afternoon and with it fed a large group of Rishis (sages), who took shelter in his Ashram on account of the famine. The blessings of the group of Hrishis increased the merit (Punya) of Gautama. Lord Indra's position became shaky because of his increased merit. So Indra ordered clouds to rain all over Trimbakeshwar, so that the famine will be over and Hrishis will go back and the increasing merits of Gautama will be weakened. Although the famine was over, Gautama urged the Rishis to stay back and kept on feeding them and gaining merit. Once he saw a cow grazing in the paddy field and he drove her away by throwing Darbha (sharp, pointed grass). The slender cow died by this. It was Jaya - Parvati's friend, who had taken the form of a cow. This news upset the Rishis and they refused to luncheon at his Ashram. Gautama requested Rishis to show a way out of this sin. He was advised to approach Lord Shiva and request him to release Ganges and a bath in the Ganges would set him free of his sins. Gautama then practiced penance by going to the peak of Brahmagiri for 1000 years. Lord Shankara was pleased by his worship and gave him the Ganges.

However, Ganges was not prepared to part with Lord Shiva, which irritated him. He made Tandav Nrutya (dance) on the peak of Brahmagiri and dashed his jata there. Frightened by this action, Ganges appeared on Brahmagiri. Later on Ganges appeared in the Trimbak Tirtha. Gautama praised her but she off-and-on appeared on the mountain at various places and disappeared in anger. Gautama could not bathe in her waters. Ganges then appeared in Gangadwar, Varaha-tirtha, Rama-Laxman tirtha, Ganga Sagar tirtha. Still Gautama could not bathe in her waters. Gautama surrounded the river with enchanted grass and put a vow to her. The flow stopped there and the tirtha thus came to be called Kushavarta. It is from this Kushavarta that the river

Godavari flows up to the sea. The sin of killing a cow by Gautama was wiped off here.

Narayan Nagbali puja is performed at Trimbakeshwar only. This puja is performed for many reasons like to cure an illness, going through bad times, killing a Cobra (Nag), childless couples, financial crisis or you want to perform some religious puja to have everything.

16.3 Kedarnath Temple, Uttarakhand

Kedarnath Temple is a Hindu temple dedicated to Lord Shiva. It is on the Garhwal Himalayan range near the Mandakini river in Kedarnath, Uttarakhand. Due to extreme weather conditions, the temple is open only between the end of April (Akshaya Tritriya) to November (Kartik Purnima - the autumn full moon). During the winters, the vigrahas (deities) from Kedarnath temple are brought to Ukhimath and worshipped there for six months. Lord Shiva is worshipped as Kedarnath, the 'Lord of Kedar Khand', the historical name of the region.

Figure 16.3: Kedarnath Temple, Uttarakhand

The temple is not directly accessible by road and has to be reached by a 18 kilometres uphill trek from Gaurikund. Pony and manchan service is available to reach the structure. One can avoid all this and take helicopter directly. According to Hindu legends, the temple was initially built by Pandavas, and is one of the twelve Jyotirlingas, the holiest Hindu shrines of Shiva. It is one of the 275 Paadal Petra Sthalams, expounded in Tevaram. Pandavas were supposed to have pleased Shiva by doing penance in Kedarnath. This temple is the highest among the 12 Jyotirlingas. Kedarnath was the worst affected area during the 2013 flash floods in North India. The temple complex, surrounding areas and Kedarnath town suffered extensive damage, but the temple structure did not suffer any "major" damage, apart from a few cracks on one side of the four walls which was caused by the flowing debris from the higher mountains. A large rock among the debris acted as a barrier, protecting the temple from the flood. The surrounding premises and other buildings in market area were heavily damaged.

The temple, at a height of 3,583 m (11,755 ft), 223 km from Rishikesh, on the shores of Mandakini river, a tributary of Ganga, is a stone edifice of unknown date. The name "Kedarnath" means "the lord of the field": it derives from the Sanskrit words kedara ("field") and natha ("lord").

According to a mythological account, Lord Shiva agreed to dwell here at the request of Nara-Narayana. After the Kurukshetra War, the Pandava brothers, came here to meet Shiva on the advice of the sage Vyasa, because they wanted to seek forgiveness for killing their kin during the war. However, Shiva did not want to forgive them: so, he turned into a bull and hid among the cattle on the hill. When the Pandavas managed to track him, he tried to disappear by sinking himself head-first into the ground. One of the brothers grabbed his tail, forcing him to appear before them and forgive them. The Pandava brothers then built the first temple at Kedarnath.

According to the hagiographies based on Madhava's Sankshepa-shankara-vijaya, the 8th century philosopher Adi Shankara died at Kedaranatha (Kedarnath); although other hagiographies, based on Anandagiri's Prachina-Shankara-Vijaya, state that he died at Kanchi. The ruins of a monument marking the purported death place of Shankara are located at Kedarnath. Kedarnath was definitely a prominent pilgrimage centre by the 12th century, when it is mentioned in Kritya-kalpataru written by the Gahadavala minister Bhatta Lakshmidhara.

The presiding image of Kedaranth in the form of lingam is of irregular shape with a pedestal 3.6 m (12 ft) in circumference and 3.6 m (12 ft) in height. There is a small pillared hall in front of the temple, that has images of Parvathi and of the five Pandava princes. There are five temples around namely Badari-kear, Madhya Maheswara, Tunganatha, Rudranatha and Kallesvara. The first hall inside Kedarnath Temple contains statues of the five Pandava brothers, Lord Krishna, Nandi, the vehicle of Shiva and Virabhadra, one of the guards of Shiva. Statue of Draupadi and other deities are also installed in the main hall. An unusual feature of the temple is the head of a man carved in the triangular stone fascia. Adi Shankara was believed to have revived this temple, along with Badrinath and other temples of Uttarakhand; he is believed to have attained Mahasamadhi at Kedaranath. Behind the temple is the samādhi mandir of Adi Sankara.

The head priest (Raval) of the Kedarnath temple belongs to the Veerashaiva community from Karnataka. However, unlike in Badrinath temple, the Raval of Kedarnath temple does not perform the pujas. The pujas are carried out by Raval's assistants on his instructions. The Raval moves with the deity to Ukhimath during the winter season. There are five main priests for the temple, and they become head priests for one year by rotation.

16.4 Somnath Temple, Gujarat

Figure 16.4: Somnath Temple, Gujarat

The Somnath temple located in Prabhas Patan in Saurashtra on the western coast of Gujarat, is believed to be the first among the twelve jyotirlinga shrines of Shiva. It is an important pilgrimage and tourist spot of Gujarat. Reconstructed several times in the past after repeated destruction by several Muslim invaders and Portuguese, the present temple was reconstructed in Chaulukya style of Hindu temple architecture and completed in May 1951. The reconstruction was completed by Sardar Vallabhbhai Patel, the then Deputy Prime Minister of India, and inaugurated by Dr. Rajendra Prasad, the then President of India.

The temple is considered sacred due to the various legends connected to it. Somnath means "Lord of the Soma", an epithet of Shiva. The Shivalinga in Somnath is one of the 12 jyotirlingas in India, where Shiva is believed to have appeared as a fiery column of light. Soma, the Moon god, is believed to have lost his lustre due to a curse, and he bathed in the Sarasvati River at this site to regain it. The result is the waxing and waning of the moon, no doubt an allusion to the waxing and waning of the tides at this sea shore location. The name of the town Prabhas, meaning lustre, as well as the alternative names Someshvar and Somnath ("The lord of the moon" or "the moon god") arise from this tradition.

The first Shiva temple at Somnath is believed to have been built at some unknown time in the past. The second temple is said to have been built at the same site by the "Yadava kings" of Vallabhi around 649 CE. In 725 CE, Al-Junayd, the Arab governor of Sindh is said to have destroyed the second temple as part of his invasions of Gujarat and Rajasthan. The Gurjara-Pratihara king Nagabhata II is said to have constructed the third temple in 815 CE, a large structure of red sandstone. Nagabhata II is known to have visited tirthas in Saurashtra, including Someshvara (the Lord of the Moon), which may or may not be a reference to a Shiva temple because the town itself was known by that name. The Chaulukya (Solanki) king Mularaja possibly built the first temple at the site sometime before 997 CE. In 1024, during the reign of Bhima I, the prominent Turkic ruler Mahmud of Ghazni raided Gujarat, plundering the Somnath temple and breaking its jyotirlinga despite pleas by Brahmins not to do so. He took away a booty of 20 million dinars. The devotees had tried to defend the temple from being vandalised and looted.

The temple at the time of Mahmud's attack appears to have been a wooden structure, which is said to have decayed in time (kalajirnam). Kumarapala (r. 1143–72) rebuilt it in "excellent stone and studded it with jewels," in 1169. During its 1299 invasion of Gujarat, Alauddin Khalji's army, led by Ulugh Khan, defeated the Vaghela king Karna, and sacked the Somnath temple. Legends in the later texts Kanhadade Prabandha (15th century) and Khyat (17th century) state that the Jalore ruler Kanhadadeva later recovered the Somnath idol and freed the Hindu prisoners, after an attack on the Delhi army near Jalore. The temple was rebuilt by Mahipala I, the Chudasama king of Saurashtra in 1308 and the lingam was installed by his son Khengara sometime between 1331 and 1351. As late as the 14th century, Gujarati Muslim pilgrims were noted by Amir Khusrow to stop at that temple to pay their respects before departing for the Hajj pilgrimage. In 1395, the temple was destroyed for the third time by Zafar Khan, the last governor of Gujarat under the Delhi Sultanate and later founder of Gujarat Sultanate. In 1451, it was desecrated by Mahmud Begada, the Sultan of Gujarat. In 1546, the Portuguese, based in Goa, attacked ports and towns in Gujarat including Somnath and destroyed several temples and mosques. By 1665, the temple, one of many, was ordered to be destroyed by Mughal emperor Aurangzeb. In 1702, he ordered that if Hindus revived worship there, it should be demolished completely. In 1782-83, Maratha king Mahadaji Shinde, victoriously brought back three silver gates from Lahore after defeating Mahmud Shah Abdati, to Somnath. After refusal from priests of Gujarat and the then ruler Gaekwad to put them back on Somnath temple, these silver gates were placed in the temples of Ujjain. Today they can be seen in two temples of India, Mahakaleshwar Jyotirlinga and Gopal Mandir of Ujjain. In 1842, Edward Law, 1st Earl of Ellenborough issued his Proclamation of the Gates, in which he ordered the British army in Afghanistan to return via Ghazni and bring back to India the sandalwood gates from the tomb of Mahmud of Ghazni in Ghazni, Afghanistan. These were believed to have been taken by Mahmud from Somnath. Under Ellenborough's instruction, General William Nott removed the gates in September 1842. A whole sepoy regiment, the 6th Jat Light Infantry, was detailed to carry the gates back to India in triumph. However, on arrival, they were found not to be of Gujarati or Indian design, and not of Sandalwood, but of Deodar wood (native to Ghazni) and therefore not authentic to Somnath. They were placed in the arsenal store-room of the Agra Fort where they still lie to the present day. There was a debate in the House of Commons in London in 1843 on the question of the gates of the temple and Ellenbourough's role in the affair. After much crossfire between the British Government and the opposition, all of the facts as we know them were laid out. In the 19th century novel The Moonstone by Wilkie Collins, the diamond of the title is presumed to have been stolen from the temple at Somnath and, according to the historian Romila Thapar, reflects the interest aroused in Britain by the gates.

When Patel, K. M. Munshi and other leaders of the Congress went to Mahatma Gandhi with their proposal to reconstruct the Somnath temple, Gandhi blessed the move, but suggested that the funds for the construction should be collected from the public and the temple should not be funded by the state. He expressed that he was proud to associate himself to the project of renovation of the temple. However, soon both Gandhi and Sardar Patel died and the task of reconstruction of the temple continued under Munshi, who was the Minister for Food and Civil Supplies, Government of India headed by Prime Minister Jawaharlal Nehru. The ruins were pulled down in October 1950 and the mosque present at that site was shifted few kilometres away by using construction vehicles. In May 1951, Rajendra Prasad, the first President of the Republic of India, invited by K M Munshi, performed the installation ceremony for the temple.

The present temple is built in the Chaulukya style of temple architecture or "Kailash Mahameru Prasad" style and reflects the skill of the Sompura Salats, one of Gujarat's master masons. The temple's śikhara, or main spire, is 15 metres in height, and it has an 8.2-metre tall flag pole at the top. The temple is situated at such a place that there is no land in a straight line between Somnath seashore until Antarctica, such an inscription in Sanskrit is found on the Bāṇastambha (Sanskrit: बाणस्तम्भ, lit. arrow pillar) erected on the sea-protection wall. The Bāṇastambha mentions that it stands at a point on the Indian landmass that is the first point on land in the north to the South Pole at that particular longitude.

16.5 Ramanathaswami Temple, Rameshwaram, Tamilnadu

Ramanathaswamy Temple is a Hindu temple dedicated to the

Lord Shiva located on Rameswaram island in the state of Tamil Nadu. It is also one of the twelve Jyotirlinga temples as well as one of the char dhams (four most sacred pilgrimages in India). The temple was expanded during the 12th century by Pandya Dynasty, and its principal shrines sanctum were renovated by Jeyaveera Cinkaiariyan and his successor Gunaveera Cinkaiariyan of the Jaffna kingdom. The temple has the longest corridor among all Hindu temples in India. The presiding deity, the Lingam of Ramanathaswamy (Shiva), is believed to have been established and worshiped by Rama, an avatar of the Lord Vishnu, to absolve the sins created during the Ramayana war at Sri Lanka. Rama prayed to Lord Shiva to absolve him of the sin committed during his war against the demon king Ravana in Sri Lanka. Rama wanted to have a large lingam to worship Shiva. He directed Hanuman, the lieutenant in his army, to bring a lingam from the Himalayas. When Hanuman was delayed in bringing the lingam, Rama's wife Sita built a small lingam out of the sand available in the sea shore, which is believed to be the lingam in the sanctum.

Figure 16.5: Ramanathaswami Temple, Rameshwaram, Tamilnadu

The primary deity of the temple is Ramanathaswamy (Shiva) in the form of lingam. There are two lingams inside the sanctum - one built by Sita, from sand, residing as the main deity, Ramalingam and the one brought by Hanuman from Kailash called Vishwalingam. Rama instructed that the Vishwalingam should be worshipped first since it was brought by Hanuman.

Like all ancient temples in South India, there is a high compound wall (madil) on all four sides of the temple premises measuring about 865 feet furlong from east to west and one furlong of 657 feet from north to south with huge towers (Gopurams) to the east and the west and finished gate towers to the north and south. The temple has striking long corridors in its interior, running between huge colonnades on platforms above five feet high. The second corridor is formed by sandstone pillars, beams and ceiling. The junction of the third corridor on the west and the paved way leading from the western gopuram to the Setumadhava shrine forms a unique structure in the form of a chess board, popularly known as Chokkattan Madapam, where the Utsava deities are adorned and kept during the Vasanthotsavam (Spring festival) and on the 6th day festival in Adi (July–August) and Masi (February–March) conducted by the Setupati of Ramnad.

The outer set of corridors is reputed to be the longest in the world, measuring about 6.9 m in height, 400 feet each in the east and west and about 640 feet in the north and the south. The inner corridors are about 224 feet each in the east and the west and about 352 feet each in the north and the south. Their width varies from 15.5 feet to 17 feet in the east and west about 172 feet on the north and south with width varying 14.5 feet to 17 feet. The total length of these corridors is thus 3850 feet. There are about 1212 pillars in the outer corridor. Their height is about 30 feet from the floor to the centre of the roof. The main tower or rajagopuram is 53 m tall. Most pillars are carved with individual compositions.

There are sixty-four Tīrthas (holy water bodies) in and around the island of Rameswaram, Tamil Nadu, India. According to Skānda Purāṇa, twenty-four of them are important. Bathing in these Tīrthas is a major aspect of the pilgrimage to Rameswaram and is considered equivalent to penance. Twenty-two of the Tīrthas are within the Ramanathaswami Temple. The number 22 indicates the 22 arrows in

Rama's quiver. The first and major one is called Agni Theertham, the sea (Bay of Bengal).

The temple in its current shape is believed to have been built during the 17th century. The temple is said to have been sanctioned for construction by King Kizhavan Sethupathi or Raghunatha Kilavan. The contribution of the Jaffna kings of the Sethupathy dynasty to the temple was considerable. King Jeyaveera Cinkaiariyan (1380 — 1410 CE) shipped stone blocks from Koneswaram temple, Trincomalee to renovate the temple's sanctum sanctorum. Jeyaveera Cinkaiariyan's successor Gunaveera Cinkaiariyan (Pararacacekaran V), a trustee at Rameswaram who also oversaw structural development of this temple and the promotion of Saivite beliefs donated part of his revenue to Koneswaram. Especially to be remembered are the immense sums that were spent during the tenure of Pradani Muthirulappa Pillai towards the restoration of the Pagodas which were falling into ruins and the splendid Chockattan Mantapam or the cloistered precincts of the temple at Rameswaram that he finally completed. The rulers of Sri Lanka also contributed to the temple - Parakrama Bahu (1153-1186 CE) was involved in the construction of the sanctum sanctorum of the temple.

16.6 Kashi Vishwanath Temple, Varanasi, Uttar Pradesh

Figure 16.6: Kashi Vishwanath Temple, Varanasi, Uttar Pradesh

Kashi Vishvanath Temple is one of the most famous Hindu temples dedicated to Lord Shiva. It is located in Varanasi, Uttar Pradesh. The temple stands on the western bank of the holy river Ganga, and is one of the twelve Jyotirlingas, the holiest of Shiva temples. The main deity is known by the name, Vishvanatha or Vishveshvara, meaning Ruler of The Universe. Varanasi city is also called Kashi, and hence the temple is popularly called Kashi Vishvanath Temple. The temple has been referred to in Hindu scriptures for a very long time as a central part of worship in the Shaiva philosophy. It was destroyed and re-constructed a number of times in history. The last structure was demolished by Aurangzeb, the sixth Mughal emperor who constructed the Gyanvapi Mosque on its site. The current structure was built on an adjacent site by the Maratha ruler, Ahilya Bai Holkar of Indore in 1780.

The temple has been mentioned in the Puranas including the Kashi Khanda (section) of Skanda Purana. The original Vishwanath temple was destroyed by the army of Qutb-ud-din Aibak in 1194 CE, when he defeated the Raja of Kannauj as a commander of Mohammad Ghori. The temple was rebuilt by a Gujarati merchant during the reign of Delhi's Sultan Iltutmish (1211-1266 CE). It was demolished again during the rule of either Hussain Shah Sharqi (1447-1458) or Sikandar Lodhi (1489-1517). Raja Man Singh built the temple during Mughal emperor Akbar's rule, but orthodox Hindus boycotted it as he had let the Mughals marry within his family. Raja Todar Mal further re-built the temple with Akbar's funding at its original site in 1585. In 1669 CE, Emperor Aurangzeb destroyed the temple and built the Gyanvapi Mosque in its place. The remains of the erstwhile temple can be seen in the foundation, the columns and at the rear part of the mosque.

In 1742, the Maratha ruler Malhar Rao Holkar made a plan to demolish the mosque and reconstruct Vishweshwar temple at the site. However, his plan did not materialize, partially because of intervention by the Nawabs of Lucknow, who controlled the territory. Around 1750, the Maharaja of Jaipur commissioned a survey of the land around the site, with the objective of purchasing land to rebuild the Kashi Vishwanath temple. However, his plan to rebuild the temple did not materialize either. In 1780, Malhar Rao's daughter-in-law Ahilyabai Holkar constructed the present temple adjacent to the mosque. In 1828, Baiza Bai, widow of the Maratha ruler Daulat Rao Scindhia of

Gwalior State, built a low-roofed colonnade with over 40 pillars in the Gyan Vapi precinct. During 1833-1840 CE, the boundary of Gyanvapi Well, the ghats and other nearby temples were constructed. A 7-feet high stone statue of Nandi bull, gifted by the Raja of Nepal lies to the east of the colonnade. Many noble families from various ancestral kingdoms of Indian subcontinent and their prior establishments make generous contributions for the operations of the temple. In 1841, the Bhosales of Nagpur donated silver to the temple. In 1835, Maharaja Ranjit Singh donated 1 tonne of gold for plating the temple's dome.

The Manikarnika Ghat on the banks of Ganges near to the Kashi Vishwanath Temple is considered as a Shakti Peetha, a revered place of worship for the Shaktism sect. The Daksha Yaga, a Shaivite literature is considered as an important literature which is the story about the origin of Shakti Peethas. The original holy well—Gyanvapi in between the temple and Gyanvapi Mosque. The temple complex consists of a series of smaller shrines, located in a small lane called the Vishwanatha Galli, near the river. The linga of the main deity at the shrine is 60 cm tall and 90 cm in circumference housed in a silver altar. The main temple is quadrangle and is surrounded by shrines of other gods. There are small temples for Kaalbhairav, Dhandapani, Avimukteshwara, Vishnu, Vinayaka, Sanishwara, Virupaksha and Virupaksh Gauri in the complex. There is a small well in the temple called the Jnana Vapi also spelled as Gyaan vapi (the wisdom well). It is believed that the Jyotirlinga was hidden in the well to protect it at the time of invasion. It is said that the main priest of the temple jumped in the well with the Shiva Linga in order to protect the Jyotirlinga from invaders.

Located on the banks of the holy Ganges, Varanasi is regarded among the holiest of the Hindu cities. The Kashi Vishwanath temple is widely recognized as one of the most important places of worship in Hindu religion. Inside the Kashi Vishvanath Temple is the Jyotirlinga of Shiva, Vishveshvara or Vishvanath. The Vishveshvara Jyotirlinga has a very special and unique significance in the spiritual history of India.

Many leading saints, including Adi Sankaracharya, Ramakrishna Paramhansa, Swami Vivekananda, Bamakhyapa, Goswami Tulsidas, Swami Dayananda Saraswati, Sathya Sai Baba and Gurunanak have visited the site. A visit to the temple and a bath in the river Ganges is one of many methods believed to lead one on a path to Moksha (liberation). Thus, Hindus from all over the world try to visit the place at least once in their lifetime.

16.7 Mahakaleshwar Temple, Ujjain, Madhya Pradesh

Figure 16.7: Mahakaleshwar Temple, Ujjain, Madhya Pradesh

Mahakaleshwar Jyotirlinga is a Hindu temple dedicated to Lord Shiva and one of the twelve Jyotirlingams, shrines which are said to be the most sacred abodes of Lord Shiva. It is located in the ancient city of Ujjain in the state of Madhya Pradesh. The temple is situated on the side of the Rudra Sagar lake. The presiding deity, Lord Shiva in the lingam form is believed to be Swayambhu, deriving currents of power (Shakti) from within itself as against the other images and lingams that are ritually established and invested with mantra-shakti.

The idol of Mahakaleshwar is known to be dakshinamurti, which means that it is facing the south. This is a unique feature, upheld by the tantric shivnetra tradition to be found only in Mahakaleshwar among the 12 Jyotirlingas. The images of Ganesh, Parvati and Karttikeya are installed in the west, north and east of the sanctum sanctorum. To the south is the image of Nandi, the vehicle of Lord Shiva. The idol of Nagchandreshwar on the third storey is open for darshan only on the day of Nag Panchami. The temple has five levels, one of which is underground. The temple itself is located in a spacious courtyard surrounded by massive walls near a lake. The shikhar or the spire is adorned with sculptural finery. Brass lamps light the way to the underground sanctum. It is believed that prasada (holy offering) offered here to the deity can be re-offered unlike all other shrines.

The temple is also glorified in 7th century C.E, Tamil tiara hymns of tirugnanasambandar, sundarar, tirunavukkarasar, and they refer to the same as tiru oonjai maakalam, oonjai being Tamil name of word ujjain. The shrine is revered as one of the 18 Maha Shakti Peetham.

Shakti Peethas are shrines that are believed to have enshrined with the presence of Shakti due to the falling of body parts of the corpse of Sati Devi, when Lord Shiva carried it. Each of the 51 Shakti peethas has shrines for Shakti and Kalabhairava. The Upper Lip of Sati Devi is said to have fallen here and the Shakti is called as Mahakal.

Kalidasa (c. 4th–5th century CE), the great Sanskrit poet of the times during the regime of king Vikramaditya, belonging to the Gupta period, has mentioned about the rituals of the temple in his works in his work 'Meghaduta'. He mentions about the nada-aradhana, the performance of art and dance during the evening rituals.

The temple complex was destroyed by Sultan Shams-ud-din Iltutmish during his raid of Ujjain in 1234-5. The present structure was built by the Maratha general Ranoji Scindia in 1734 CE. Further developments and management was done by other members of his dynasty, including Mahadji Scindia (1730–12 February 1794) and Daulat Rao Scindia's wife Baiza Bai. (1827–1863). During the reign of Jayajirao Scindia (until 1886), major programs of the then Gwalior State used to be held at this temple.

16.8 Naina Bhagwati Temple, Manikaran, Himachal Pradesh

It is a small beautiful wooden temple, located in Manikaran, Himachal Pradesh. The importance of this temple lies is in the story of naming the place as Manikaran. It's a temple of goddess which is named after the ***third eye of Lord Shiva***.

Figure 16.8: Naina Bhagwati Temple, Manikaran, Himachal Pradesh

The Himalayan range of hills at Manikaran are called Shivalik range. The Parvati river flows beside the Shiva temple. It is said in the story that Goddess Parvati loses her precious stone (Mani) from the ear (karan) while being inside the river (hence the name Manikaran). Lord Shiva comes to know about the loss of the jewel and opens his third eye (Naina) on not finding it anywhere on the earth. To rescue the world, Sheshnag, who had this jewel returned this along with other precious jewels too. This temple is dedicated to that third eye of Lord Shiva.

B. SOME SHIVA TEMPLES OUTSIDE INDIA

16.9 Pashupatinath Temple, Kathmandu, Nepal

Figure 16.9: Pashupatinath Temple, Kathmandu, Nepal

The Pashupatinath Temple is a famous and sacred Hindu temple complex that is located on the banks of the Bagmati River, approximately 5 kilometres north-east of Kathmandu in the eastern part of Kathmandu Valley, the capital of Nepal. This temple complex was inscribed on the UNESCO World Heritage Sites's list in 1979. The temple is one of the 275 Tamil Paadal Petra Sthalams (Holy Abodes of Shiva) on the continent. Kotirudra Samhita.

The temple was erected anew in the 5th century by Lichchavi King Prachanda Dev after the previous building was consumed by termites. Over time, many more temples have been erected around this two -storied temple. These include the Vaishnava temple complex with a Rama temple from the 14th century and the Guhyeshwari Temple mentioned in an 11th-century manuscript.

Pashupatinath Temple is the oldest Hindu temple in Kathmandu. It is not known for certain when Pashupatinath Temple was built. But according to Nepal Mahatmaya and Himvatkhanda, the deity here gained great fame there as Pashupati, the Lord of all Pashus, which are living as well as non-living beings. Pashupatinath Temple's existence dates back to 400 B.C. The richly ornamented pagoda houses the sacred linga or holy symbol of Lord Shiva.

Legend says that Lord Shiva and Parvati once took the form of an antelope and sported unknown in the forest on the Bagmati river's east bank. The gods later caught up with him and grabbing him by one of his horns, forced him to resume his divine form. The broken horn was worshipped as a Sivalinga but over time it was buried and lost. Centuries later astonished herdsmen found one of his cows showering the earth with milk. Digging deep at the site, he discovered the divine linga of Pashupatinath.

Another chronicle states that Pashupatinath Temple was in the form of Linga shaped Devalaya before Supuspa Deva constructed a five-storey temple of Pashupatinath in this place. As the time passed, the need for repairing and renovating this temple arose. It is learnt that this temple was reconstructed by a medieval King named Shivadeva (1099-1126 AD). It was renovated by Ananta Malla adding a roof to it.

It is said that the wish-fulfilling cow Kamadhenu took shelter in a cave on the Chandravan mountain. Everyday Kamadhenu went down to the place the lingam was sunken into the soil and poured her milk on top of the soil. After a few thousand years some people saw Kamadhenu pouring milk on that same spot every day, and started to wonder what that would be. So they removed the soil and found the beautiful shining lingam and started worshiping it.

The area of Pashupatinath encompasses 264 hectares of land including 518 temples and monuments. Main pagoda style temple is located in the fortified courtyard within the complex guarded by Semi-Military Nepal Police and Military Force Nepal Army and has a police outpost along with living quarter within. In front of the western door, there is a huge statue Nandi bull, in bronze. Along with many temples and shrines of both Vaishnav and saiva tradition.

The sacro sanctum, or the main idol is a stone Mukhalinga with a silver yoni base bound with the silver serpent. The lingam is one metre high and has faced in four directions. These faces represent various aspects of Shiva; Sadyojata (also known as Barun), Vamadeva (also known as Ardhanareshwara), Tatpurusha, Aghora & Ishana (imaginative). Facing West, North, East, South and Zenith respectively representing five primary elements namely earth, water, air, light and ether.[10] Each face has tiny protruding hands holding rudraksha mala on right hand and a kamandalu on the other. Unlike other Shiva lingams in India and Nepal this Pashupati Shiva lingam is always Dressed in its golden vastram except during abhisheka, so pouring milk and Ganga Jal is only possible during abhisheka through the main priests.

The unique feature of this temple is that only 4 priests can touch the idol. Daily rituals of Pashupatinath are carried out by two sets of priests ; one being the Bhatt priests and other Bhandari. Bhatta or Bhatt are the one who performs the daily ritual and can touch the lingam, whereas Bhandaris are the helper and temple caretaker priests who are not qualified to perform pooja rituals or to touch the deity.

The temple courtyard has 4 entrances in the cardinal directions. The western entrance is the main entrance to the temple courtyard and the remaining three entrances are open only during festivals. Practising Hindus and Buddhists of Nepali diaspora are only allowed into Temple courtyard. Practising Hindus of Western descent are not allowed into the temple complex and must go no further than other, non-Hindu visitors. An exception is granted to Sikhs and Jainists; if they are of

Indian ancestry they may enter the temple complex. Others can look at the main temple from the adjacent side of the river[12] and have to pay a nominal fee of $10 (1000 Nepali rupees) for visiting the hundreds of small temples located in the external premises of the temple complex.

The inner temple courtyard remains open from 4 am to 7 pm for the devotee but the Inner Pashupatinath Temple where the Lingam of Lord Pashupatinath is established is open from 5 am to 12 pm for the morning ritual and viewing and from 5 pm to 7 pm for the evening ritual. Unlike many other Saiva temples, devotees are not allowed to enter in the innermost Garbhagriha premises but are allowed to watch from the exterior premises of the outer Garbhagriha.

The inner sanctum where the Shiva Linga is placed, has four entrances: east, west, north, south. Normally devotees will have the Shiva Lingadarshan through western door entrance only. From 9:30 to 1:30 devotees can worship from all the 4 doors. All the four doors are also opened during the Abhisheka time. All the four sides of the Shiva, Lingadarshan is possible during this period.

16.10 Prambanan Temple, Java, Indonesia

Prambanan or Rara Jonggrang is a 9th-century Hindu temple compound in Special Region of Yogyakarta, Indonesia, dedicated to the Trimūrti, the expression of God as the Creator (Brahma), the Preserver (Vishnu) and the Transformer (Shiva). The temple compound is located approximately 17 km northeast of the city of Yogyakarta on the boundary between Central Java and Yogyakarta provinces. The temple compound, a UNESCO World Heritage Site, is the largest Hindu temple site in Indonesia, and one of the biggest in Southeast Asia. It is characterized by its tall and pointed architecture, typical of Hindu architecture, and by the towering 47-metre-high (154 ft) central building inside a large complex of individual temples.

The Prambanan temple was most likely started by Rakai Pikatan as the Hindu Sanjaya Dynasty's answer to the Buddhist Sailendra Dynasty's Borobudur and Sewu temples nearby. Historians suggest that the construction of Prambanan probably was meant to mark the return of the Hindu Sanjaya Dynasty to power in Central Java after almost a century of Buddhist Sailendra Dynasty domination. The construction of this massive Hindu temple signifies that the Medang court had shifted its patronage from Mahayana Buddhism to Shaivite Hinduism. According to the Shivagrha inscription of 856 CE, the temple was built to honour Lord Shiva, and its original name was Shiva-grha (the House of Shiva) or Shiva-laya (the Realm of Shiva). Some archaeologists propose that the statue of Shiva in the garbhagriha (central chamber) of the main temple was modelled after King Balitung, serving as a depiction of his deified self after death.

Figure 16.10: Prambanan Temple, Java, Indonesia

The temple compound was expanded by successive Mataram kings, such as Daksa and Tulodong, with the addition of hundreds of perwara temples around the chief temple. Prambanan served as the royal temple of the Kingdom of Mataram, with most of the state's religious ceremonies and sacrifices being conducted there. At the height of the kingdom, scholars estimate that hundreds of brahmins with their disciples lived within the outer wall of the temple compound. The temples collapsed during a major earthquake in the 16th century. Although the temple ceased to be an important centre of worship, the ruins scattered around the area were still recognizable and known to the local Javanese people in later times. The statues and the ruins became the theme and the inspiration for the Loro Jonggrang folktale. After the division of Mataram Sultanate in 1755, the temple ruins and the Opak River were used to demarcate the boundary between Yogyakarta and

Surakarta (Solo) Sultanates, which was adopted as the current border between Yogyakarta and the province of Central Java.

The Trimurti open-air and indoor stages on the west side of the temple, across the Opak River, were built to stage the ballet of the traditional Ramayana epic. This traditional Javanese dance is the centuries-old dance of the Javanese court. Since the 1960s, it has been performed every full moon night in the Prambanan temple. Since then, Prambanan has become one of the major archaeological and cultural tourism attractions in Indonesia.

The temple was damaged during the 2006 Yogyakarta earthquake. Early photos suggested that although the complex was structurally intact, the damage was significant. Large pieces of debris, including carvings, were scattered over the ground. The temple was closed to visitors until the damage could be fully assessed. Eventually, the head of Yogyakarta Archaeological Conservation Agency stated that it would take months to identify the full extent of the damage. Some weeks later in 2006, the site was re-opened for visitors. There is great interest in the site. In 2008, 856,029 Indonesian visitors and 114,951 foreign visitors visited Prambanan. On 6 January 2009 the reconstruction of Nandi temple finished. As of 2009, the interior of most of the temples remains off-limits for safety reasons.

Shiva Temple

The Shiva temple is the tallest and largest structure in Prambanan Loro Jonggrang complex; it measures 47 metres tall and 34 metres wide. The main stairs are located on the eastern side. The eastern gate of Shiva temple is flanked by two small shrines, dedicated to guardian gods, Mahakala and Nandhisvara. The Shiva temple is encircled with galleries adorned with bas-reliefs telling the story of Ramayana carved on the inner walls of the balustrades. To follow the story accurately, visitors must enter from the east side and begin to perform pradakshina or circumambulating clockwise. The Shiva shrine is located at the centre and contains five chambers, four small chambers in every cardinal direction and one bigger main chamber in the central part of the temple. The east chamber connects to the central chamber that houses the largest temple in Prambanan, a three-metre high statue of Shiva Mahadeva (the Supreme God). The statue bears Lakçana (attributes or symbol) of Shiva such as skull and sickle (crescent) at the crown, and third eye on the forehead; also four hands that holds Shiva's symbols: prayer beads, feather duster, and trisula (trident).

The architecture of Prambanan temple follows the typical Hindu architecture traditions based on Vastu Shastra. The temple design incorporated mandala temple plan arrangements and also the typical high towering spires of Hindu temples. Prambanan was originally named Shivagrha and dedicated to Lord Shiva. The temple was designed to mimic Meru, the holy mountain, the abode of Hindu gods, and the home of Shiva. The whole temple complex is a model of the Hindu universe according to Hindu cosmology and the layers of Loka.

16.11 Arulmigu Sri Raja Kaliamman Temple, Johor Baru, Malaysia

The Arulmigu Sri Rajakaliamman Glass Temple is a major Hindu temple in Johor Bahru, Malaysia. The temple was listed in the Malaysian Book of Records as the first and only glass temple in the nation on 12 May 2010. The temple started in 1922 as a simple shelter on land presented by the Sultan of Johor. In 1991, Sri Sinnathamby Sivasamy, current temple chairman and chief priest, also known as

Figure 16.11: Arulmigu Sri Raja Kaliamman Temple, Johor Baru, Malaysia

Guru Bhagawan Sittar inherited the administration of the temple from his father. Transformation of the temple with glass fittings started in 2008 and was completed in October 2009. Since then, it has become one of the state's major tourist attractions.

Light from crystal chandeliers is reflected on doors, pillars, walls and ceilings in a bright blaze that's quite blinding initially. At least 90 per cent of the temple is embellished by a mosaic of 300,000 pieces of red, blue, yellow, green, purple and white glass.The centre-piece in the Athma Lingam sanctuary is a lotus for Lord Shiva, on which devotees can pour rose water and perform their prayers. At a glance, the walls appear to have an unusual embossed texture. Each Rudraksha bead is embedded in the walls with a chanted prayer.

There are 10 gold-finished sculptures close to the ceiling. Of the two figures on the left, one appears to be lying down and the other crawling, while the one on the far right seems to be reclining too. These sculptures portray the cycle of life, from birth, youth, adulthood, to old age and death. There are 10 white marble statues standing 120 centimetres (47 in) tall each. According to the name plaques, these are Gautama Buddha, Guru Nanak Dev Ji, Sai Baba and Mother Teresa. On the left wing, there are two large panels on the ceiling painted by specially commissioned artists to convey a universal message of social and racial harmony.

16.12 Katas Raj Temple, Chakwal, Pakistan

The Katas Raj Temples, located in Chakwal, Pakistan, is a complex of several Hindu temples connected to one another by walkways. The temple complex surrounds a pond named Katas which is regarded as sacred by Hindus. The temples' pond is said in the Puranas to have been created from the teardrops of Shiva, after he wandered the Earth inconsolable after the death of his wife Sati. The pond occupies an area of two kanals and 15 marlas, with a maximum depth of 20 feet.

The temples play a role in the Hindu epic poem, the Mahābhārata, where the temples are traditionally believed to have been the site where the Pandava brothers spent a significant portion of their exile. It is also traditionally believed by Hindus to be the site where the brothers engaged in a riddle contest with the Yakshas, as described in the Yaksha Prashna. Another tradition states that the Hindu deity Krishna laid the foundation of the temple, and established a hand-made shiva linga in it.

The name of the temple complex is believed to derive from the Sanskrit word kataksha, meaning "tearful eyes." The pond was originally referred to as Viskund, or "poison spring", but was later referred to as Amarkund, Chamaskund, and finally Katakshkund, meaning "Spring of tearful eyes."

Figure 16.12: Katas Raj Temple, Chakwal, Pakistan

The complex was a popular pilgrimage site for Hindus prior to the 1947 Partition of British India, with large numbers visiting for Shivratri. Following Partition, the local Hindu community left the region for the newly established Republic of India. The relationship of Hindus with local Muslim population was good, and local Muslims accompanied Hindus to the nearby town of Choa Saiden Shah, from where the local Hindu population departed for India. Indian pilgrims continued to visit the temple for the Shivratri festival until the Indo-Pakistani War of 1965, after which Indian pilgrims were barred from visiting again until 1984.

The complex consists of several temples and associated structures. The pond at Katas Raj is said to have been created from the teardrops of the Hindu deity Shiva, following the death of his wife Sati. The temples are considered to be the second most sacred site in the historic Punjab region, after the temple at Jwalamukhi in modern Himachal Pradesh.

The temples derive their holiness from the legend that following the death of his wife Sati, the Hindu god Shiva wandered inconsolably, while some of his tears collected in two ponds, one of which is the pond around which the Katas Raj Temples are set, while the other is at Pushkar, near the famous Sufi pilgrimage centre of Ajmer. Another version of the legend mentions the two pools at Katasraj and Nainital. Another version of the Shiva legend involves the death of Shiva's horse Katas instead of that of Sati his consort.

Some legends also state that very first Shiva Ling (Sihv-Ling) was in Kattas. some old manuscripts also consider Katas as the janam bhoomi (birthplace) of Hindu incarnation Rama, as well as that of Ayodhya; but this has become quite controversial. The oral tradition by local Hindus never mentioned it as being Rama's birthplace or celebrated in annual rituals.

Temples at Katas Raj display characteristics of Kashmiri Hindu temples. The Katas site houses the Sangria, a group of seven ancient temples, remains of a Buddhist stupa, five other medieval temples, hovels scattered around a pond considered holy by Hindus. The temples at Katas are mostly constructed on square platforms. The elevation of the sub shrines seems to form a series of cornices with small rows of pillars, crowned by a ribbed dome. The seven temples were built in an architectural style similar to Kashmiri temples, with dentils, fluted pillars, trefoil arches, and rooflines that are pointed. The Shiva temple is also built on a square platform. Its entrance is a recessed round arch with faint cusps and a rectangular opening to the north.

C. 'THIRD EYE' SHRINES OUTSIDE INDIA

16.13 Swayambhu Temple, Kathmandu, Nepal

Swayambhunath (Devanagari: स्वयम्भू स्तूप; Nepal Bhasa: स्वयंभू; sometimes Swayambu or Swoyambhu) is an ancient religious architecture atop a hill in the Kathmandu Valley, west of Kathmandu city. The Swayambhunath Temple got its name "monkey temple" due to a large presence of resident sacred monkeys all over the temple. They are holy because Manjushri, the bodhisattva of wisdom and learning was raising the hill which the stupa stands on. He was supposed to leave his hair short but he made it grow long and head lice grew. It is said that the head lice transformed into these monkeys. The area around the Swayambhunath Temple has a Tibetan name which refers to sublime trees because of the abundance of an assortment of trees on the hill. The Swayambhunath Temple is also one of Kathmandu's oldest and most holy temples. For the Buddhist Newars, Swayambhunath occupies a central position, it is probably the most sacred among Buddhist pilgrimage sites. For Tibetans and followers of Tibetan Buddhism, it is second only to Boudha.

Figure 16.13: Swayambhunath Buddhist Temple, Nepal depicting the Third Eye of Buddha

The complex consists of a stupa, a variety of shrines and temples, some dating back to the Licchavi period. The stupa has Buddha's eyes and eyebrows painted on. Between them, the number one (in Devanagari script) is painted in the fashion of a nose. The site has two access points: a long staircase leading directly to the main platform of the temple, which is from the top of the hill to the east; and a car road around the hill from the south leading to the south-west entrance. The first sight on reaching the top of the stairway is the Vajra. Behind this Vajra is the vast, round, white dome of the stupa, like a full solid skirt, at the top of which are two giant Buddha eyes wisely looking out over the peaceful valley which is just beginning to come alive.

According to Swayambhu Purana, the entire valley was once filled with an enormous lake, out of which grew a lotus. The valley came to be known as Swayambhu, meaning "Self-Created." The name comes from an eternal self-existent flame (svayaṃbhu) over which a stupa was built later. Manjusri had a vision of the Lotus at Swayambhu and traveled there to worship it. Seeing that the valley can be a good settlement and to make the site more accessible to human pilgrims, he cut a gorge at Chovar. The water drained out of the lake, leaving the valley in which Kathmandu now lies. The Lotus was transformed into a hill and the flower became the stupa.

Swayambhunath is among the oldest religious sites in Nepal. According to the Gopālarājavaṃśāvalī, it was founded by the great-grandfather of King Mānadeva (464-505 CE), King Vṛsadeva, about the beginning of the 5th century CE. This seems to be confirmed by a damaged stone inscription found at the site, which indicates that King Vrsadeva ordered work done in 640 CE. However, Emperor Ashoka is said to have visited the site in the third century BCE and built a temple on the hill which was later destroyed.

Although the site is considered Buddhist, the place is revered by both Buddhists and Hindus. The stupa was completely renovated in May 2010, its first major renovation since 1921and its 15th in the nearly 1,500 years since it was built. The dome was re-gilded using 20 kg of gold. The renovation was funded by the Tibetan Nyingma Meditation Center of California, and began in June 2008. At around 5 a.m. on 14 February 2011, Pratapur Temple in the Swayambhu Monument Zone suffered damage from a lightning strike during a sudden thunderstorm. The Swayambunath complex also suffered damage in the April 2015 Nepal earthquake.

The stupa consists of a dome at the base, above which is a cubical structure painted with eyes of Buddha looking in all four directions. There are pentagonal Toran present above each of the four sides with statues engraved in them. Behind and above the Torana there are thirteen tiers. Above all the tiers there is a small space above which the Gajur is present. The stupa has many artefacts inside it.

The dome at the base represents the entire world. When a person awakes (represented by eyes of wisdom and compassion) from the bonds of the world, the person reaches the state of enlightenment. The thirteen pinnacles on the top symbolize that sentient beings have to go through the thirteen stages of spiritual realizations to reach enlightenment or Buddhahood.

There is a large pair of eyes on each of the four sides of the main stupa which represent Wisdom and Compassion. Above each pair of eyes is another eye, **the third eye**. It is said that when Buddha preaches, cosmic rays emanate from the third eye which acts as messages to heavenly beings so that those interested can come down to earth to listen to the Buddha. The hellish beings and beings below the human realm cannot come to earth to listen to the Buddha's teachings. However, the cosmic rays relieve their suffering when Buddha preaches. Between the two eyes (also called Wisdom Eyes), a curly symbol, symbolizing the nose, is depicted which looks like a question mark, which is a Nepali sign of number figure one. This sign represents the unity of all things existing in the world as well as the only path to enlightenment through the teachings of Buddha.

There are carvings of the Panch Buddhas (five Buddhas) on each of the four sides of the stupa. There are also statues of the Buddhas at the base of the stupas. Panch Buddhas are Buddha in a metaphorical sense in Tantrayana. They are Vairochana (occupies the centre and is the master of the temple), Akshobhya (faces the east and represents the cosmic element of consciousness), Ratna Sambhava (faces the south and represents the cosmic element of sensation), Amitabha (He represents the cosmic element of Sanjna (name) and always faces the West) and Amoghsiddhi (He represents the cosmic element of confirmation and faces the north).

16.14 Angkor Wat, Cambodia

Angkor Wat was first a Hindu religion temple and then later it was turned into a Buddhist temple. It is located in Cambodia and was first built by Khmer King Suryavarman II in the early 12th century in Yasodharapura, the capital of the Khmer Empire. It is the world's largest religious monument and one of the most visited religious sites in the world. Below are a few interesting facts that you need to know about Angkor Wat.

Figure 16.14: Angkor Wat, Cambodia

1. 50% of international tourists visit Cambodia to see this religious monument. As if to show how proud they are of their heritage, the monument is featured on their national flag. Afghanistan's current flag is the only other national flag to feature a national monument.
2. Angkor Wat is the best representation of classical style of Khmer architecture.
3. The temple has been built to represent Mount Meru, the home of the Hindu Mythology lord of Brahma and the demi-god devtas.
4. Unlike other temples in the region that are aligned facing to the east, this temple was aligned to the west. It faces sunset and the evening sun adds to its beauty in the evening.
5. It is not until the 16th century that the temple came to be known by its present name. Prior to this, it was known as Pisnulok, the official title of the Khmer king Suryavarman II that built it.
6. In recognition of the important part it played in both the Hinduism and Buddhism, UNESCO declared it a World Heritage Site in 1992.

7. Although most tourists know of the Angkor Wat temple complex, the city comprises of Angkor Thom and the Bayon Temple which are equally intriguing.
8. Unlike his predecessors who belonged to lineage of kings who practiced 'Shaivism' and thus their supreme God was Lord Shiva; Suryavarman II broke ranks with them and built this temple that is dedicated to Lord Vishnu.
9. The decorations on the walls of the temple have a uniquely Hindu story telling characteristics. They have fables and myths pictures that tell of the temple's origin in Hindu religion.
10. The site receives more than 2 million visitors annually for a reason - It ebbs an aura of divinity that can only be found in Incan and Mayan holy shrines.

Angkor Wat is a sight to behold. It forms a nice picture backdrop that one treasures forever.

16.15 Temple of Isis, Philae, Egypt

Built to honour the goddess Isis, this was the last temple built in the classical Egyptian style. Construction began around 690 BC, and it was one of the last outposts where the goddess was worshipped. The cult of Isis continued here until at least AD 550.

In the central court of the Temple of Isis, the mammisi (birth house) is dedicated to Horus, (well known for his eye or 'the third eye') son of Isis and Osiris. Successive pharaohs reinstated their legitimacy as the mortal descendants of Horus by taking part in rituals celebrating the Isis legend and the birth of her son Horus in the marshes. The second pylon leads to a hypostyle hall, with superb column capitals. Note also the reuse of the temple as a Christian church, with crosses carved into the older hieroglyph reliefs, and images of the Egyptian gods carefully defaced. Beyond lie three vestibules, leading into the Inner Sanctuary of Isis. Two granite shrines stood here, one containing a gold statue of Isis and another containing the barque in which the statue travelled, but these were long ago moved to Florence and Paris, and only the stone pedestal for the barque remains, inscribed with the names of Ptolemy III and his wife, Berenice. Take a side door west out of the hypostyle hall to the Gate of Hadrian where there is an image of the god Hapi, sitting in a cave at the First Cataract, representing the source of the river Nile. East of the second pylon is the delightful Temple of Hathor, decorated with reliefs of musicians (including an ape playing the lute) and Bes, the god of childbirth. South of this is the elegant, unfinished pavilion by the water's edge, known as the Kiosk of Trajan ('Pharaoh's Bed'), perhaps the most famous of Philae's monuments and one that was frequently painted by Victorian artists, whose boats were moored beneath it.

Figure 16.15: Temple of Isis, Philae, Egypt

Figure 16.16: Relief of the Eye of Horus in the Temple of Isis, Philae, Egypt

The whole complex was moved from its original location on Philae Island, to its new location on Agilkia Island, after the flooding of Lake Nasser. A major multinational UNESCO team relocated Philae, and a number of other temples that now dot the shores of Lake Nasser. You can see the submerged original island a short distance away, punctuated by the steel columns used in the moving process.

CHAPTER - 17

Where exactly is the Third Eye located and How to open it?

17.1 Where exactly is the location of the third eye?

In this book we have described various locations of the third eye depending on the faith and religion of the people. In Hinduism, it is said that the third eye is located at the position of the 'Ajna Chakra' (in the middle of the eye brows). Some schools of thought, which are in majority, claim that the third eye is located at the point of Pineal gland (the same position as that of the Ajna Chakra). Some of these groups go to the extent that the Pineal gland itself is the third eye. Then there are people (though in minority) who claim that the third is located in the place where the Pituitary gland is found. Some other group of people claim that the Thalamus is the third eye. Then there are some mystics who claim that the third eye is not located at either of these positions but elsewhere in the head, may be at the back of the head, or may be in the middle of the head.

But a single question which can be addressed to all the above-mentioned claimants. The question is, "If you dissect the dead body of a seer or a saint, whose third eye was believed by you as opened, will you actually find any third eye anywhere in his body?" The obvious answer is 'No'. So the third eye does not have a physical location as many people think. Because they have two eyes here, they assume the Third Eye has to be located somewhere in the body. Then if there is no physical form of the third eye, the question of its location does not arise. The third eye (also called the mind's eye, or inner eye) is a mystical and esoteric concept of a speculative invisible eye which provides perception beyond ordinary sight. At the best, to give concessions to the above mentioned claimants is: if one focuses one's attention on the location of the third eye (as claimed by them) the third eye power (a spiritual power) will get awakened. So the third eye does not imply that there is a single or unitary place in the mind or brain where clairvoyance or where the inner awakening occurs.

The third eye is simply the spiritual power (Shakti), not a physical entity. The third eye is a spiritual concept that refers to a person being able to achieve perception beyond ordinary sight. Also known as the 'inner eye', it is the gateway to inner realms and states of higher consciousness, beyond the physical world. The third eye is often associated with religious visions, clairvoyance, the ability to observe chakras and auras, precognition, and out-of-body experiences. The person with the opened third eye can see through the past, present and future of his own or another person in front of him.

17.2 Preparations for opening one's third eye

Actually the third eye chakra is never closed fully in any person; it is just working below its actual potential. In fact you would experience major problems if any chakras were closed; they function with the body and organs and play an important role in maintaining life by correctly distributing/filtering/changing energy. The Third-Eye-Chakra is under-working due to various reasons such as preset conditioning of the mind, energy blockages, negative energy, limiting beliefs, and the calcification of the pineal gland.

The third eye is regarded as the main centre point of source of energy in human body. To retrieve this power of your body you need to be focused on advanced mediation level of third eye. To activate the third eye, you need to concentrate on meditations and need to take care of following given points:

(i) Time

The best time of day to do your sadhana (practice) is early in the morning, within the two hours before dawn. This is known ***as brahma-muhurta*** in Sanskrit, 'the divine time'. At this time the spiritual energy is high and there are likely to be fewer disturbances, both external and internal, than at any other period of the day. However, if you are unable to practice during brahma-muhurta, choose some other time when the stomach is not loaded.

(ii) Place of practice

Try to practice in the same place every day. This will gradually build up a positive atmosphere which will be helpful for your sadhana. Your place of practice should be clean, peaceful and well ventilated. It should be dry and neither neither too hot nor too cold. Do not practice on the bare floor; place a blanket or mat beneath you. If necessary, wrap a blanket or sheet around you. Try to avoid the use of fans, unless absolutely necessary.

(iii) Clothing

Clothing will depend on the prevailing climate, but it should be as light, loose and comfortable as possible.

(iv) Regularity

Try to practice daily at a fixed time, without fail, following the step-by-step program that is given in this book. On certain days, the mind may give justification for not practicing, or it may be upset, disturbed or restless. Providing there is no illness, you should endeavour to do your practice as normal.

(v) Preliminary practices

Before starting the third-eye-awakening technique,, try to empty the bowels and take a cold shower. If you live in a cold climate, then at least wash the face with cold water. This is essential in order to remove sleepiness.

It is a good idea to do a few asanas before commencing the sadhana. If time does not permit, then at least do 5 to 10 rounds of surya namaskara, starting slowly and then accelerating the pace. This should be followed by a short rest period in shavasana until the breathing rate returns to normal.

(vi) Awareness

If the mind wanders here and there like a wild monkey, do not worry. Let thoughts and emotions arise without suppression. Watch them with the attitude of a witness and continue your practice. Gradually the mind will become one-pointed. Whatever happens, your practice should continue. This attitude of witnessing the mind without interfering, can be defined as awareness or mindfulness.

(v) Posture

Most of the practices for specific chakras and the third-eye-awakening techniques are done in a sitting position, or meditative asana. The best sitting asana is **siddhasana (for males) and siddha yoni asana (for females).**

Figure 17.1: Siddhasana for men Figure 17.2: Siddha yoni asana for women

Not only do these two asanas apply direct pressure on muladhara chakra, but this pressure, when applied correctly, brings about an awakening and redirection of nervous energy and blood circulation upwards from the pelvic and abdominal regions to the brain. The perineal pressure awakens the source of energy and actively distributes prana upwards to the higher centres.

Figure 17.3: Padmasana posture

Padmasana is also utilized for sadhana techniques. Though siddhasana is generally preferred in most of the other techniques, padmasana can also be used as an alternative. The disadvantage is that it does not apply a direct pressure on muladhara chakra.

In case one is not physically comfortable in sitting continuously in Siddhasana or in Padmasana, 'Sukhasana' (a more comfortable sitting posture) is alright for this practice. This is depicted in the following picture:

Figure 17.4: Sukhasna posture

17.3 Techniques for awakening the third eye

17.3.1 Guidelines that will help you develop your third eye:

(i) Cultivate silence

Foster the silence of the mind, whether it is through meditation, just sitting calmly in nature, or being absorbed in your favourite art or sport practice.

Why? Because the third eye perception elevates your senses to more subtle levels. Some call it "the space in between", psychic abilities, the realm of the invisible. To be able to listen to the messages and information that comes through your third eye, you should be ready to perceive the whisper of its wisdom. If your mind is busy or noisy, you might miss its main message.

(ii) Hone your intuition

There are many ways to cultivate your intuition. The third eye is the centre of insight, vision, and higher wisdom. So what about getting acquainted with your dreams and their meanings, perhaps giving a try at lucid dreaming, etc.? Find new ways to intuit into your daily life activities.

Why? Because the third eye is the main seat of higher levels of perception and intuition. Be curious, learn about these intuitive techniques. With the passage of time, these otherwise esoteric practices will appear more familiar, and you will gain more confidence in your own abilities. You don't need to take this seriously – actually, the opposite is recommended. Have fun, explore, and most importantly, keep your mind and chakras open to possibility and wonder.

(iii) Nurture your creativity

Let your creativity flow freely by focusing on specific activities or letting your imagination loose. For instance, start learning a new art or craft; don't try to be perfect, just let your inspiration run through your hands and be ready to be surprised by the results.

Why? Creativity is a very efficient way to loosen your rational mind. This is to discourage the mental chatter that comments every step you make to see whether it is right or wrong, that tends to control every action with a specific agenda and intended outcome. When you calm the part of your mind that wants to be in charge of how reality should be and leverage your creativity to open up possibilities, your third eye capacity has more space to unfold and blossom.

(iv) Ground yourself to better soar

For most of us, it might not be obvious that in order to open our third eye abilities, we need to first land both our feet on the ground. Also note the importance of opening up gradually, building reliable foundations first that will allow you to have proper discernment and interpret your extrasensory perceptions with as much clarity as possible.

Why? Because we need to have enough energy running through our whole body and energetic system to support a healthy opening of subtle channels of perception. When the third eye gets activated, the information that comes through might appear rather unusual, unfamiliar, or simply disturbing to the common mind. Being grounded and having enough energy allows us to expand into subtle dimensions of perception. It can help us open up unhindered and avoid the common negative symptoms of third eye opening, such as feeling disoriented or confused.

(v) Exercise your intuition

- Rest under the moon light and reflect; the moon light resembles the quality of light of your intuitive centre;
- Nurture silence to hear the wisdom of the third eye; listen, the third eye's sound is more like a whisper;
- Strengthen the energy of your first chakra, as well as your throat chakra; both are useful anchors for unlocking the energy of your third eye in powerful and balanced ways;
- Commune with nature and the energy of the elements;
- Enjoy creative crafts;
- Feel free to try and enjoy the exploration. It is the best way to get energy flowing in the third eye after all.

17.4 How to Open Your Third Eye?

The third eye symbolizes an enlightened state of consciousness through which one can perceive the world. The following paragraphs will discuss how to open your third eye so that you can have a deeper sense of intuition about the world around you. Awakening or opening of the third eye means ensuring the path in which you are walking is aligned with the vision of the universe

The following points, although discussed earlier, are summarized once again:

(i) Find some place which is peaceful. (ii) Sit down comfortably. (iii) Focus on your ajna chakra. (iv) Pick a mantra and use it. (v) Become more mindful.

17.4.1 Learning the Third Eye Meditation

- When you meditate, try to focus your mind on this third-eye chakra. It is responsible for helping you to see the world more clearly.

Figure 17.5: Awakened Third Eye

- If you simply cannot be comfortable sitting, don't worry. You can try what is known as walking meditation. For some people, the rhythmic sounds of their footfalls can be very soothing. Walk slowly, and have a clear path so that you don't have to think too much about where you are going. Labyrinth walking can be force multiplier in the process.
- Your mantra should be something that you want to integrate into your mind, or your awareness.
- Meditation is a practice. That means that the first time to sit down to meditate, it might not be a big success. Your mind might wander, or you might even fall asleep. Learning to successfully meditate is a process and it takes time. Make meditation a part of your everyday life.

17.4.2 More on Mindfulness

- Being mindful means that you are more actively aware of what is going on around you. You are consciously paying attention to your emotions and physical sensations. Being more mindful will help you to get in tune with yourself and the world around you.
- As you are becoming more observant, avoid being judgmental. Just observe and acknowledge without forming an opinion about whether something is "right" or "wrong".
- Being mindful can allow you to get more in touch with your creative side. Research suggests that mindful meditation is a great cure for writer's blocks and for blocks those artists and

other creative types of experience. Being more mindful can allow you to open up your creative pathways.

- Pay attention to each aspect of your surroundings and your routine. For example, when you are taking a shower, consciously observe the physical sensations. Take note of how the warm water feels on your shoulders. Appreciate the refreshing scent of your shampoo.
- When you better understand your emotions, you will feel more capable of dealing with them.
- Opening your third eye is very likely to reduce your stress levels. You will feel more peaceful and self-aware. There are many physical benefits from reduced levels of stress. People with less stress are less likely to have high blood pressure and symptoms of depression.

17.5 How to Awaken your Third Eye (Another Technique)?

By raising the energy through the third eye and up to the crown chakra at the top of the head increases our sensitivity to the spirit and expands the aura. As this happens the aura also opens—that is, it becomes sensitized to subtle vibrations, to other people, and also to the spirit communicators. At this time other people's thoughts and feelings of jealousy, anger, hatred, and so on can deeply affect us. The auric body and the third eye centre are sensitive to these vibrations. We are also subject to depletion of energy if we are in contact with people who are ill. During our daily life, we are unaware of the vibrations surrounding us. If our auras were expanded and open all the time, or our third eye active, then negative vibrations would soon deplete us. Intense people or those with severe mental problems project their thought waves that would influence our auras and could affect us deeply and undermine our inner harmony. Our auric energy may also be sapped by the "psychic vampires". This is why a medium, on finishing work, allows his or her aura to quiet down and "close." Furthermore, an expanded aura requires high energy levels that cannot be sustained by the novice. Only the advanced spiritual adept, such as a yogi who has renounced worldly activity, would be safe remaining in this state all the time.

17.5.1 How to Open the Third Eye in Six Steps

Step 1:

Sit comfortably and with your eyes closed, notice how your breathing is slowing down. Enjoy watching the breath for a while as your mind enters a peaceful state of contemplation.

Step 2:

See below you an ocean of brilliant white light. This is the infinite prana energy that is tapped during meditation. You are floating above this ocean of light. Now draw this energy toward the first chakra, which lies at the base of the spine. As the light comes to this base centre, feel it swirling with energy. The chakra opens like a flower of light.

Step 3:

Now draw the light up to each chakra one at a time, moving through the third eye and finishing with the crown chakra at the top of the head. This opens in a mandala of light—like a brilliant jewelled fan of peacock's feathers. Return each time to the sea of light below and draw energy. This is the way of opening the third eye. As the light enters each chakra see them open like flowers of light. They vibrate with brilliant lights in the colours associated with each chakra. The charkas are now vitalized. The prana energy is drawn upward from the base of the spine, through the third eye and to the top of the head.

Step 4:

Now that the chakras are open, visualize a glorious sun of light above you. Its golden rays shine through you and shower you with light. As the light floods through your body it washes away all negativity. This process purifies the aura and prepares the astral body for communication with the spirit.

Step 5:

Once you feel the light has done its job, allow the light from above to fill your whole body with light. You may imagine it as liquid light pouring in through the crown chakra and filling the body like a vessel from the soles of the feet to the top of the head, which is now open like a glorious mandala of light.

Step 6:

As the cosmic light fills your body you will feel the energy moving into your aura. This now expands and links with the others meditating with you. The merging of the lights flowing up through the base chakra and down from the crown chakra create a powerful spiritual force. At this point, you may become aware of how your auric light is at one with the omnipresent divine light. You may merge with the light and experience the wonderful inner peace and joy that accompanies this realization. If done properly, this aura meditation will naturally induce a state of inner peace. You will feel energized and relaxed and spiritually in bliss.

17.6 How to Open your Third Eye? (Yet another Way)?

We have discussed above two types of methods to open one's third eye. Likewise there could be numerous permutations and combinations of techniques for opening the third eye.

It is best to practice your third eye meditation after having recently woken up from a state of sleep. So the best time is either in the morning or after an afternoon nap. The reason for this is that the brain is already in a state conducive to meditation, that is, it is relaxed in the theta state, with heightened inner-awareness and intuition and low stress/anxiety levels. It is also possible to enter third eye meditation as you are falling asleep, however, this takes some practice and it is best to start the other way around first.

Herebelow is given yet another technique in the following steps:

(i) Sit in the lotus position to ensure your chakras are aligned.

(ii) Begin by relaxing each muscle in your body, starting with your toes and working all the way up to your head. Visualize each muscle, bone and ligament relaxing.

(iii) After this, see the wave of calm energy come over your body. Feel its warmth as it rises up through your body.

(iv) Slowly draw the energy to the centre of your head, in between your eyebrows. Don't hold onto any one though process or image.

(v) Neither welcome other thoughts nor reject them forcefully. These thoughts will come and go during meditation and after sometime they will automatically subside.

(vi) Feel yourself becoming lighter and lighter, as gravity falls away.

(vii) Stay with your breath and visualize a white ball of light rotating 360 degrees at the centre of your mind. See this ball expanding and fully accept its presence. Invite this to come into your ownership.

(viii) As this ball of white light expands, let the light stream out through the centre of your forehead.

(ix) Let the light in and remain open to seeing whatever is put before you be it pictures, colours or information.

(x) If you're seeking to connect with God (Mother Nature), or a spirit guide, this is the time to call out and connect. This can be done vocally (calmly and peacefully) or internally. Recite by calling through your favourite mantra until you receive a sign of response. You'll know when it comes.

(xi) Try not to be alarmed when it does; any shock or sudden movement may break the meditation.

(xii) You may simply choose to just be and take what comes from this enlightening experience.

(xiii) This experience may appear as dream-like, but in time you will familiarize yourself with the experiences and learn to cultivate and manifest higher knowledge into your physical existence.

17.7 Signs of 'Third Eye Awakening'

Following are some of the signs to know that the third eye is being awakened:

(i) Tingling sensation or pressure: One may begin to develop this in the "third eye" area (between the eyebrows), at the crown of the head. This happens for two reasons: (a) One is picking up energetic signals; (b) One's chakras are opening up. In the initial stages of development, this sensation can be very strong.

(ii) Connection with Spirit: One might find that one is having a stronger connection with the spiritual world. In other words, it may become easier for one to sense the presence of

Spirit: angels, and one's own loved ones in heaven. One may also begin to feel the presence of other people's loved ones around.

(iii) **Desire to be away from negativity:** One may also find that one is picking up on the emotions and feeling of others quite easily. This is known as being empathic. Because of one's sensitivity, one might feel drained being the surrounding people who are very negative or dramatic. One should accept what one is feeling, and stay away from the drama whenever possible.

(iv) **Desire to eat healthier foods:** One might suddenly be reaching for a salad instead of a junk food! Here's why: When you are doing intuitive work, you vibrate at a higher frequency (remember, we are all vibrational beings). So, without realizing it, you could be instinctively reaching for "higher vibrational" foods, such as fruits, vegetables, etc. These foods help keep one from being weighed down and keep the vibrations light. Some people even choose to adopt a psychic diet.

(v) **Desire to learn and be more spiritual:** Most of the time one who experiences the 'third eye awakening' has an appetite to learn. As we open up, we are shedding our old skins and subconsciously remembering the luminance of our soul. To that end, it is natural to wish to read everything we can get our hands on, learn as much as possible, and walk a more spiritual path.

(vi) **Frequent or vivid dreams:** Vivid dreaming, or dreaming more often, is another common symptom of 'third eye awakening'.

(vii) **Heightened sensitivity of your physical senses:** If you find that your hearing is heightened, you are seeing twinkles of light, or "something" out of the corner of your eye, it means that your psychic senses, or "clairs," are opening up and getting stronger. This is a normal part of the third-eye-awakening process.

(viii) **Intuitive "Hits":** Having a sense that something is going to happen or receiving a third eye vision, is another sign.

(ix) **Losing old friends, making new ones:** The path of third-eye awakening is exciting! Your soul will grow tremendously during this time. You may find that you are outgrowing some friends and things that were once important to you, no longer are. It is okay; the Universe will put new people in your path. Continue to trust.

Chapter - 18

Benefits of Awakened Third Eye of Lord Shiva

Third Eye Vision is a clear siddhi, a divine power, which comes to you by the awakening of your Third Eye with a proper process. It is not street magic. It can be reproduced on thousands or millions. There is no fraudulence involved in it. There is no magic involved in it. It is the pure spiritual power, a mystical science. Once your Third Eye is awakened, it is permanent.

Once you learn to open your third eye, you will be able to experience the benefits that go along with it. Part of this is due to achieving a greater sense of self-compassion. Being more aware of yourself generally causes you to practice more self-kindness. Being kinder to yourself offers many benefits. You will feel more self-confident and less anxious. One of the reasons many people want to open their third eye is because it is thought to make you more knowledgeable. Since it increases your perception of the world around you, it makes sense that you will be able to learn more about the world around you. People who have opened their third eye report that they feel like they have more wisdom. Opening the third eye allows a meditator to clear energy blocks and self-limitations and releases negative karma.

18.1 With Third Eye awakening you will have these benefits:

- **It will improve your Physical and Mental Health:** It will guide you to understand your physical or mental ailments and bring your body back to health because the Third Eye is the seat of intuition and will-power. As your third eye opens more and more, your physical, mental, and emotional health multiplies, while new and higher level souls begin to naturally enter your life.

- **Improvement in Inter-Personal Relations:** It will help you have beautiful relationships with colleagues, friends, relatives, and immediate family members because you will just know the person, not his/her actions.
- **You will achieve what you deservingly deserve:** You will be easily able to achieve anything you want from yourself, from the society and from other people.
- **Better Understanding of Perspectives of Life:** With each session of meditation, it shifts your consciousness into higher and higher states, automatically releasing anxiety and worry of the future and stress of the past. With an open and activated third eye, everything comes into perspective. Life's petty worries go to the wayside while you get a clear picture of your true life purpose.
- **Higher level of consciousness free from stress, anxiety or worry:** We are all human, and while we all want to have a fear-free life, worrying about how we'll accomplish our daily tasks, only perpetuates more worry. After all, like attracts like, especially true with our thoughts. When we set a time each day to practice third-eye-meditation, changing the nature of our thoughts from the root, we begin to have fewer and fewer worries, anxieties, and negative thoughts. And when they go, what will take their place will be stronger and more in-tune with the omnipresent law of attraction. An open third eye chakra will increase the vibration of your thoughts and higher vibrational thinking is cantered on the present moment. Anxiety and worry is cantered on the future and stress is cantered on the past. The chains of anxiety and stress will no longer drag you down and you will instead experience the bliss of being in the present moment.
- **Development of Intuitive Wisdom:** Just as meditation holds the benefit of reaching higher states of consciousness, allowing you to become more self-aware, achieving mastery

of your emotions while easily handling the stress of your day, meditation also tunes you into a natural born gift we all hold – intuitive wisdom. Your third eye intuition knows how to restore damaged relationships. Your third eye intuition knows how to attract people. Your third eye intuition knows precisely why you have chosen this life at this time.

- **You will see beyond the Unseable:** By activating your third eye, meditation allows you to see, understand, and enjoy the sights and sounds of the previously hidden world, allowing you to optimize and perfect your present life using this vast reserve of new information.
- **It awakens your higher intuition:** Opening the third eye is like unveiling another layer of reality you didn't know was there. You have probably heard that you would be able to see astral entities and auras but will you also understand what these entities communicate and what these auras say about someone. The third eye chakra is also the seat of the intuition and grants you access to a higher level of understanding. Everything is essentially known to your spirit and an awakened third eye bridges the connection between your spirit and your conscious mind. Granted this higher level of understanding, you will begin to realize how we are all connected and a part of a universal consciousness. Your intuition will reveal the reasons why certain events in your life happened and how you became the person you are today. But most importantly, you will know about your future as well.
- **You will be directed to your true path:** With direct access to your intuition, you will know exactly what you need to do at this moment to progress in life. Better yet, you will be in your soul's direction and directed onto the path that will bring you the most fulfilment. No more confusion. No more searching for answers. They are all within as they always have been. But now you will know how to find them. As your activated third eye makes the correct path to success as clear and obvious as the staircase leading to your higher floor apartment, third-eye-meditation will help you manifest abundance as easily and naturally as breathing.

- **You will tap into your hidden psychic abilities and obtain razor sharp instincts:** All of history and everything that will happen in the future has happened in the present moment. Everything is here now. Our third eye chakra transcends space/time and is attuned to this truth. This is why psychics (with open third eyes) are often able to tell what will happen in the future. The future is intuitive knowledge that can be tapped into with the third eye chakra. You will be to sense danger approaching. You will know the right answer. You will do the right thing. That is what a heightened intuition will result in. You will also be able to see people's auras and astral entities that dwell around. You will be able to peel away a layer of reality and see it for what it truly is. We are energetic beings and are all interconnected. Our thoughts manifest in the astral. These are some of the things you will begin to understand and experience for yourself with an open third eye.
- **You will harness the power of the law of attraction and manifest the life you desire:** Higher vibrational thoughts exert more power and manifest much more quickly. You will begin to notice many synchronicities with an open third eye chakra as your thoughts frequently manifest into 'coincidences'. This level of thought is centred on the present moment and the present is the source of all the energy in the universe. If you have ever tried to manifest your desires by imagining you have it, you may have failed because your imagination was overshadowed by your anxiety to obtain what you desired and stress of not having it. In fact, you may not have even been able to clearly visualize what you wanted. You can expect a much more vivid imagination that is centred on the present moment with an open third eye and finally take advantage of the law of attraction.
- ***A*wakenyour childlike imagination and enjoy boundless levels of creativity:** Generally, people with active third eye chakras (not necessarily fully open) are able to visualize very clearly and have a great imagination. This is because the third eye is able to see into the astral realm and our thoughts are manifested in the astral. An open third eye grants you absolute

clarity with your imagination and enables you to experience your thoughts like you did as a child. With your conscious mind more in tune with the astral, it is more in tune with the endless possibilities of reality. Connecting with the source of creation activates the imagination.

- **You will perceive the 'Real Truth':** The opened third eye allows us to begin to perceive the "Truth" that surrounds us. What this means is that you begin to see the world as it its: with its inequality and misery. And once that occurs, you will not want to close your eyes for what is happening. You will feel a desire to be free and live in a world filled with love, compassion and truth. Eventually, you will feel and see the interconnectedness with everything around you in nature and develop a strong bond with the Universe. This is a deep sense that allows you to see the beauty in all things and to realize that your physical 'I' is not your true nature.
- **Laws of Attraction / Space Order:** As a result of awakening the Muddy Pellet (another name of the 3rd eye), the Brow chakra is activated, which in turn facilitates to align your seven chakra system. When you are energized and in harmony with the Universe, you are like a giant magnet for events, people, situations etc. By harnessing the power of the positive intent, gratitude and love, you can manifest much more beauty in your life. You will become aware that the number of useful "coincidences" will increase number of times.
- **Vivid Dreams / Lucid Dreaming:** You will find that you sleep cycle is much better and that your dreams are more vivid. You could also be lucid dreaming. This means that you will feel that you can control your dreams and you will be able to realize your true infinite self and the infinite possibilities that exist in a state of sleep. Additionally, you will realize that this world of dreams is the same as the "real world" in which we live. The third eye allows you to consciously glimpse the astral when you see entities, auras or even when you vividly see what you imagine. It will also grant you the ability to consciously visit the astral realm in your etheric body. An awakened third eye results in a higher level of awareness that goes beyond the egoistic mind that is attached to the body.

Awareness of your energy body can keep you awake even when your body falls asleep and allow you to enter the astral as your astral self. This level of awareness often allows you to remain conscious in your dreams as well.

- **Astral Travel / Astral Projection:** When the third eye connects to this level of existence where there is no time and space, our soul is able to rise above the physical body and astral travel in time and space. Astral projection is one of the benefits coming with the activation of your third eye. It has the ability to go anywhere in the universe and at any time in the universe. Many people believe that when we dream, we actually astral travel, and with wide opened third eye we are able to consciously astral travel while we are awake, for example, when we are in a state of meditation.
- **Incredible Imagination / Creativity:** With activated third eye, you are continuously connected to the plane of existence where our souls reside. In this plane of existence, there is no time or space, just an endless love and truth – everything that has happened and will ever happen already exists in the plane of existence. After connecting to it, you will find that your imagination and creativity are super charged. You gain the ability to find quick solutions to problems much easily because all the solutions to all possible problems in the world exist in the higher planes of Consciousness.

So you should become an experienced observer of the unseen, make the impossible, possible. Third-Eye-Meditation is the key to unlock your infinite potential. You will see transformation in every area of your life.

18.2 Beneficial effect of 'third eye meditation' on the prefrontal cortex resulting into relaxation of mind

Neuro-imaging or the brain scans done with PET (Positron Emission Tomography) imaging equipment show that when a person meditates there is a lot of activity triggered in the prefrontal cortex. The medial prefrontal cortex lies in the same general area of the **"third eye"** of occult and eastern spiritual literature. Brain research informs us that people who regularly meditate actually physically evolve their brain structures with neural changes that promote higher consciousness.

The pre-frontal cortex is thought by neuroscientists to be part of the cognitive (mental) processing system of humans and appears to play an inhibitory calming or influencing role over the emotional or limbic part of the brain. This part of the brain also has been found to mediate and down-regulate the production of the stress hormone known as cortisol, that is produced via the Hypothalamic-Pituitary gland-Adrenal gland axis (HPA axis) when a person is stressed.

This effect on the prefrontal cortex appears to regulate and control the fear and can dampen an overall increase in escalation of fear mediated by the Amygdala, which is the part of the brain that evokes a "fight or flight" response in us all. This is believed to be partly why meditation practices can assist anxiety and trauma sufferers to "calm" down arousal symptoms in their nervous system and brain function.

A part of the brain known as the Orbitofrontal Cortex lies just above the orbit of the eyes and forms part of the frontal lobe in the area that correlates to the **"third eye".** This piece of brain facilitates direct inputs from many other cortical and sub-cortical areas of the brain. It also sends or signals outwards other forms of information and signals to the same and different cortical and subcortical regions of the brain. This wealth of incoming information from outside provides a snapshot of what is happening in the external environment as well as what reactions and plans are being organized by other parts of the brain. Critically, its output communication affects a variety of behaviours and physiological responses, including emotional and ANS (Autonomic Nervous System) responses organized by the Amygdala part of the brain.

It is this mediating function that apparently helps us integrate external experience with internal states, and also allows us to influence states of being in the body and to raise our window of tolerance of arousal from internal and external sources of discomfort. This is speculated as being the vehicle by which the spiritual people can alter their own body functions such as heart rate, blood flow, pain thresholds etc when you see them demonstrating unusual "tricks" that appear painful or which would signal injury or death in the rest of us.

The Orbitofrontal Cortex is also an area of brain that "lights up" in brain scans when meditation and visualization occurs. If one notices that the "outputs" go to mental centres, emotional centres, physiological processes, and memory areas of the brain, then an interesting correlation should be noted. In meditation it is stressed that one should develop the correct logical thoughts or reasoning (mental), develop a strong feeling (emotional), create a stable visualization (memory), and have correct meditative posture (physiological posture) when doing so.

In effect it may be a speculation but perhaps this is the critical reason why advancing one's spiritual realizations require the alignment of each of these key areas. The implication is that the Orbitofrontal Cortex may "update" our body-mind reality across these different cortical and subcortical areas of brain function. A comprehensive set of new information may in turn shape our operative reality, which is the basis for the creation of "realisation" in humans as a deep personal experience, as against just a mental conceptual knowledge of the same object.

Neuro-imaging not only shows that meditators shrunk their Amygdala over time, but also that their Hippocampus increases over time. The Hippocampus is commonly associated with memory function, and is part of the temporal lobe of the brain. It appears that the Hippocampus plays a key part in consciousness by shaping conscious or declarative thinking and also mediating learnt responses from past associations with incoming sensory data.

It is known that trauma and continued stress can damage Hippocampus cells via the action of the stress hormone Cortisol, which causes cell damage and shrinkage of the Hippocampus. Apparently meditation can reverse or repair some of this damage and facilitates growth of the Hippocampus area of the brain. Meditation has been shown to have a calming effect on the body-mind system and promote a relaxed feel-good, parasympathetic state of the ANS outcome. Immune system repair of the body needs such a state to exist for healing to occur and be sustained. So it can be seen that there is now more evidence emerging that the point in the body known as the **"third eye"** correlates to the same physical location of brain and gland functions which have direct impacts on our physical, mental, emotional and spiritual states of being, as well as states of consciousness.

Our third eye is the bridge between our soul and the universal consciousness. Let us walk on the bridge before it is too late.

|| Om Shanti Shanti Shanti Om ||

Bibliography

Books /Monographs / Theses / Dissertations

- Sadguru and Arundhathi Subramaniam, "Adiyogi: The Source of Yoga", HarperCollins Publishers, India, 2018.
- Sri Swami Sivananda, "Kundalini Yoga", Divine Life Publication, 4th edition, 1998, Chapter 2.
- Paramahamsa Nithyananda, "Secrets of Third Eye Awakening", Nithyananda
- University Press, 2015.
- Satchidanand, "Opening the Third Eye", www.energyenhancement.org, 2018.
- Master Del Pe, "The Third Eye: A Universal Secret Revealed", MDP BElife, India, 2010.
- Samuel Sagan, "Awakening the Third Eye", www.clairvision.org, Third Edition, 2007.
- Ammon-Wexler, Dr. Jill, "Pineal Gland & Third Eye: Develop Your Higher Self", Quantum Self Group, Inc. expanded 7th edition, 2012.
- Swami Satyananda Saraswati, "Kundalini Tantra", Yoga Publication Trust, Munger, Bihar, India. ISBN: 9788185787152.
- Philippe L. de Coster, "Shiva Yoga of Meditation", Satsang EBook Publications, Ghent, Belgium, 2017.
- Pattanaik , Devdutt, "The Third Eye", First Delhi, 2008.
- O'Russel, Kate, "Third Eye Awakening Mastery: 7 Techniques to Open the Third Eye Chakra, Deactivate and Decalcify Your Pineal Gland, 2018.

- Shumsky, Susan, "Awaken your Third Eye", New Age Books, New Jersey, USA, 2015.
- Sri Swami Sivananda, "The Science of Pranayama", A Divine Life Society Publication. 17th edition, 1997.
- Blavatsky, Helena P., "The Secret Doctrine", Vol. 2, Theosophical University Press.
- Baker, Douglas Dr., "The Opening of the Third Eye", Claregate, 1993.
- Bailey, Alice Ann, "A Treatise on Cosmic Fire" Lucis Publishing Company, 1925.
- Barsotti, Tiffany Jean, "A Proposed Spiritual Axis of the Bodymind: How the Reticular Activating System (RAS), Vagus Nerve and the Alta Major Chakra Axis May Be the Nexus of Bodymind/Spirit Consciousness" Master's Degree Thesis, Holos University, 2010.
- Dudeja, Jai Paul, "Maha Mrityunjaya Mantra: An Invincible Armour for Conquering Death", ISBN: 9789386397973, Kalpaz Publications, New Delhi, 2018.
- Dudeja, Jai Paul, "Gayatri Mantra: A GPS to Enlightenment", ISBN: 9788184356038, Adhyayan Publishers and Distributors, New Delhi, 2018.
- Dudeja, Prof. (Dr.) Jai Paul, "Ajapa-Japa Sohum-Humsa Mantra: An Eternal Mantra for Inner Consciousness", ISBN: 9788170848103, Chaukhamba Sanskrit Pratishthan, Delhi, 2019

Articles / Papers / Web links

- Padma V, N Anand and C. Ramakrishnana, "Pineal Gland: The Third Eye", J. App. Medicine & Surgery, Vol. 4, Issue 1, 2015, pp 9-14.
- Jain, Dr. Teena, and Dr. Sunil Kumar Yadav, "A study of third eye w.s.r pineal gland", International Ayurvedic medical Journal, Volume 4; Issue 06; June- 2016, pp 980-986.
- Lahiri, Srabona, Nikhil C. Shah, and Dhrubo Jyoti Sen, "Inner Eye or Third Eye: Both originate from Theosophy followed by Meditation", European Journal of Pharmaceutical and Medical Research (ISSN: 2394-3211), Vol. 4, Issue 4, 1-8, 2017.
- www.Tantra-Kundalini.com

- http://www.chakras.info/12-chakras/
- https://crystalclearchakras.com/the-12-chakra-system
- https://ffmt.fr/articles/kundalini/ajna/ajna-rev161103.pdf
- http://umich.edu/~umjains/jainismsimplified/chapter12.html
- Cassaro, Richard, "Discovery Of The Third Eye In The Ancient Americas", https://www.richardcassaro.com/discovery-of-the-third-eye-in-the-ancient-americas/
- Osborn, Gary, "The Gate of God", Idea Solar, Oct 2012.
- https://www.mindbodygreen.com/0-25407/what-is-an-aura-and-how-can-you-see-yours.html
- Hamilton-Parker, Craig, "How to Open the Third Eye" https://psychics.co.uk/blog/third-eye/
- "A Treatise on White Magic - Rule Six - The Work of the Eye", http://www.light-weaver.com/LW-old/magic/magic/magi1090.html
- Frater Apollonius, "Theosophical Anthropology of the Third Eye", http://www.astronargon.us/Theosophical%20Anthropology%20of%20the%20Third%20Eye.pdf

Index

D

J

K

L

M

N

O

P

Q

R

S

List of Figures